POLICING A DEMOCRACY

A Comparative Study of India and the US

POLICING A DEMOCRACY

A Comparative Study of India and the US

R.K. RAGHAVAN
Indian Police Service

MANOHAR
2023

First published 1999
Reprinted 2021, 2023

ISBN 978-81-7304-261-4

Published by
Ajay Kumar Jain *for*
Manohar Publishers & Distributors
4753/23 Ansari Road, Daryaganj
New Delhi 110 002

Printed at
Replika Press Pvt. Ltd.

Contents

Foreword

ALTHOUGH interest in policing is international, there are few genuinely comparative books about the police. Countries cooperate with one another in law enforcement; regional institutional integration of policing is growing; police officers exchange visits internationally for social and professional purposes; they attend international conferences and belong to the same professional organizations. But there are only a handful of books that compare police structures, strategies, and practices across international borders. The reason, I suspect, is that police officers don't write books and scholars aren't particularly interested in the police. Police are preoccupied with the operational responsibilities of their demanding profession, whereas scholars tend to regard policing as an unimportant and, sometimes, unsavoury activity.

When I say that there are few genuinely comparative books on the police, I am making a distinction that needs stressing. There are a host of books describing the police of individual countries. When they are written by foreigners—non-natives—they are sometimes lumped under the heading of comparative studies. But they aren't, in the sense that they do not keep more than one country in view at the same time. They are really single country monographs. What is noticeably lacking are books that keep in view similar features of police organization and activity in two or more countries at the same time.

Mind you, it is difficult to write comparative books. The people who know most about policing, namely police officers, are unlikely to have the time to familiarize themselves with foreign practices, whereas people who may have a professional interest in studying foreign countries are unlikely to have developed a substantial interest in the police. The reason, then, that scholarship on the police is parochial is because comparison requires unusual expertise.

R.K. Raghavan's book is, therefore, both ambitious and unique. It is ambitious because it systematically compares policing in two countries. It is unique because it is the first book treating India and the United States. Considering how natural such a comparison is, it is remarkable that it hasn't been done before. India and the United States are the world's two largest democracies; both have constitutions incorporating guarantees of human rights; both distribute power among levels of government according to federal principles; both achieved independence from the same colonial power; and both have very heterogeneous populations.

At the same time, of course, India and the United States are notably different on a host of dimensions—economic development, population density, educational attainment, technology, health and well-being, social stratification, and military power. These obvious differences will cause many people to question the value of comparing police practices as Raghavan has done. 'You can't compare India and the United States', they will say, 'they are so different'. They are wrong. People tend to think that their own countries are unique. Perhaps this is a matter of national pride. It is also a case of parochialism masquerading as common sense. Social and historical differences among countries are not a bar in principle to productive comparison, any more than are among individual people. The point is that one cannot determine whether comparison is valuable until it is tried.

In the case of the police, is it true that the pattern of its police evolution is different from the American? Were different causative factors involves in each case? Does the presence of civil unrest affect police similarly or differently in the two countries? Could community policing solve some of the same problems in both countries? Are the causes of police misbehaviour, such as brutality or corruption, wholly different in each country? Are there devices for increasing public accountability of the police that could work equally well in both India and the United States? Could raising educational level of police officers in India produce benefits similar to what has occurred in the US? Could India and the United States learn from one another about how better to mediate communal differences?

None of these questions can be answered until someone goes and looks. Perhaps it matters that India has a few state police forces whereas the United States has thousands of local forces. Perhaps it matters that India has a caste system whereas the United States has pronounced racial divisions. But perhaps it doesn't. One should not make up one's mind until the attempt at comparison has been made.

For my part, I am convinced that India and the United States have a great deal to learn from one another about both the usefulness of current practices and the factors that shape police development.

R.K. Raghavan has taken on the daunting task of finding out whether India and the United States can learn from one another about how policing should be organized and conducted. His knowledge of both systems is encyclopedic. I doubt if there is anyone who knows as much about both systems as R.K. Raghavan. At the same time, his book is selective, as it must be, and reflects his own interests. Fortunately, these interests are important to anyone concerned with modern policing. Raghavan focuses on crime, civil unrest, science and technology, community policing, and personnel management. His success in comparing these complex dimensions of police activity should, I hope, embolden others to study other shared aspects of policing, not only between India and the United States but many other countries.

Although policing is as old as civilization, its comparative study is in its infancy. This book should help to show the way.

DAVID H. BAYLEY

Preface

HAVING SPENT more than three decades in the Indian Police, fundamental issues of policing—professionalism, effectiveness and public image—agitate my mind constantly. In terms of these, police forces in India have generally fallen short of even the most modest of expectations. Several factors—especially the complexities of the polity and society, a lack of faith in professionalism, and the forbidding dimensions of the population and geographical area covered—explain this unfortunate situation only to an extent. The blame perhaps lies more in the ethos of the forces and of those who lead them.

For long, I have been curious to find out how the police in other countries, with somewhat similar problems and a rich democratic tradition, have performed. Fortunately, a stint in a US university gave me the access to people and information helpful to comprehend the basic police problems in a country that had many similarities with India: a democratic form of government, a vibrant press and other media, and growing economic inequalities, with consequent fissures in society. I had the advantage of interacting closely with academics—Professors David Bayley, Ron Clarke and Jack Greene—and police officers—Willie Williams, McLaughlin, Jack Murphy and Gus Carrie, all of Philadelphia—to name only a few. Conversations with them helped considerably in gaining an insight to the police ethos in that country. I have tried to reflect this to an extent in my description of the US scene.

I have presented material under each major head—law and order, crime, community policing, use of science and technology and human resource management—relating to both countries, and concluded with a brief analysis of the overall scene. This approach may not exactly stand the scrutiny of orthodox experts in comparative policing, who would prefer describing an operational problem, and then and there examine how the countries compared have sought to handle it. Notwithstanding this apparent technical flaw, I am confident that this work will provoke police officers with an academic bent of mind to delve deeper into a fascinating area of knowledge that is of vital interest to public policy.

I am aware that I may not have made any original contribution to the thinking on the subject. I can, however, claim credit for long hours of labour, spread over six years, and for locating most of the available credible material on policing in the two countries. With the help of such material, I have woven together facts which should facilitate a broad understanding of how the two police systems work.

I look upon the present volume only as a fairly reliable reference work which could support serious research. If it fulfils this objective, I will have been more than justified in taking many hours off my valuable leisure time.

This has been an ambitious and difficult book to write. My attempt has been to address two diverse audiences—Indian and American. I am naturally concerned about the idiom. Despite my reasonable familiarity with the American lingo, I am not sure whether I am fully intelligible to the average American reader. I leave the verdict to him.

R.K. RAGHAVAN

Acknowledgements

I STARTED working on this book in 1991 immediately following my return from the US after my graduate studies. A traumatic incident intervened soon. I somehow managed to collect myself to resume my labours in late 1992. During the six years since then, I have had the affection and consideration of many of my colleagues in the Indian Police, particularly those in Delhi and Tamil Nadu, making it possible for me to assemble the enormous material that has gone into this book. My friends in the US were no less forthcoming.

I do not know how exactly I can describe my relationship with David Bayley who now heads the School of Criminal Justice at State University of New York (SUNY), Albany. I first met him briefly in 1980 in India. I had the good fortune later to get to know him and his charming wife, Chris, during my visits to the US.

David has been my friend, philosopher and guide. He went through every chapter of the manuscript after it had attained a reasonable shape. His perceptive comments have imparted a definite direction to this book. This would not have been possible if he had not laboured as hard as he did. I owe him a huge debt of gratitude not only for this, but also for his delightful 'Foreword' which distinctly embellishes the end-product.

The School of Criminal Justice, Rutgers at Newark awarded to me a Visiting Library Fellowship in the Spring of 1994. This gave me the valuable opportunity to work at the School's unrivalled library and ferret out the latest information on the US Police. I should thank Dr. Ronald Clarke for the award and for looking after me so well when I was in Newark. Associate Dean Allan Futernick was equally warm and responsive. Library Director Phyllis Shultze is a remarkable person. Her speed and accuracy in locating whatever I needed were incredible. She continues to help me.

A special mention of Mangai Natarajan is very appropriate here. From being my unpretentious student at the Madras University way back in the early 1980s, she went on to complete her Ph.D. from

Rutgers. Apart from collaborating with Dean Clarke in various research projects at Rutgers, she now teaches at John Jay, New York. Mangai played a positive role in my going to Rutgers. Apart from this, she has been of great assistance in getting me a lot of data on the US Police. My friend of Temple University days, Professor Sankaran Raghunathan of the School of Management at Rutgers, was another source who came to my rescue whenever I was badly in need of some information.

Professor Douglas Verney of the Centre for Advanced Study of India (CASI), University of Pennsylvania, Philadelphia read the first few chapters at their formative stage. His suggestions were pointed and extremely relevant.

A number of police officers in the US helped me with current data on community policing, personnel management and computerization. These include Barbara B. McDonald (Chicago), Captain M.I. Montalvo (Houston), Director of Systems Charles Drescher and Sergeant Alan J. Atkins (LAPD), Chief Paul M. Walters and Lt George Saadeh (Santa Ana), and Deputy Commissioner Michael J. Farrell (NYPD). I thank all of them for their prompt response to my enquiries.

I am obliged to a number of individuals and institutions in India. Foremost among them is N. Krishnaswamy, retired Inspector-General. His affection and consideration for me have always been overwhelming. He went through the manuscript in great detail and imparted more than a sense of direction. In fact, I relied heavily on him for the chapter on science and technology, an area in which N.K. is an authority. I cannot adequately thank him. My guru, C.V. Narasimhan, was another source of valuable help. He pored over the entire manuscript and offered extremely perceptive comments. His labour greatly improved the quality of almost all the chapters. I am beholden to him for this.

The National Police Academy, Hyderabad has become a recognized centre for excellence in the area of policing. My frequent visits to the NPA gave me access to its well-stocked library and courteous staff. Joint Director Prasad and his officers were never wanting in their anxiety to rush me with the information sought so frequently. In the same way, Librarian Damodaran of Police Training College, Ashok Nagar, Madras and Gnanamurthy of the CID, Library, Madras stood by me all the time.

I should thank N.S. Saksena, former DG, CRPF for having allowed me to use his exhaustive notes on various subjects, which were meant for the National Police Commission.

Satish Sahney, L.C. Amarnathan and 'Bobby' Balachandran were other IPS colleagues whom I should thank for their generous assistance during the course of the present work.

I have nothing but admiration for the staff of the American Library, Madras. Very often they went out of the way to meet my short-notice requirements. Mrs Soman, Jagdish, Ratna, Meena Reddy, Krishnakumari and Gayatri are names I will always remember.

A word about the Jain brothers. My relationship with them transcends one between an author and his publishers. P.P. and Ramesh brought out my first book in 1989. Ever since then, it has been an enduring friendship, in which I have received more than what I have given. This book would not have been possible without their encouragement. Thanks are due to my good friend Prabir Bhambhal of the Oxford University Press for having put me on to the Jains.

Finally, I have to acknowledge the unstinted assistance of my personal staff. Vijayan and Ramesh helped with the graphs and other computer work. Gopal, Velu, Kandaswami and Pattan were spontaneous in their response in various odd ways.

My family—Shanti, Rajesh and Sona—bore the brunt of my tantrums when I was working against a self-imposed deadline. I should acknowledge their forbearance! At this moment, I cannot forget my beloved parents (Jaya and Kitchi), but for whose care in my early years, I would not have imbued the values and attained the goals I was to set for myself later on in life.

1

A Profile of the Two Nations

> To state that the US and India have much in common is to state the obvious. It is that commanality that has sustained their relations these two hundred years.
>
> M.V. Kamath, *The US and India 1776-1976,* Washington: Embassy of India, 1976

A COMPARATIVE STUDY of policing in two different countries gains focus mainly against the backdrop of prevailing socio-economic and political/administrative trends. Background material on such trends lends a valuable insight into the environment in which each system operates and the pressures generated by the environment on that system. This chapter seeks to present a panoramic view of the polity, economy and the society in India and the US, so that the reader gains an idea of the ambience in which a policeman operates in either country. Table 1.1 which gives a few basic statistics should be illustrative to the reader.

A note of caution is, however, warranted. The narrative here has been deliberately made simple in order to serve the limited purpose of providing some basic information to the outsider. I crave the indulgence of the insider in each system, if he or she finds my presentation too elementary and, in some respects, also inexact to a critical eye.

THE INDIAN SCENE

The Political System

After wresting Independence from the British in 1947, India became a republic in 1950 and gave herself a comprehensive Constitution. Borrowing selectively from many Western democracies, this established a Westminster model of government as a legacy of the British past.

TABLE 1.1: INDIA AND THE US AT A GLANCE

	India	US
Land mass	3,287,263 sq km	9,372,610 sq km
Population	950 million	252.5 million
Sex distribution	51.9 % male 48.1 % female	51.4 % female 48.6 % male
Major religions	Hindu, Islam, Sikhism & Christianity	Christianity & Judaism
Languages	18 (officially recognized)	English (Spanish also widely spoken and understood)
Literacy	52.2 %	97 %

The head of State is the President, chosen by an electoral college comprising the Parliament and State Assemblies. He holds office for five years and is eligible for re-election any number of terms. While the Constitution vests enormous authority in him—the prime minister and other ministers of the Union Cabinet hold office at his pleasure—the president exercises all his powers only on the advice of the Council of Ministers. He is, therefore, a titular head, comparable in many respects to the British Crown. In a few crisis situations in the past, some presidents are, however, known to have asserted themselves, giving rise to the belief that a strong personality, with a mind of his own, could give this essentially ceremonial office connotations of power not probably intended by the constitution-makers.

The Constitution of India lays down a quasi-federal system. The 25 states forming the Indian Union share power with the central government in a variety of spheres. A schedule to the Constitution specifically lists subjects which fall within their respective law-making competence. There are a few subjects mentioned in the Concurrent List in respect of which both the central and state governments may make laws.

What tilts the balance substantially in favour of the central government are two articles. Under Article 256, on any matter pertaining to laws made by the Union Parliament and to any existing laws which apply in a state, the central government may issue a directive that is obligatory for that state to implement. Again, under Article 356, the President of India may, on the advice of the Governor of a state or otherwise, dismiss a state government on grounds of a breakdown of the constitutional machinery. This is popularly referred to as the imposition of 'President's Rule' in a state.[1] This particular article has been invoked several times in the recent past, generating a public debate on the wisdom of persevering with a provision that upsets the equation between central and state governments. When a state is brought under President's Rule, all executive powers are exercised by the State Governor—a nominee of the central government—who may appoint a few advisers (usually serving or retired civil servants) to help him in day-to-day administration.

The Indian Parliament is bicameral. The lower chamber—Lok Sabha (House of the People)—comprises 543 members, directly elected by the people once in five years.[2] Each state sends a certain number that is proportionate to its population. The Upper Chamber—Rajya Sabha (House of the States)—has 250 members, of whom, 238 are elected by members of State Assemblies and 12 are nominated by the President of India.

The Union Council of Ministers, headed by the prime minister, is collectively responsible to the Lok Sabha, making this body more powerful than the Rajya Sabha. A vote of no-confidence, if adopted by the Lok Sabha against the Council of Ministers, leads to its resignation and paves the way for a new government.

Part II of the Constitution deals with the 'fundamental rights' available to citizens. Equality before the law, prohibition of discrimination on grounds of religion, race, caste, sex or place of birth, equality of opportunity in matters of employment, right to free speech, assembly and to movement throughout India, and protection of life and property are some of the fundamental rights guaranteed. Every citizen has the right to move the Supreme Court or the High Court of a state for enforcing these rights.

Article 368 lays down an elaborate procedure for bringing about any amendment to the Constitution. Either house of the Union Parliament is competent to initiate a bill in the matter, which, when supported by two-thirds of the members of both the houses present and voting, is presented to the President of India for his assent. However, in respect of certain subjects (such as election of the President, matters pertaining to the Union and State judiciary, representation of states in Parliament and provisions of Article 368) an amendment requires to be ratified by at least one-half of the states before being sent to the President for his assent. Till now, the Constitution has been amended 76 times.

The Administration of States in India

In addition to the 25 states, there are 6 Union Territories, and the National Capital Territory of Delhi, which are administered directly by the Ministry of Home Affairs (MHA) of the central government.

The head of the state administration is the Governor appointed by the central government.[3] Real executive power, however, vests in the popularly elected Council of Ministers led by the chief minister who enjoys enormous administrative and political authority. The Assembly is the lower House of the State Legislature to which the Council of Ministers is collectively responsible. A majority of states have an Upper House called the Legislative Council which represents varied interest groups and is elected indirectly by the Assembly and other constituencies.

A state is divided into districts for providing decentralized administration. Each of these is headed by a Collector—known as Deputy Commissioner/District Magistrate in some states—who is a civil servant belonging to the Indian Administrative Service (IAS), to whom all other specialist functionaries of the district, such as the Superintendent of Police, report. Each district is divided into three or four sub-divisions (headed by a Sub-Collector) whose policing needs are supervised by a Sub-Divisional Police Officer (SDPO) in the rank of Deputy/Assistant Superintendent.

Civic needs of major cities are looked after by an elected council called the Corporation, which is headed by a Mayor, who has the executive assistance of a Commissioner belonging to the civil service, normally the IAS. In smaller cities, this is the responsibility of a Municipality with an elected council headed by a Chairman whose principal administrative assistant is the Municipal Commissioner. Village needs are met by the *Panchayats,* which are elected bodies assisted by lower civil service functionaries. Significantly, none of these civic bodies has any control over the police which comes under the district administration, even at the grassroots level.

The Civil Service in India

The seeds of the civil service in its present form in India were sown by the British. The Indian Administrative Service (IAS), which resembles the generalist Administrative Class of the UK, functions as the leader of the civil service. It came into being following Independence in 1947, as successor to the Indian Civil Service (ICS), which formed the 'steel frame' that buttressed the foreign rule. Similarly, the Indian Police Service (IPS) succeeded the Indian Police (IP) in 1947. It provides the leadership for police forces and organizations under the central and state governments. Interestingly, to begin with, the ICS and IP were almost the exclusive preserve of Englishmen, with recruitment being done only in England. Gradual Indianization began only around early 1900s.

IAS and IPS officers are appointed by the central government and allotted to the various states to meet the latter's requirements at the state capital and in the districts spread all over the state. Members of the two services also man senior positions in the central government, on being deputed by the state governments, at the former's request, but only for a specified tenure.

Initially, the IAS and IPS alone constituted the All India Services (AIS). A third All India Service—the Indian Forest Service (IFS)—was formed in 1966. The combined All India strength of the three services is about 10,000. A typical state, such as Tamil Nadu, has 323 in the IAS, 200 in the IPS and 145 in the IFS.

Besides the three All India Services, there are more than 20 Central Services to lead departments such as Income Tax, Customs, Central Excise, Posts, etc. While the Central Services are exclusively meant to cater to central subjects in administration, the All India Services are required to handle both central and state subjects.

The Union Public Service Commission (UPSC) conducts an annual competitive examination all over the country for the positions notified by the central government. The examination for the IAS, IPS, Indian Foreign Service and other non-technical Services, such as Civil Accounts, Customs, Income Tax, etc., is common. This is in two stages; a preliminary examination which weeds out a majority of the more than one million aspirants, and a final examination at which three candidates compete for every available slot. About 700-800 candidates are appointed each year to all the services put together. Over the years, the number has come down in pursuance of the government's policy to cut down civil service costs.

The head of the civil service in the central government is the Cabinet Secretary, who is a career civil servant belonging to the IAS. He attends meetings of the Union Cabinet (comprising a select group of the Council of Ministers) and implements decisions taken. A senior civil servant, normally from the IAS (or sometimes, from other superior civil services, like the Indian Civil Accounts Service, the Indian Revenue Service or the Indian Police Service), called Secretary, heads the administration of each ministry and reports to the minister holding charge of a particular portfolio (such as Home, Finance, Defence, Commerce, Industry, etc.).

The head of the state civil service is the Chief Secretary, who is a career civil servant belonging to the IAS. He is assisted by a number of secretaries, mostly belonging to the IAS, each of whom handles a subject, such as finance, education, health, etc.[4]

The Judiciary in India

The highest court of law in the country is the Supreme Court of India in New Delhi. Headed by a Chief Justice, it has a strength of 24 judges. Serving normally as an appellate court, it devotes most of its time to interpreting the country's Constitution. The highest court in a state is the High Court, which confirms or modifies the orders of its lower courts called District & Sessions Courts. There is a Chief Judicial Magistrate (CJM) in every district, who handles essentially criminal matters. The District Collector and some of his deputies, as also the Commissioner of Police in major cities, enjoy limited judicial powers pertaining to the maintenance of public peace. This enables them to prohibit or regulate public meetings, processions, etc., so that these do not lead to a breach of public peace.

The Indian Economy

India is a planned economy. There is a Planning Commission at the national level which gives direction to all the economic activity in the country through its Five Year Plans. Since 1951, when India launched its First Plan, there have been eight Plans, each carrying a distinct thrust.

From a predominantly agricultural economy till Independence (1947), India is well on the road to becoming a highly industrialized nation. Overall, the nation's output of goods and services went up from a mere $50 billion in 1950 to $250 billion in 1995. Impressive achievements have been registered in the fields of steel, chemicals, machinery, rail equipment and defence goods (Adams 1996). The basic strength of the nation rests however on agricultural production which remains high at 198 million tonnes. As a result, the country's food imports are selective and limited, causing the minimum dent on the country's foreign exchange reserves. What dips heavily into these reserves are oil imports. During the year 1996-7, the country produced 33 million tonnes of crude oil. Imports were of the order of 34 million tonnes. Whenever international prices of oil go up, the economy suffers markedly (CMIE December 1997).

1991 may be described as a watershed in Indian economic history. A massive liberalization of controls operating on entrepreneurship was undertaken that year, permitting freer flow of foreign capital into the country. Initially, the industrial output did not match the gains in GDP and agricultural production. However, in course of time, especially after mid-1994, industrial growth picked up. The latter registered an 8 per cent rise in 1995 against a GDP rise of 6 per cent.[5]

Per capita GDP is as low as Rs.10,460 (US $ 300 approximate). More distressing, however, is the fact that nearly 40 per cent of the population are estimated to be below the poverty line.[6]

It is painful that much of India's economic success is diluted by its massive population. A nearly 25 per cent growth is recorded in every decade. According to the last census (1991), the population was 846.3 million. Since then, it is believed to have crossed the 950 million mark. A UNDP report of 1996 predicts that, in about three decades, the figure will go up to 1.8 billion. This has serious implications for poverty levels and, generally, for the quality of life.[7]

Population control measures sponsored by central and state governments and supported by non-governmental organizations (NGOs) have brought down the rate of population growth only slightly. A high-decibel propaganda promoting the small family norm offers hopes that this norm will gradually gain wider acceptance.

The Indian Society

Four aspects of Indian society call for some understanding by an outsider. These are:

(i) the role of religion;
(ii) the strong and significant presence of the caste system;
(iii) the role of family; and
(iv) the place of women in society.

Role of Religion in India

India is a secular State where all religions are equal. None is a State religion that is entitled to favoured treatment. The Constitution of India (Article 25) confers on all persons the fundamental right 'freely to profess, practise and propagate religion'. Article 26 embodies the right of every religious denomination or any section thereof 'to establish and maintain institutions for religious and charitable purposes' and 'to manage its own affairs in matters of religion'. Articles 29 and 30 protect the rights of religious and linguistic minorities to conserve their script or culture and to create and manage educational institutions of their choice. Courts in the country are extremely sensitive to actions, by the State or others, which, even by implication, infringe minority rights.

Religion plays an important role in the average Indian's daily life. Hindus are the dominant majority (82.64 per cent). The next single largest group is of the Muslims (11.35 per cent). Those who follow are Christians (2.43 per cent), Sikhs (1.96 per cent), Buddhists (0.71 per cent) and Jains (0.48 per cent) (Census 1991).

Early accounts of Hinduism are available from the Vedas (Books of Knowledge) attributed to the period prior to fourth century BC. Islam came to India in eighth century AD as a fall-out of repeated invasions by Muslim armies from Arabia into the northern region of Sind. Doctrinal differences between those practising the two religions, ignited by those in control of the polity, have unfortunately rendered Hindu-Muslim relations over the years extremely fragile. Violent exchanges between the two groups, provoked by the flimsiest of grounds, have marred Indian history, posing problems of great complexity and magnitude to law enforcement agencies. More of this later in the book.

Places of worship of the different persuasions may be found even in the remotest parts of the country. In many centres, they are situated close together, pointing to the high level of religious tolerance that still prevails amidst apparent discord.

Such physical proximity is also a source of tension on major festive occasions when the ostentation and exuberance displayed, sometimes deliberately by one group, offers grave provocation to the other. There are also controversies which ignite religious feelings and lead to major law and order situations.[8] These happenings have more than an echo on the politics of the country as well. As a result, very few sections of the population may be said to be unaffected by religion.

The Caste System in India

This is a prominent characteristic of the Indian society and an area of acute controversy. It has received extensive scholarly attention, both at home and abroad.

Mentioned even in the Hindu Vedic literature, the caste system splits the society into various major and minor groups, each with many sub-divisions. The original rationale for the arrangement was the need to recognize groups by the occupation—the royal or ruling class, priesthood, military and commerce—with which each was generally associated. In course of time, the castes acquired several other identifiable features, such as hierarchy, restrictions on food, drinking and smoking, distinction in custom, dress and speech, rituals, etc. (Srinivas 1979).

Perhaps the most unfortunate feature of the system was the arrangement of the hereditary groups in a hierarchy that placed the priestly class—the Brahmins—at the top. This has been the cause of extreme resentment and acrimony to this day. It has generated many social justice movements, especially in the south of the country. What is most relevant here is that, although the concept was essentially Hindu in origin, in course of time, the caste system found acceptance by the other religions as well. This is true especially of the Indian Muslims and Christians. Like the Hindus, these groups also suffer from marked inter-caste disputes based on rival claims to superiority, which very often restrict marriages between members of different castes and the partaking of food at the homes of one another.

Looking at the positive side of the system, Srinivas (1979:1) writes:

> The institution of caste may be mentioned as a typical example of the paradox that is Indian society. Each caste stands for a way of life that is to some extent distinctive, but, at the same time, castes of a region form part of a single social framework. . . . Caste is ubiquitous, and this has resulted in an ideology tolerant of diversity.

Even fifty years after Independence, there are no signs of the caste system losing its hold. There are no doubt strong trends suggestive of a change of perceptions on the part of many opinion leaders. Nevertheless, the fact that one belongs to a particular caste is embedded in the mind of even the most liberal and modern Indian citizen and erupts in conversation at the most unexpected moment. Scholars like Andre

Beteille (1996:152-3) recognize this as a certain 'ambivalence' that is 'easy to recognise and not difficult to describe, but . . . not received the scholarly attention it deserves. . . . [E]ducated Indians know that caste exists, but they are unclear and troubled about what it means for them as members of a society that is a part of the modern world.'

India is a highly politicized nation and political cross-currents stare at you wherever you go. While concluding this brief section on the caste system, one has therefore necessarily to try and answer the question: How does the Indian polity react to castes?

It is widely known that all political parties are extremely sensitive to caste pulls while choosing candidates at elections. Behind-the-scene activities are invariably focussed on garnering the support of caste blocks. This has been the situation since 1952, when free India held its first countrywide elections for the Central Parliament and State Legislative Assemblies. Nevertheless, there is one change which is visible from about the late 1970s.

The support to the caste system by political parties has moved from a concession to *realpolitik* to a passionate faith in the need to render social justice to large sections of the population who did not have access to higher education and, therefore, to responsible positions in the bureaucracy (Beteille 1996). It is this, which has ushered in a quota system—popularly known as the reservations policy—the subject of bitter public debate and long drawn-out judicial battles.[9] In view of the large numbers in the population who are benefited by this policy of reservation, all political parties have found it expedient to fall in line with it. Beteille (1996:169) identifies a paradox here:

> caste has, at least for the time being, strengthened its grip over politics. But it still is an unsteady grip, for neither the supporters nor the opponents of caste quotas say that caste itself should be revitalised. In fact, the strongest supporters of caste quotas are, paradoxically, also the strongest opponents of caste as a hierarchical system.

The Indian Family

It is very difficult to exaggerate the impact of the family as an institution on the average Indian. He or she acquires a faith in religion and imbibes most of his or her values from within this closely-knit institution.

The joint family, where at least two generations, if not three, lived together was the norm of the Indian society till recently. In the traditional Hindu household, the eldest male—father or the eldest brother/son—managed the affairs of the joint family. He wielded considerable authority which went almost unquestioned. Perhaps most distinct was the relationship between the mother-in-law and the daughter-in-law who lived under the same roof. Total obedience, bordering on servility, was expected of the latter. This often led to discord that had an impact on the stability of the marriage itself (Srinivas 1980).

Stanley Wolpert's (1991:134-5) observations on the system should be quite illuminating to the American reader:

> The family head—the father or the grandfather—is generally treated almost as a god, approached by children who bow to touch his feet, given deference and respect virtually unknown any longer in the West, empowered to make decisions that must be obeyed at the risk of ostracism. . . . The typical Indian family live together under a single roof and eat food prepared in the same kitchen. There is very little privacy in an Indian household, nor does it seem to be missed or much desired. Indians as a rule appear to have less-developed privacy needs than do Americans, and usually miss the bustling human contact if they opt to leave their joint-family home to establish an isolated nuclear family in some modern apartment. Most Indians find life in America much too 'lonely', even as Americans usually find India much too 'crowded'.

Except in parts of rural India, the joint family has now given way to the nuclear family. One major factor is urbanization that has forced many to abandon the traditional vocation of agriculture and move to the cities to take up jobs in industry. This phenomenon has also led to brothers/sisters locating themselves at different and far-flung centres rendering the joint family a physical impossibility. They get together for brief periods, once in a while, during a festive occasion, such as a wedding in the family, or in times of bereavement. One consequence is the slight dilution of an effective support system for a family member in distress, such as loss of employment or grave illness, that was available in the joint family system. Notwithstanding this, family loyalties in India, like caste loyalties, are strong and manifest themselves when the occasion demands it.

Women in Indian Society

This is again a controversial area that has produced many treatises. What should strike a casual visitor is the ambivalence that characterizes male attitudes. While women are still expected to be subservient, large blocks of the electorate have not hesitated to vote women leaders to high office. Apart from a woman prime minister—Mrs. Indira Gandhi—several have been chief ministers in states and members of Parliament and State Assemblies.

Tradition over centuries had assigned a purely domestic role to the Hindu woman. She had no existence apart from her husband, so much so that, on the death of her husband, she was required to jump into the funeral pyre to put an end to herself. Known as *sati*, this social evil, though not widespread, has been nearly wiped out.

Another age-old source of harassment of women is the sometimes exorbitant demand for dowry, made on the bride's family by the groom's parents, at the time of marriage. Very often, out of an anxiety to get their daughter married to a boy in good position, parents pledge their belongings to make up the resources required. Where they are unable to meet the demand in full before the wedding day, a promise is made to hand over the remainder in course of time. Whenever this is not fulfilled, the bride is invariably harassed, not only by her in-laws but by her husband as well.

Torture of the daughter-in-law is not an unusual occurrence, and this often drives her into suicide. Known widely as 'dowry deaths', this phenomenon persuaded the government to frame the Anti-Dowry Act of 1961, which punished both the giving and taking of dowry and their abetment. Exclusive anti-dowry cells have been created in many state police departments.

The traditionally lower status accorded to women renders the girl child an unwelcome addition to a family. This state of mind accounts for another evil, viz., female infanticide. In the rural areas of some states, there is the cruel practice of murdering girl babies immediately after birth.

One piece of statistic of the Indian demography is relevant here. In 1901, there were 972 women for every 1000 men living in India. In 1991, the ratio became 929:1000. While six states in the country had more women than men during the previous census (1981), in 1991, this came down to just one (Kerala) (Kaushal 1996).

THE US SCENE[10]

THE US POLITICAL SYSTEM

Somewhat like India, the US was born out of a struggle for independence fought by the 13 British colonies against their English masters. The War of Independence broke out in 1775 and lasted six years. Even as this was being waged, the colonies declared their independence in 1776 and gave themselves an 'Articles of Confederation and Perpetual Union' at a Congress of the States in 1777, which was formally signed in July 1778. The Articles brought about a loose association of the states and established a Federal Government with extremely limited powers. The ineffectiveness of the arrangement was evident from the anarchy that prevailed, in what was basically a new nation. It was against this backdrop that the Continental Congress, the legislative arm of the new republic, met at Philadelphia on 25 May 1787. Although they had been empowered only to bring about needed amendments to the Articles, the delegates went beyond this to draft a Constitution that envisaged a centralized form of government. The document was officially adopted on 4 March 1789.

The US Federal Government

The Constitution ensures that the three branches of government—executive, legislature and judiciary—are separate and distinct from one another. Executive power rests in the US President who is chosen by an electoral college formed out of a popular vote. He holds office for four years and is eligible for only one more term.

Reckoned as the world's most powerful political executive, the American President enjoys considerable executive, legislative and judicial authority. He proposes bills to the Congress and has also the authority to enforce federal laws. Noteworthy is his power to veto any bill passed by the legislature, unless it is reversed by a two-thirds vote. The President is the chief of the cabinet, each of whose members, titled Secretary, heads a department, such as State, Defence, Commerce, etc.

The US Constitution provides for a bicameral legislature—the Congress—comprising the Senate and the House of Representatives. Every state, irrespective of its size, has two members in the Senate, making up a total of 100. Representation in the House is, however, determined by population. The six smaller states have each only one Representative, while the largest, California, has 45. The current strength of the House is 435.

A major characteristic of the American legislative system is the dominant role of the Committees—16 in the Senate and 22 in the House—which deal with specific areas such as foreign affairs, defence, agriculture, commerce, etc. Every bill introduced in either house of the Congress will have to go through a committee that can approve, revise, kill or ignore any measure referred to it.

Provisions of the Constitution may be amended from time to time through a prescribed procedure. An amendment requires the approval of two-thirds of each house of the Congress. Alternatively, the legislatures of two-thirds of the states may ask Congress to call a national convention to discuss and draft an amendment. In either case, an amendment requires the ratification of three-fourths of the states in order to become law.

There have been 26 amendments to the US Constitution since 1789. The most significant of these are the first 10 amendments, collectively known as the Bill of Rights. While the first guarantees freedom of worship, speech and press, the right of peaceful assembly and the right to petition government, the second amendment confers the right to bear arms.

The Administration of States in the US

Each state also has a written Constitution that has almost the same features as the US Constitution. Matters lying within the competence of state governments include internal communications, regulations relating to property, industry, business and public utilities and the State Criminal Code. While there are many overlapping areas, the Federal Government has, in the recent past, started taking up increased responsibility in sectors such as health, education, welfare and transportation. On the same lines as the Federal Government, each state has three branches.

The executive is headed by the Governor, who is elected by popular vote and enjoys a four-year term. States have a bicameral legislature, except Nebraska which has only one house.

Being a highly urbanized country, the administration of civic needs (including policing) of large cities is a multi-dimensional task. City governments, though chartered by states, enjoy a lot of autonomy. Their composition and tasks vary widely. However, each has a kind of popularly elected central council and an executive officer, assisted by various departmental heads, who include the Police Chief.

There are three broad forms of city government: the Mayor-Council, the Commission and the City Manager.

The most popular of these is the first one, in which an elected Mayor is the chief of the executive branch, and the elected council representing the various neighbourhoods forms the legislative branch. The Mayor appoints heads of city departments and can veto ordinances passed by the council.

In the Commission form, the legislative and executive functions are entrusted to a group of elected officials called Commissioners, each of whom oversees the work of one or more of the city departments.

In the third form, a small elected council makes the law but hires a paid administrator, called the City Manager, to execute the decisions. This form of local government is in recognition of the fact that modern urban problems require management expertise which may not be possessed by elected public officials.

The civic needs of a group of townships or villages are met by a County administration, which has a board of commissioners or supervisors that levies taxes, borrows and appropriates money, builds and maintains highways and bridges and administers welfare programmes. Thousands of other municipal jurisdictions, which are too small to be city governments, are called towns or villages. Their civic needs are managed by elected boards or councils headed by a chairman or president or sometimes by an elected Mayor.

The US Civil Service

Three distinct periods, each marked by a particular organizing concept, can be identified in the history of the US civil service (Rosenbloom 1994).

In the first (1789-1829), the 'era of gentlemen', recruitment was from the upper classes, the criterion for selection being 'fitness of character'. The second phase (1829-70s) was dominated by President Andrew Jackson's dictum that the civil service had to be socially and politically representative of the public. In his view, its upper class composition rendered it insensitive to popular needs. He therefore proposed that civil servants should be selected from a broad spectrum and be rotated from time to time, thus providing the basis for the much-abused spoils system which was to dominate the US scene for nearly four decades. The third phase (1870s to 1920s) could be looked upon as a 'reaction to the excesses of the spoils system' and was characterized by a strong reform movement that placed faith in merit, political neutrality and scientific management (Rosenbloom:219).

A formal recognition of the three principles was found in the Civil Service Act of 1883 (popularly known as the Pendleton Act). This paved the way for the gradual extension of merit as the criterion for selection to the civil service. By 1919, 70 per cent of the jobs came under the competitive classified civil service. The 1883 Act had also ensured the creation of a Federal Civil Service Commission to ensure that merit and neutrality dictated the norms for civil service recruitment and functioning.

The next landmark in the history of the civil service was the Reform Act of 1978 which was in response to three developments: the Watergate scandal, the growing concern over ethnic imbalances in the civil service and the regard for the concept of equal employment opportunity, and, finally, the popular perception, which was shared by President Jimmy Carter, that the federal bureaucracy was 'bloated, inefficient and badly in need of reform' (Rosenbloom: 221). This Act did away with the Federal Civil Service Commission, and created in its place, a Merit Systems Protection Board (MSPB). An Office of Personnel Management (OPM) was also formed to discharge most of the management functions of the Civil Service Commission. Another innovation was the establishment of a Senior Executive Service (SES), a group of higher civil service, considered for long, a needed adjunct to the Federal Government.

The SES is unique among the many federal civil service classes, in that it confers the rank on a person and not the position held by him (Rosenbloom 1994). Senior civil service officials in the GS-16 to GS-18 levels are among the others eligible to join the SES whose members are liable for re-assignment between different organizations. What they lack in terms of job security, they make up through liberal cash bonuses (*Congressional Quarterly Guide*, 1989).

The OPM issues guidelines on how to classify jobs within the General Schedule (GS). This ensures a certain uniformity between agencies in the Federal Government. Basically, each job gets a grading according to its level of difficulty. The low grade positions are from GS-1 to GS-6 and the middle ones from GS-7 to GS-12. The highest are in GS-13 to GS-18.

Popular expectation countrywide, since the beginning of the twentieth century, has been one that favours the government undertaking more and more citizen services. As a result, the bureaucracy has grown in numbers. This is much more marked in the case of the state and local governments; from 6.4 million in 1960 to 15.2 million in 1990, a 137.5 per cent rise. Federal employees, however, grew only by 20 per cent during this period (USIA 1991). The current strength of the federal civil service is around three million (Rosenbloom 1994).

The US Judiciary

The country's apex court is the Supreme Court in Washington, which has a strength of nine judges. All cases, except those involving a foreign dignitary and those in which a state is a party, come to it only on appeal. Judges appointed to the Supreme Court need not be lawyers. The second tier of the federal judiciary comprises the 11 Courts of Appeals serving geographical regions. Below them are 89 District Courts spread over the 50 states, which try, through a jury, federal offences, such as misuse of mail, theft of federal property, etc.

The highest judicial body in a state is the State Supreme Court, which, along with the Supreme Court of Appeals and Supreme Judicial Court, constitutes the judiciary of appellate jurisdiction in a state. Below them are the intermediate appellate courts (Appeals Court, Superior Court and Court of Criminal Appeals). In the next tier are the major trial courts, viz., the Circuit Court, District Court and Superior Court. Finally, there are the lower or inferior courts with limited jurisdiction, such as the Magistrate's, Justice of the Peace, Municipal and Country Courts (Inciardi 1987).

The US Economy

The US economy has had many ups and downs. Contrary to popular fears, the post-World War II period saw an upsurge. Most remarkable was the rise of the automobile industry which quickly adapted itself to the change-over from making tanks and bombers. Also significant was the rise of new industries, such as aviation and electronics. This marked growth of the economy, however, slowed down in the late 1960s and early 1970s at the time of the Arab oil embargo (1973-4). High inflation, unemployment and stagnant demand were the characteristics of the times. Till about 1982, the nation went through a recession.

The drop in oil prices and the strict fiscal discipline imposed by the Federal Reserve brought down inflation, and, by 1983, the economy had recovered substantially. There were, however, problems in the period that followed.

Serious droughts in 1986 and 1988 aggravated the farmers' plight. The rising federal deficits were also of great all-round concern. A recession gripped the economy again in 1991 (USIA 1991). This was, however, short-lived, and from all accounts, the economy has recovered substantially.

Although it is a 'dynamic free-market economy', the US may be more accurately described as a mixed economy in which the Federal Government also has a significant role in the marketplace. According to one estimate, the public sector accounts for one-fifth of all economic activity. The size of the economy may be gauged from the fact that, with less than 5 per cent of the world's population, the country produces more than 25 per cent of the world's output. The GNP has been steadily rising. From more than $3400 thousand million in 1983, it went up to $ 5500 thousand million (USIA 1991 and 1992).

Agriculture has always played a significant role in the US economy. Apart from the bounties of nature, huge capital investments, use of scientifically-developed seeds and trained-labour have all ensured a high yield from farm land. This is noteworthy if one reckons the fact that the number of farms has come down to 2.1 million as against 6 million in 1940, and the labour force has dropped to 3 per cent of all workers in the country as against 50 per cent a century ago (USIA 1991).

The US produces approximately 65 million tonnes of wheat annually. Other important grains include corn (250) and soyabeans (70) (US Department of Agriculture Economic Research Service).

The country has abundant oil reserves extending from the Gulf of Mexico to Alaska's North Slope. Production value of crude oil is about $ 4.2 thousand million each year (USIA 1991).

A major characteristic of the current US society is the galling disparity in levels of income. A number of economists identify the mid-1970s to the early 1980s as the period from which such inequality became noticeable.

The wealthiest 1 per cent of households in the US now own nearly 40 per cent of the nation's wealth. Also, the top 20 per cent of American households report 55 per cent of all after-tax income. Further, the lowest-earning 20 per cent households record only 5.7 per cent of after-tax income.

Among the many reasons cited for this phenomenon are the falling wages of unskilled workers, low tax rates on the rich under Reagan, low minimum wages, the loss of influence of labour unions and the rapid rise in the 1980s of the stock and bond markets in which rich people invested heavily (*Times of India*, 27 April 1995 quoting *New York Times*).

Incidentally, as per the definition of 'poverty' by the National

Academy of Sciences, there are 40 million 'poor people' in the US. This works out roughly to 16 per cent, a 1.5 per cent increase since the last census in 1990 (*Times of India*, 1 May 1995).

The American Society

The US is a multi-ethnic society. According to the Harvard Encyclopaedia of American Ethnic Groups, it has 106 major groups. Of these, whites (73.6 per cent) are the largest. The two significant minorities are the African-Americans (blacks) (11.1 per cent) and Hispanics (8.3 per cent).

Irrefutable is the division between the white and black. This has a historical basis. The first group of about 20 blacks, captured on the Caribbean Sea by a Dutch ship from a Spanish ship bound for South America, arrived in North America in 1619. They provided the much-needed labour for clearing land and building houses. They were followed at frequent intervals by many other batches of blacks who landed in the English colonies. In course of time, black labour was very much sought because it was cheap. The seeds of antagonism between the two races were sown two or three decades later when the black labour was brought into a formal system of slavery. US history since then has been marked by many violent black-white clashes. More of this in Chapter 3.

The civil rights movement spearheaded by Martin Luther King, Jr. in the early 1960s and the subsequent Civil Rights Acts of 1964, 1965 and 1968 substantially altered the situation in favour of blacks. However, the average black still nurses many grievances.

Blacks complain of poverty that the State has not chosen to tackle. (Although there is now an identifiable black middle class which is growing in strength, the average income of blacks is markedly lower than that of the whites.) They believe that they are being discriminated against in the matter of public employment. (It is true that black unemployment is higher than the white and the Equal Employment Clauses have not greatly helped.)

Perhaps the most bitter of complaints by the blacks is that the whole criminal justice system is arrayed against them. They quote statistics of their involvement in police cases to buttress the complaint that this is disproportionate to their numbers in the population. (This subject is dealt with in some detail in Chapter 4.)

The American Family

During its infancy, when the US was an essentially farming nation, sheer economic necessity brought about marriages between partners, who could both work on their farm and produce enough for the market to earn a decent income. The concept changed in the 1800s, when the US became an industrial nation. Since a person could work outside his home in a factory, the basis for marriage became one of love and not economic need. In course of time, especially at the beginning of the twentieth century, this had its own impact on the stability of a marriage. A rise in divorce rate was seen around this time, because livelihood did not depend wholly on family cohesion, as it did during the earlier farming days (USIA 1991).

The 1950s saw a re-emphasis of the benefits and glory of the family as an institution. Significantly, this was the 'baby boom' time when birth rates escalated. The 1960s-70s again saw a change in attitudes, especially that of the women, who believed that they should live a life that was not burdensome with rearing children and looking after them. Female employment went up about this time. There was soon the phenomenon of couples living together outside marriage. Simultaneously, one saw a rise in the divorce rate, from 47 per 1000 in 1970 to 114 in 1980. A rough estimate is that 50 per cent of marriages in the US still fail (USIA 1991). Interestingly, the refrain of 'family values' has been frequently heard in recent Presidential campaigns directed at the average American distressed by the fragile nature of marriage as a social institution.

One significant feature of the US society is the rising number of working women. It is estimated that 60 per cent of all women are employed outside their homes. Apart from growing opportunities for women, work has become an economic necessity. Relevant here is that 80 per cent of women who work have to support their children without the help of a man (USIA 1991).

Role of Religion in the US

Christianity is the dominant religion. Protestants (79 million) out-number the Roman Catholics (54 million). Jews account for nearly 6 million.

There is no State religion. The First Amendment to the Constitution prohibits any law 'respecting the establishment of religion' or 'prohibiting the free exercise thereof'. This has ensured total religious freedom. Interestingly, churches have managed to survive purely on private support (Kosmin and Lachman 1993).

Remarkable is the pervasive Protestant influence on almost all the other faiths. Alongside this is the effort of the many denominations to innovate and fit their practices into the American mainstream. As a result, one can perceive considerable differences between them and their counterparts in other countries. Kosmin and Lachman (1993: 279) look upon America as 'a greenhouse for religious formation, adaptation, and change'.

Although it is widely believed that the Founding Fathers had successfully kept the Church and State apart, the influence of religion on American politics is perceptible during Presidential election campaigns.

For instance, when John F. Kennedy contested the 1960 election, his Roman Catholic background came into public gaze. The question that was frequently aired on the occasion was: 'Can a President adhering to the Roman Catholic faith remain true to the constitutional principle of separation of Church and State?' (Kosmin and Lachman 1993:169). To appease Protestant attacks on him, Kennedy had to declare his position openly thus: 'I believe in an America where the separation of Church and State is absolute . . . where no man is denied public office merely because his religion differs from the President who might appoint him or the people who might elect him' (ibid.).

Again, in 1964, Republican candidate Barry Goldwater's apparent 'lack of commitment to Christian social action' was a subject of concern even among moderate Protestants (Kosmin and Lachman: 171). When Lyndon Johnson won the election, it was known that many among his voters were conservative evangelists who were traditionally known for supporting the Republican cause. It was believed that a majority of white Protestants voted Democratic—'a feat that no subsequent Democratic Presidential candidate had been able to achieve' (ibid.: 175).

During the 1992 Presidential campaign also, there was evidence that both the candidates—President Bush and Bill Clinton—were conscious of the power of an appeal to 'Christian values', and they so repeatedly invoked the name of God that political commentator William Safire humorously said: 'never has this or any other nation been so thoroughly and systematically blessed, as in the 1992 campaign' (ibid.: 158).

NOTES

1. There is no such provision for imposition of President's Rule at the Central Government level, if there is a breakdown of the constitutional machinery following the fall of the ruling central government or under any other circumstance. This is a subject of animated discussion during political instability at the national level. The concept of a national government, in which diverse political parties sink their differences and agree to govern the nation collectively at the instance of the country's President, has been mooted very often. This is yet to take formal shape. The nearest to this concept is a coalition government of left and centrist parties like the one that was installed in 1996.
2. Mid-term elections are not unknown, when the Lok Sabha is dissolved before it completes its life of five years following a loss of majority by the ruling party/coalition in the House. For instance, the Lok Sabha constituted after the 1996 elections was dissolved in late 1997 and fresh elections held in February-March 1998.
3. The Governor could be an active politician or a retired civil servant. There have been occasions in which retired police officers have been appointed to the position. Currently, Governors of two states (Nagaland and Manipur) are former members of the Indian Police Service.
4. In some states, a senior police officer functions as the Secretary to the Home Department, which handles subjects such as police, fire service and prisons. This experiment has worked out satisfactorily, and it fulfils the demand of IPS officers that they should be considered for non-police assignments as well for improving their career prospects.
5. For a more detailed analysis of India's present economic scene, I would commend John Adams' 'Reforming India's Economy in an Era of Global Change' in *Current History* (April 1996). Adams identifies three phases in the country's economic growth: the Planning Era of 1950-80, the Golden Decade of the 1980s and the Post-1991 period of reforms. He predicts that the economy will grow at or above 6 per cent in the years to come, backed up by a 'dynamic' private sector.
6. This is based on the norms prescribed in the report of the Expert Group on Estimation of Proportion and Number of Poor (Lakdawala Committee) (*Business Line,* 14 December 1996).
7. According to the *Human Development Report 1996* published by the UNDP, India ranked one hundred and thirty-fifth in Human Development Index based on a study of health standards, sanitation, treatment of women and other indicators related to the quality of life. This annual report carried for the first time a new Capability Poverty Measure (CPM) that attempted to link economic growth with employment and economic well-being. The report believed that, in most South Asian nations, capability poverty was more widespread than economic poverty. The report placed 554 million and 229 million Indians respectively in the two categories. (*Times of India*, 17 July and *Hindu,* 18 July 1996)
8. One major controversy that rocked the nation in 1992 was in the northern state of Uttar Pradesh, where Hindu fundamentalists razed to the ground a

mosque, saying that a Hindu temple had been brought down several centuries ago to give place to this mosque. The incident sparked off a debate on many other issues, including the role of the State Police and that of central government's police placed under the command of the former, in such situations.

9. The Mandal Commission appointed by the Central Government in 1979 to go into the question of the need to reserve certain percentages of seats in professional courses, such as engineering, medicine, law, etc., and jobs in government, gave its recommendations in 1980. However, this was implemented only in 1990. As a result, a 27 per cent quota in government jobs and in admission to educational institutions, run by the government or receiving government financial assistance, is now available to those castes recognized by government as Other Backward Classes (OBCs). This is in addition to the 22.5 per cent quota earmarked for the Scheduled Castes (SCs) and Scheduled Tribes (STs). Significantly, the Supreme Court, while upholding the central government's notifications to implement the Mandal Commission Report, laid down that the more advanced sections (among the OBCs), which constituted the 'creamy layers', were to be excluded from the Mandal concessions.
10. Most of the material for this section was culled out from the *Outline* series published by the United States Information Agency (USIA) on several aspects of the country. Also useful was the *About the United States* series prepared by the USIA.

2

A Historical Perspective

> Rapid growth is another sure sign of crisis in an organization's theory. Any organization that doubles or triples in size within a fairly short period of time has nesessarily outgrown its theory. . . . To continue in health, let alone grow, the organization has to ask itself again the question about its environment and core competencies.
>
> Peter F. Drucker, 'The Theory of Business', *Harvard Business Review,* September-October 1994

As we saw in the previous chapter, the US and India share the heritage of a strong British link. It is not illogical, therefore, to look for a few common influences on their political and administrative institutions. Against this contextual similarity, it will be interesting to explore how much the two systems resemble or differ from each other.

A Brief History of the Indian Police

A semblance of what is now regarded as the police existed in India even during the Vedic times, viz., prior to fourth century BC. The Laws of Manu (200 BC to AD 200) carry some references to what may be identifiable as a police function. The Maurya administration (324 BC to 183 BC) encompassed aspects of an intelligence machinery. Policing was mostly rural, intimately linked to land holding. This envisaged the owners of large pieces of land keeping a watch on whatever was happening in areas under their possession and taking up responsibility for apprehending whoever was guilty of disturbing peace or stealing any article that lawfully belonged to another individual. Outside such large private territory, there was the hierarchy of a village headman and a few watchmen under him performing similar functions (Curry 1932, Griffiths 1971 and Trivedi 1993).

Historical research of the evolution of the Indian Police is greatly hampered by a period of darkness between the end of the Maurya dynasty in the second century BC and the establishment of the Mughal Empire around fifteenth century AD. A general presumption that the village and land-based police style, with minor refinement, survived this period appears tenable. 'Not until Moghul times do we see anything like a definite police organization, and even then, we must beware of translating the medieval Moghul arrangements into modern terms. The villages were still responsible for their own safety and that of travellers within their limits' (Curry 1932:20).

By all accounts, the Mughals laid the foundation for a system of governance that served as the base from which the British East India Company was to stabilize itself and pave the way later for the Crown to take over. Unfortunately, the abundant administrative literature on this period is very sketchy with regard to policing. There were separate sets of officials for the rural area and for the towns. Some of them combined police and civic duties. One such official was the *faujdar* who, as the chief executive of a division, was responsible for ensuring peace and security. He was to look after policing in the rural areas through *thanas* (police stations) headed by *thanedars*. Another functionary figuring frequently in despatches was the *kotwal*, who, besides attending to his civic chores, was the urban policeman (Griffiths 1971 and Trivedi 1993).

British entry into India in early 1600s was for the ostensible purpose of trade under the banner of the East India Company. Assiduously filling the vacuum caused by the break-up of the Mughal Empire, the Company prepared its ground before the ultimate take-over in 1858 of the entire subcontinent by the British Crown. The alien ruler worked to a plan and spent considerable time in administrative experiments, including those relating to the police, many of which were unsuccessful (Curry 1932).

The History of the Bombay Police, 1672-1916 by S.M. Edwardes is a valuable source that offers a glimpse of the justice administration of the times. It refers to the formation (1672) of a body of militia that functioned as a night-watch. This was styled in 1771 as the *Bhandari Militia* and reorganized to perform specific police duties. In 1779, a Superintendent of Police and a Lieutenant of Police functioned as chiefs in Calcutta and Bombay respectively.

The next document of some significance available to us is the proceedings dated 19 April 1774, issued by Warren Hastings, the Governor-in-Council of Bengal (who subsequently became the first Governor-General of the East India Company). According to it, the Province was full of dacoits who were in fact protected by landowners (*zamindars*). Warren Hastings attributed this to the disappearance of *faujdars* and their deputies, the *thanedars*—a system created by the Mughals to look after rural policing. He therefore contemplated an extraordinary legislation for their revival and a directive to landowners to assist them in tackling violent crime. He also proposed the creation of a separate body that would receive and collate all the information received from the *faujdars.* According to Curry (1932:25), this was 'the germ from which sprang the fully developed police system of modern India'.

A review of the situation by Warren Hastings on 9 December 1775 indicated that the cooperation of *zamindars* and the tax-farmers was not yet spontaneous. Gradually, the system fell into disuse, and by 1781, all the four *faujdars* appointed in the Province were withdrawn (Curry 1932).

It was to the credit of Lord Cornwallis, who succeeded Warren Hastings as the Governor-General, that he gave the country, through the Police Regulations of 1792 and the Code of 1793, a 'well defined system of administration . . . a body of definite laws and procedures (and) . . . wholetime paid police officers, at a time when such an agency (was) unknown anywhere else in the world except Dublin' (Gupta 1974:46). These well-meaning reforms by Cornwallis did not, however, greatly alter the 'deplorable state of affairs' (Curry 1932). His successors, Wellesley and Bentinck, made their own efforts to tackle the 'flood of crime' that was seen in Bengal and Madras Provinces. On the report of a committee (1813) appointed by Bentinck, the Court of Directors of the East India Company ordered (1814) the reversion to the traditional village-based policing system. Significant was the transfer, at this point of time, of control over the police from the District Judge to the District Collector, who headed the revenue administration (ibid.).

This was broadly the position till 1843, when the Sind Province adopted the Royal Irish Constabulary model, which was to be extended first to Bombay in 1853, with the appointment of a Superintendent of Police for every district, and later to Madras and other parts of the country (Curry 1932). While doing so, the anxiety was not to throw overboard whatever had been experimented with by the Mughals, but to refine or improve on them. This was why one saw the Company, first abandoning the traditional village policing, only to revert to it in 1814 after finding that a newly-introduced functionary *daroga*—appointed by a Magistrate and armed with several police powers, including the recording of offences and arresting of offenders—was a poor substitute for the earlier *zamindar*, who was responsible for dealing with all the crime occurring in his holdings and was supervised by the *faujdar* (Curry 1932).

A Police Commission was constituted by the Government of India in 1860 mainly with a view to bringing down costs and enhancing police efficiency. The commission recommended abolition of the military police as a separate wing and the formation of a single homogeneous corps of civil constabulary, which would perform chores not normally assignable to the military wing. Further, there was to be an Inspector-General for each Province who was responsible for the general management of the police (Police Commission 1902).

The 1860 Commission also gave a draft bill based on the Madras Police Act for giving effect to its recommendations. This became the Police Act 1861 which placed the police on a firm footing.[1] The subsequent commissions, such as the Second Police Commission (1902), also known as the Fraser Commission—called after its Chairman, the Chief Commissioner of Central Provinces—concentrated on structural and personnel matters, including the throwing open to Indians an opportunity to be drawn into the higher ranks, which had till then remained the Englishman's preserve.

India attained freedom from the British in 1947. During the 50 years since then, there has been a manifold increase in the numerical strength of the police all over the country (Table 2.1).

There are now 39.5 policemen per 100 sq km and 137 for a population of 100,000 as against 27.3 and 131 respectively in 1981 (*Crime in India*, 1995).

No history of policing in India will be complete without a reference to the landmark study of the system by the National Police Commission (NPC) appointed by the Central Government on 15 November 1977. The six-member commission, headed by a retired ICS officer and a former Governor of Karnataka, Dharma Vira, submitted eight reports between February 1979 and March 1981.

The NPC's first report almost exclusively concentrated on the plight of the constabulary and gave several recommendations for improving

TABLE 2.1: GROWTH OF POLICE IN SOME STATES OF INDIA

States	1960	1970	1980	1995
Andhra Pradesh	36,200	42,500	49,300	72,800
Assam	15,100	29,100	32,000	48,700
Bihar	32,600	41,900	61,500	80,100
Gujarat	28,600	40,700	47,100	65,600
Madhya Pradesh	40,600	53,500	64,400	89,700
Maharashtra	62,200	76,000	93,700	1,29,300
Orissa	14,200	23,200	26,500	34,000
Tamil Nadu	29,300	41,700	49,600	73,700
Uttar Pradesh	63,700	87,100	1,26,400	1,55,200
West Bengal	49,000	63,600	66,400	78,800

Note: Figures rounded off to the nearest hundred.
Source: R.K. Raghavan (1985) and *Crime in India* (1995).

their working and living conditions, including the setting up of a full-fledged grievance redressal mechanism. Also significant was the proposal for a machinery—the District Inquiry Authority (DIA)—that would look into the more serious complaints of misconduct against the police. (This has not been implemented so far.)

The second report was pathbreaking in that it addressed itself to the task of how to prevent the police from being misused for narrow political ends, and how to confer greater operational autonomy on the policemen in the field without diluting their accountability. Two recommendations made in this connection, namely, a fixed tenure of four years for the Police Chief, and the constitution of a State Security Commission headed by the State Minister in charge of the police, are yet to be implemented. The commission went on to give a draft Police Act that would replace the 1861 Act and provide for more focussed and professional policing. This draft is also yet to find government acceptance.

The most pronounced phenomenon of post-Independence India is the birth of many new forces managed by the central government to meet the ever-increasing policing needs of the country and the growth of those already in existence (Table 2.2). This is significant because, according to the distribution of powers enumerated by the Constitution of India, 'police' and 'public order' are within the legislative competence of the state governments alone. Prominent among the forces created after Independence are the Border Security Force and the Central Industrial Security Force.

TABLE 2.2: GROWTH OF CENTRAL POLICE ORGANIZATIONS

1986	1988	1990	1992	1995
458,170	463,304	520,485	567,851	560,896

Source: *Crime in India*, 1995 and Memorandum (1994) of the IPS Central Association to the Fifth Central Pay Commission.

A noteworthy feature of recent years is the growing accent on technological sophistication in police operations. State-of-the-art wireless communication equipment (including static, mobile and walkie-talkie sets) and expansion of computerization projects form the core of on-going country-wide projects. Many of these are funded by the central government under a 'modernization scheme'.

EVOLUTION OF THE US POLICE

The US does not have a national police force, although there are several organizations working under the Federal Government. This situation is not very different from the early days when, each colony, in assertion of its autonomous status, developed its own style of administration, particularly the law enforcement machinery (Sweatman and Cross 1989). There was nevertheless a common strand, a watch system, that formed the basis for policing in each colony.

Constables and Watchmen constituted the system. Their functions were threefold. These were: maintenance of order through night patrolling and looking for strangers, performance of services such as putting out fire, lighting street lamps and clearing garbage and enforcing criminal law (Samaha 1988). There was no conscious attempt to combat crime. The philosophy was one of responding to a complaint about crime that had already taken place, rather than pre-empting it.

In essence, it was reactive rather than proactive policing. Lacking in professionalism, the colonial policeman was a small-time local functionary picked from the able-bodied citizenry and chosen in some cases by election (Walker 1983 and Samaha 1988).

Such an arrangement was adequate as long as life in the colonies was uncomplicated and centred around a rural economy. The advent of industry and urbanization in the nineteenth century exposed the limitations of an unprofessional body of watchmen who had no training to equip themselves nor a career to look forward to.

The trend prominent in England during the first half of the nineteenth century, namely, increasing crime and public disorder flowing from drunkenness, led to the creation of full-fledged forces, particularly the London Metropolitan Police. The message to police forces on the other side of the Atlantic, especially those in big cities, such as New York, Philadelphia and Boston, was not lost. Between 1845 and 1855, several American cities opted for a constabulary of the British model (Samaha 1988). New positions such as Chief and Deputy Chief, among others, were created, and police stations called 'precincts' came into being.

Notwithstanding all these developments, policing remained essentially a local affair. There was no urge or initiative to seek information on crime and public misdemeanour. The changes in the police organization were merely cosmetic. One factor that contributed to this was the resistance of the local politician who was intent on retaining his control over the department. This was the 'spoils era' in American history when the Police Chief was one 'whose sole qualification was that he would do the bidding of the politician or politicians who gave him the job' (Trojanowicz and Bucquroux 1990:48). Corruption was the order of the day, and standardization of recruitment and promotion policies through the Civil Service Act of 1883 had only a marginal impact on police image and performance (ibid.).

The transformation of the American Police from a politicized and venal body into the present modern professional force is traceable to two distinct phases of reform. First, towards the end of the nineteenth century, agitated by what they believed was the corrosive influence of politics, a group of Progressives, mainly private individuals forming the elite in society who were actuated by a strong community sentiment, pleaded for centralization of each force and upgradation of personnel. They wanted to see a stronger chief who kept the department away from the petty politician and ensured minimum standards of recruitment and performance. As a sequel, the management of many city forces was removed from the Police Board and vested in a single chief. This did not, however, bring about the much-wanted professional leadership, as the Chief invariably happened to be a non-policeman who had no equipment for the job (Trojanowicz and Bucqueroux 1990).

The second reform movement, which began around 1910 and continued until the late 1960s, owed its origin to a group of enlightened police chiefs, such as August Vollmer of Berkeley and O.W. Wilson of Chicago, among others, who successfully pressed forward a scheme to introduce science and technology into operations. Their slogan was 'professionalism', and this paved the way for improved mobility and communication in police departments, as also the induction of a corps of educated police officers.

Of the several police reform bodies set up by the Federal Government in the twentieth century, at least two deserve a mention. The first is the National Commission on Law Observance and Enforce-ment, popularly known as the Wickersham Commission—after its chairman Attorney-General George W. Wickersham—formed in 1929. Two of its fourteen reports were devoted to the police. The emphasis was on professionalism. Towards this end, it demanded improved quality of leadership, greater central control and enhanced personnel standards. Perhaps, most striking was the call for an end to brutality— a plea that had the desired impact on policemen all over the country (Fogelson 1977 and Walker 1983). The Wickersham Commission may be rightly regarded as a watershed in the history of American Police.

Police handling of the civil rights movement in the early 1960s and the serious riots in New York (1964) and in the Watts section of Los Angeles (1965) provoked a nationwide debate on police relations with the community. The appointment of a President's Commission on Law Enforcement and the Administration of Justice—also known as the Crime Commission—in 1965 was a logical sequence. Apart from reiterating most of what Wickersham had stated three decades earlier, the President's Commission was unequivocal on the need for a greater use of science and technology in day-to-day police work. It took note of the unhappy relations between the police and the community, and suggested team policing as one way to bring about a qualitative change in the scene (Fogelson 1977 and Walker 1983).

The President's Commission was closely followed by the National Advisory Commission on Civil Disorders (popularly known as the Kerner Commission, after its chairman) which repeated many of the former's recommendations. It desired a change in the style of police patrolling, especially motorized patrolling, which introduced a certain antagonism between the police and the community. Greater protection for the ghettos and increased employment of minorities were its other suggestions aimed at enhancing community confidence in the police (Walker 1983).

The Police Structure in India

Till the Mughals gave a nearly formal structure to their administrative apparatus, police functions presumably did not have the benefit of being organized on hierarchical lines. Undoubtedly, there were a few officials charged with this responsibility. It was unlikely however that they were bound by a code of discipline that we normally associate with the modern police.

The Mughal administration had the *kotwal* to police towns. He was 'paid a large salary from which he was required to defray the expenses of a considerable establishment of police' (Indian Police Commission 1902:4). In the rural area, policing was the responsibility of the *foujdar*, who had a large army of *chaukidars* to assist him locally in every village (Griffiths 1971).

The police structure has undergone only a few cosmetic changes since the British left India in 1947. 'Police' and 'Public Order' being two distinct subjects within the law-making competence of the state governments, police departments in the states account for a bulk of the police personnel in the country. Each of the 25 states has a force headed by a Director-General of Police (DGP) belonging to the IPS.

The DGP reports to the Home Secretary, a career civil servant belonging to the IAS. The Home Secretary is accountable directly to the Chief Secretary, the head of the civil service, and, subsequently, to the Minister in charge of the Home Department, an elected functionary who forms part of the Cabinet that is responsible to the State Assembly.[2]

Till a few years ago, an officer of the rank of Inspector-General of Police headed each force. The level was upgraded to Director- General mainly to widen the career prospects of IPS officers and, incidentally, to take into account the greater responsibility thrust on the higher echelons in the context of heightened political and social tensions.[3]

At the bottom of the pyramid is the Police Constable (PC), who constitutes the 'cutting edge' of the force. Between him and the DGP, there are nine levels of officers (Table 2.3).

As we saw in Chapter 1, each state is divided into a number of districts for convenient civil administration. The head of the District Police force is the Superintendent of Police (SP) who is accountable to the District Collector in matters of preservation of peace and control of crime.

TABLE 2.3: RANK STRUCTURE IN A TYPICAL STATE POLICE FORCE IN INDIA

Director-General
Additional Director-General
Inspector-General
Deputy Inspector-General
Superintendent of Police
Additional Superintendent
Assistant/Deputy Superintendent
Inspector
Sub-Inspector/Assistant Sub-Inspector
Head Constable
Constable

The SP controls a large number of police stations (PS)—the lowest formation of the local police machinery. Each station is headed by a Station House Officer (SHO) who could be of any rank, but is invariably a Sub-Inspector (SI) in a rural area, and an Inspector or Deputy Superintendent (DSP) in a town. The extent of geographical area covered by each police station varies from state to state. On an average, a rural station covers 100 sq. miles and an urban station, 25 sq. miles.

While there is no division of work in a rural police station, in the essentially urban ones, work is distributed among three distinct sections, viz., law and order, crime and traffic. Law and order personnel handle all matters concerning preservation of public peace such as patrolling, mob control, etc. Those constituting the crime section investigate all offences listed in the Indian Penal Code (IPC) and special enactments.[4]

The traffic section looks after the regulation of vehicular traffic in public places. Apart from manning specific points at road intersections, its personnel in some states, also handle investigation of road accidents.

While the staff of a town police station work in shifts, those in a rural station do not enjoy this benefit. They are expected to be available all the time, although, on paper, they are entitled to off-duty once a week.

A distinctive feature of the Indian Police is the commissionerate system that prevails in major cities. Before Independence, this was available only in the three Presidency towns of Bombay, Calcutta and Madras. Gradually, this has been extended to several others, including the nation's capital, New Delhi. This system provides for a greater freedom to the police from the Executive Magistrate (usually the District Collector and his deputies) in the matter of crowd control and issue of licences, such as those required for buying arms and running cinema houses and hotels. In a typical commissionerate, the Commissioner (normally of the rank of Additional DGP in major cities and IGP/DIG in the smaller ones) is assisted by one Additional and several Joint Commissioners, each of whom looks after a geographical area or a specific function, such as law and order, crime, traffic, etc. Next come the Deputy Commissioners (equivalent to a District SP) who have Assistant Commissioners, Inspectors and Sub-Inspectors and the constabulary working under them.

Police stations in the big cities have a much smaller area to cover, as compared to their rural or small town counterparts. The number of stations varies with cities. For instance, Madras City (now called Chennai), the capital of Tamil Nadu, with a population of nearly 6 million, has 82 police stations and 4 outposts. The largest of the Commissionerates is Delhi, which has about 41,000 personnel, a bulk of whom perform VIP Protection duties. Bombay (30,000), Calcutta (15,000) and Madras (11,000) follow (*Crime in India*, 1995).

The Armed Police in India

Grave incidents which threaten public peace require dexterous handling. They demand extreme physical fitness and mental toughness. A special group, called the Armed Reserve (AR), is available for this purpose at the headquarters of each district under the operational control of the SP. There are situations, when even the AR is unequal to the task. It is to tackle such really serious happenings that there is a Special Armed Police in every state at the disposal of the Director-General.[5] Consisting of a number of battalions, this special force is deployed in disturbed areas for assisting the District Police.

The Criminal Investigation Department (CID) in India

In the same manner, a special group of ace investigators called the Criminal Investigation Department (CID) is available at every State Police Headquarters to take over the investigation of grave occurrences, such as a political murder, large-scale riots, bank robbery involving large sums of money or theft of a precious piece of art. This wing is also used for conducting sensitive enquiries into allegations of misconduct by police personnel or other public agencies.

The Intelligence Wing in Indian Police

Every government requires an agency that keeps track of the activities of anti-social and anti-national elements, who aim at fomenting disaffection against the lawfully constituted government and disrupting normal public life. Also needed is a facility to monitor public opinion on the performance of the government so that quick corrective action is initiated to prevent a breakdown of law and order or economic stability. This twin role is fulfilled by the Intelligence branch at district and state levels. It is a sensitive group, which has to be manned by personnel of proven integrity and ability for collecting information in an unobtrusive manner. On matters of mutual interest, such as terrorism, VIP security, religious feud (especially Hindu-Muslim conflict), the State Intelligence coordinates with the Intelligence Bureau (IB) of the central government.[6]

In many states, there are also a few other specialized agencies such as Training, Railways, Home Guards, etc. Each of these is headed by an officer of the rank of Additional Director-General or Inspector-General reporting to the Director-General at the police head-quarters (Table 2.4).

Police Forces under the Central Government in India

Prior to Independence (1947), agencies under the central government, which were either fully or partially police in character, were the Intelligence Bureau (originally the Central Criminal Intelligence Department set up in 1904) and the Delhi Special Police Establishment formed in 1941 (which was to become the Central Bureau of Investigation in 1963), the Assam Rifles (born out of the Cachar Levy formed in 1835) and the Central Reserve Police (called the Crown Force to start with) formed in 1939. Since Independence, there has been a mushroom growth of central forces. These include the Border Security Force (BSF), Indo-Tibetan Border Police (ITBP), Railway Protection Force (RPF), Central Industrial Security Force (CISF) and the National Security Guards (NSG).

TABLE 2.4: TAMIL NADU POLICE ORGANIZATION

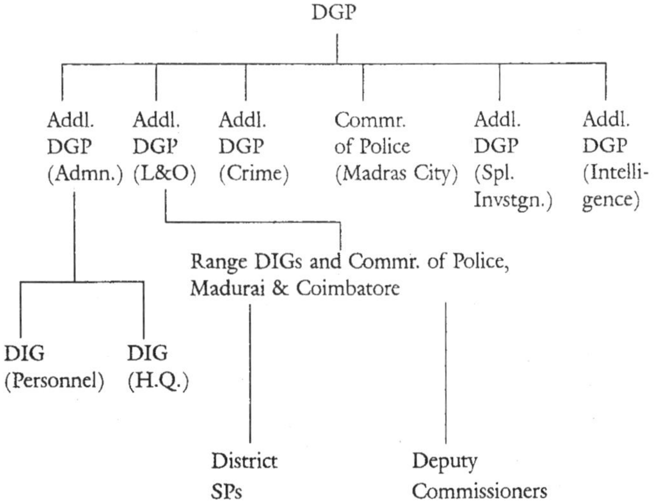

Perhaps the most useful to the states has been the Central Reserve Police Force (CRPF), which serves as a standby for them to tackle major law and order situations. It has been growing steadily with the public order situation becoming more and more complicated and state governments finding it difficult to raise their own battalions in quick time.

Phenomenal also is the expansion of the Central Bureau of Investigation (CBI), initially called the 'Special Police Establishment', that was meant only to look into allegations of corruption of civil servants working under the central government. It has now three wings: general crime, economic offences and anti-corruption. With the special consent of state governments, the CBI is now empowered to investigate matters which are normally under the domain of state police agencies.

THE POLICE STRUCTURE IN THE US

While a police force in India is either under the central or state Government, its American counterpart could fall into one of four slots—municipal, county, state or federal. This is why the US Police is so badly fragmented, making application of uniform standards problematic.

There are nearly 17,000 law enforcement agencies in the US.

About 75 per cent of these are local. The state and federal agencies account for 14 and 11 per cent respectively. More than 10,000 police departments are those operating in small towns, each employing ten or fewer personnel. There are about 155 large departments which employ 300 or more personnel. Some of the large departments include New York City (37,090), Chicago (13,032), Los Angeles (9148), Philadelphia (6,455) and Houston (5252). (The figures do not include civilian employees.) Nationally, there are about 2.3 sworn officers, i.e., non-civilians, per 1000 citizens. 90 per cent of all sworn employees are males (UCR 1996 and Samaha 1988).

A prominent feature of the US system is the substantial civilianization of the departments. Civilians make up 28 per cent of the police workforce of which 62 per cent are females (UCR 1996).

Municipal Police in the US

The municipal police, otherwise called the local police department, dominates the US scene. It performs a bulk of the police chores in small towns and big cities. Appointed by the Mayor, the Police Chief is not necessarily the one who has grown with the department. Very often, he is an outsider hired after a countrywide search.

Apart from their size, the smaller and the larger departments differ on priorities. It is the experience that small town departments are preoccupied with minor street fights and domestic quarrels. '[T]hey are peace-keepers and community service agencies, not crime fighting organizations' (Samaha 1988:160). Their organization is informal and less bureaucratic than the big city police. Solving a crime is an incidental activity. Significant here is that suburban and rural areas in the US are relatively untouched by serious crime.

A typical city police department is divided into several bureaux: Patrol, Detective and Services (such as Community Relations, Crime Prevention, School Patrol, Personnel Training, Research and Development, etc.). A Deputy Chief or Deputy Commissioner (in the larger cities such as New York and Philadelphia which have a Police Commissioner) supervises each bureau. A Chief Inspector/Inspector heads each bureau. Other lower functionaries in the descending order are Captain, Lieutenant, Sergeant, Corporal, and Detective. The lowest level is a Police Officer, also called the Patrol Officer, when on patrol duty.

Tables 2.5 and 2.6 give the organizational chart of two large departments.

TABLE 2.5: ORGANIZATION OF PHILADELPHIA POLICE DEPARTMENT

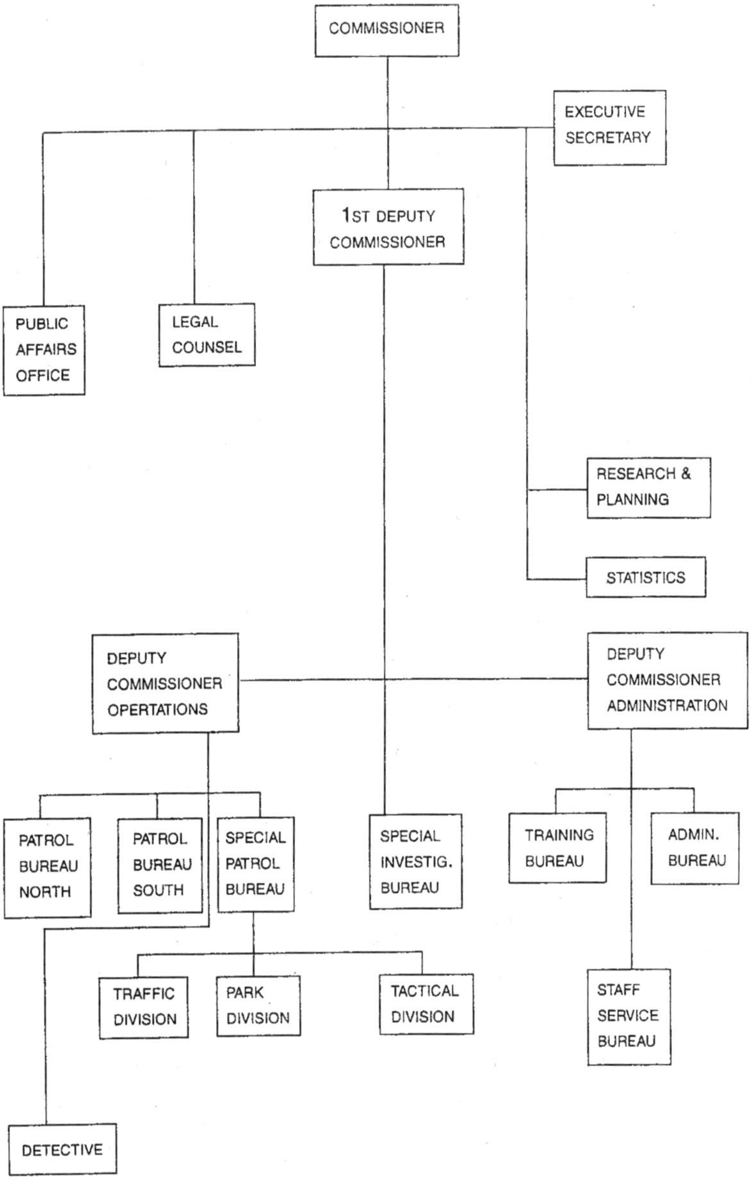

TABLE 2.6: ORGANIZATION OF ST. LOUIS POLICE DEPARTMENT

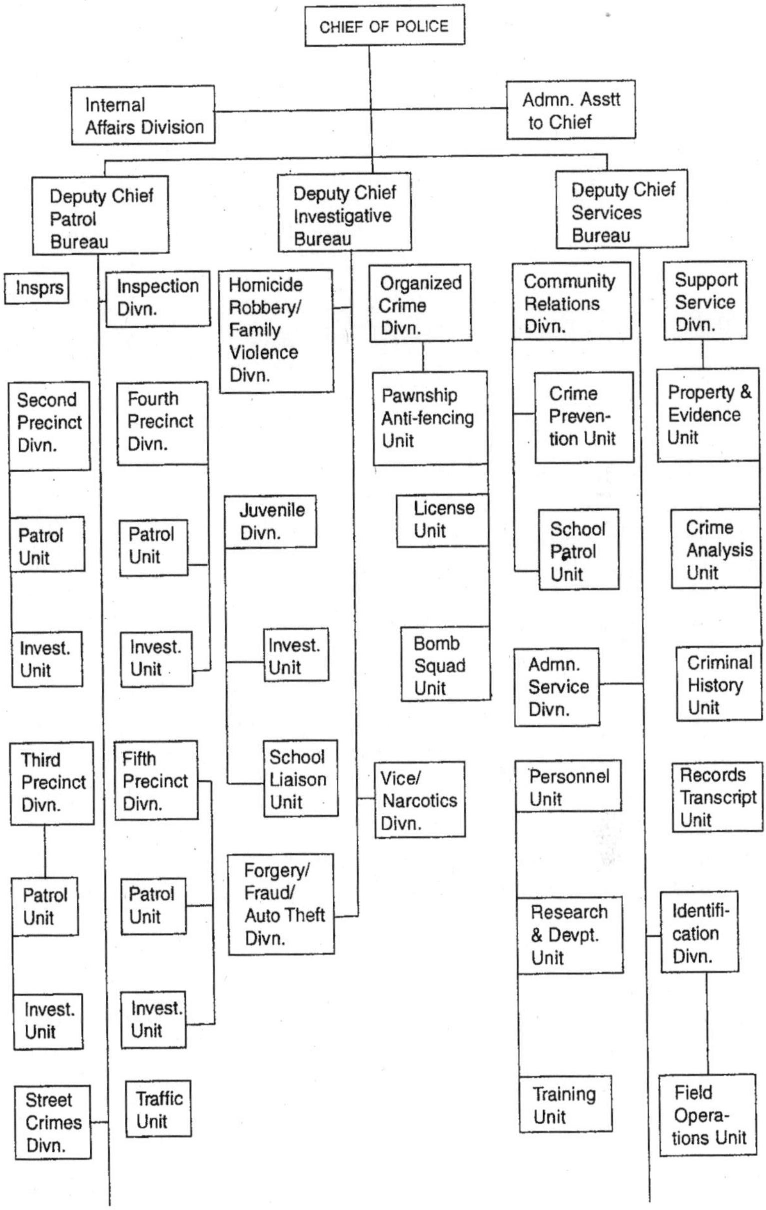

URBAN POLICING IN THE US

The Patrol Bureau is the most prominent of urban police formations. A bulk of each department's manpower is assigned to it. (New York's Patrol Services Bureau has nearly 23,350 out of a total force of about 37,000.) The bureau is divided into a number of geographical divisions. Philadelphia has nine, which are subdivided into Patrol Districts. While an Inspector commands a division, districts are looked after by Captains. There is no uniformity between districts with regard to area, population or manpower assigned. In some cities, such as Philadelphia, there is a Special Patrol Bureau, which ensures an orderly flow of traffic and investigates accident cases. It also handles special assignments, such as directed patrol of crime-prone areas, handling of explosives and rescue of hostages. Wherever they exist, marine, mounted and canine units are attached to the Special Patrol Bureau.

The Detective Bureau undertakes investigation of homicides, robberies, burglaries, assault, car thefts, etc. There is invariably a special squad that handles homicides. In Philadelphia, this squad has the responsibility for the entire city. For lesser offences, there are two squads with assigned territorial jurisdiction.

In some large cities, there is a Special Investigation Bureau working under a Deputy Chief. This takes care of very sensitive enquiries involving police misconduct and the enforcement of anti-vice law. Organized crime and narcotic offences also come under this bureau.

Counties in the US are small units of civil administration which came into existence prior to urbanization. Each of these is headed by a Sheriff, who is elected by popular vote almost everywhere, although, nomination of a citizen to this office is not entirely unknown. The Sheriff is a 'crime-enforcement agent' whose functions are threefold. As a police official, his role, like that of the local police, is primarily one of maintaining law and order. Secondly, he is a court official responsible for the execution of warrants and summonses. Finally, as a corrections officer, he is responsible for the management of county jails (Samaha 1988).

In early 1800s, there arose a need for a statewide law enforcement agency to tackle crime which cut across several towns and encompassed the jurisdiction of more than one police department. Perhaps, the first such agency so created was the Texas Rangers which was specifically charged with the task of looking after the large influx of population from other states. Several others followed suit to combat the high violence that had crept in following rapid industrialization. In course of time, the State Police acquired powers of traffic law enforcement, a development flowing from the increase in automobiles on the road (Samaha 1988).

The Highway Patrol is another statewide law enforcement agency that came into being as a logical sequel to the expansion of the highways and the subsequent phenomenal increase in automobile population. This development was seen especially during 1910-40. Highway Patrol Officers are meant primarily for traffic law enforcement. They also take cognizance of crime that occurs on or near the highways or otherwise in their presence. A distinguishing feature of the Highway Patrol Officer, often referred to as Trooper, is the extremely rigorous and sophisticated training that he receives. This is equally true of officers of the State Police (Samaha 1988).

Federal Police in the US

The concept of a national police is an anathema to the states in the US. Actually, till the beginning of the twentieth century, the Federal Government hardly played a role in law enforcement. Against the backdrop of the traditionally sanctified autonomy of the states, crime and its control were reckoned as local issues beyond its pale. It was only after an expansion of the role of the Federal Government that the concept of federal crime, such as mail fraud, came into being. This gave the impetus for action to set up police agencies which would look into the crime that transcended state borders. However, the several nationwide law enforcement agencies created during the twentieth century are hardly looked upon as police forces because they do not perform traditional police chores, including preservation of peace. Neither do they undertake any other community service (Samaha 1988, and Langworthy and Travis 1994).

Unlike the State or Municipal Police whose functions are somewhat diffused, federal agencies have a specific charter that vests in them enormous investigative authority. Perhaps the best known and the largest of national agencies is the Federal Bureau of Investigation (FBI), an arm of the Department of Justice. A near equivalent of India's Central Bureau of Investigation (CBI), the FBI has branches all over the country and a few centres abroad. Its field personnel or Agents investigate a wide spectrum of federal crime that includes organized crime and political corruption.

Another powerful national force is the Drug Enforcement Agency

(DEA), which also functions under the Department of Justice. The Immigration and Naturalization Service (INS), a wing of the Department of Justice, handles matters concerning foreign immigrants, patrols the borders and helps in deporting illegal aliens. The Internal Revenue Service (IRS), which deals with the evaders of income-tax, and the Bureau of Alcohol, Tobacco and Firearms (BATF) are two enforcement agencies which come under the Treasury Department. The Secret Service, with a strength of about 1500 agents, protects the President and also investigates counterfeiting and forgery of government security documents. Mini departments, such as the Forest Rangers and Coast Guards, perform limited criminal law enforcement activities (Samaha 1988).

Finally, there are the US Marshals who, through their deputies, effect arrests in respect of federal offences, assist in riot control, transport federal prisoners and protect federal witnesses. There is one Marshal for every federal judicial district.

A significant reserve force that has made a major contribution to tackling national calamities and widespread public violence is the National Guard, a generic term for the state-organized units of the US Army and Air Force. Originally styled the 'Militia', under Article I, Section 8 of the Constitution, it acquired its present name informally in 1824 and then formally in the 1900s (Conaway 1994 and Encyclopaedia Americana 1992).

The National Guard is composed of citizen-volunteers, who undergo a minimum required training and are available for being drafted for duty during national or local emergencies. In the mid-1970s, the total strength was 392,000 for the Army Guard and 94,000 for the Air Guard. It is funded principally by the Federal Government and, to a small extent, by state governments. It is available to the Federal Government for humanitarian missions and other peace-time engagements abroad. Within the US, it is available to the State Governor, at whose request, it is deployed to assist law enforcement agencies for restoring normalcy in a disturbed area and those hit by natural disasters.

The National Guard was frequently pressed into action in the 1960s and 1970s. For instance, 1992 was a busy year, with nearly 300 call-ups involving the drafting of 30,000 troops. During the Los Angeles riots of 1992, over 10,000 Guard members were mobilized. Interestingly, the National Guard is also used in counter-drug operations (Conaway 1994 and Encyclopaedia Americana 1992).

Comparative Analysis

Policing in India dates back to nearly two thousand years, although formal policing in its modern trapping could be said to have arrived only in the 1840s when the police in the Sind Province was reorganized on the pattern of the Royal Irish Constabulary in 1843. Interestingly, it was at about the same time that the US police moved over from a crude indigenous apparatus to an organized semi-professional force. As we have already seen, it was during the decade 1845-55 that many modern cities borrowed the British Constabulary model. It is, therefore, appropriate to say that both the Indian and US Police have had the same length of experience of ups and downs in their growth.

As we saw earlier in the chapter, there have been two distinct phases of police reform in the US during the past hundred years. While the private citizens were the moving force behind the first, the second was propelled by a few distinguished police chiefs. Their concern was to pull the system out of the quagmire of politics and corruption and make it clinically professional. To a large extent, they were at least modestly successful because of a certain willingness of the political system itself to go along with them. The contribution made by several official commissions such as the Wickersham Commission (1930), President's Commission (1967), Commission on Criminal Justice Standards (1973) and the Special Task Forces appointed by city departments, like those of Philadelphia, was more significant in bringing about several structural and other changes.

In contrast to the US, private initiatives at police reform in India have been too insignificant to record. All efforts have been government-inspired, albeit these have taken into account the public's poor perceptions of the police. It is to the credit of the British that, as early as 1860, they found it necessary to set up a reform commission that would suggest nationwide changes in the police. There was a similar endeavour, again by the government, in 1902, that led to the investigation into police organization and practices by another commission. Finally, 1977 saw a new central government appointing the National Police Commission (NPC). Again, unlike in the US, orchestrated attempts by police chiefs in India aimed at improving the quality of police services, have been marginal. Nevertheless, it is appropriate here to acknowledge the contribution to the thinking on the subject by many eminent chiefs, such as B.N. Mullik, D.P. Kohli, K.F. Rustamji, N.S. Saksena, C.V. Narasimhan and N. Krishnaswamy (especially in the field of communication).

We saw in the first chapter how the US is much more federal than India in its distribution of powers. Its fifty states enjoy what the average Indian would regard as high autonomy. Interestingly, within each state itself, abundant autonomy exists in the administrative structure. This is especially true of the police. This is why there are nearly 17,000 law enforcement units in the country; 75 per cent of them are local and free from any central control.

In striking contrast, policing in India is a highly centralized activity, with the qualification that the centralization is at the state and not at federal level. This would mean that, while the central government has constitutional authority to supersede the state government or give executive directions to it, there is no superior-subordinate relationship between their respective police agencies. They have independent areas of operation although, lately, a certain inter-dependent relationship has evolved.

While the US Police may be put into four slots—federal, state, municipal and county—its Indian counterpart has just two, viz., central and state. The State Police in India, with a single head, the Director-General of Police (DGP), encompasses all functions, including those discharged by the municipal and county departments in the US. The trend seen increasingly in India is one of making the State Police Headquarters more and more powerful. This has been the result of technological improvements ushered in during the past three decades. Sophisticated radio communication (UHF/VHF telephones, both stationary and mobile) and computer networks have given so much of control to the DGP and his staff officers that the autonomy of field officers has been severely eroded. (The situation is partly explained also by the pressure exerted on the police leadership by the executive, in their anxiety to ensure that even trivial grassroots incidents do not get blown up and affect larger geographical areas.) This is a phenomenon that may be difficult for an average American police executive to comprehend, because he is accustomed to a vast area of discretion in decision-making.

An interesting point for comparison is the size of police forces. While the larger cities in the two countries enjoy near parity in terms of strength of personnel, there is a noticeable disparity in the manpower allotted to the smaller formations. For instance, in the most populous state of the US, California, if the strength of the Los Angeles police is excluded, the rest of the state has about 14,700 policemen spread over 344 departments (UCR 1993). The Indian counterpart, Uttar

Pradesh (which does not have a large metropolis anywhere near to Los Angeles) has 155,183 policemen. This would give an idea of the dimensions of manpower management in the Indian Police.

A more meaningful comparison perhaps is the one between the smaller US departments and the grassroots police units in India, the police stations. (To an extent, police departments of the large cities in US, such as Los Angeles, New York, Houston and Philadelphia, can be equated with the city police forces in India.) An average rural police station in India has about fifteen to twenty personnel. This is about the size of a very large percentage of the seventeen thousand and odd law enforcement agencies in the US.

One striking feature of the Indian Police is the near unity in the number (11) and the nomenclature of the ranks constituting the state police forces. An analysis of the structure of the US Police reveals a marked divergence in practices. While the head of Los Angles Police Department (LAPD) is called the Chief, his New York counterpart is the Commissioner, and, in Chicago, he is known as the Superintendent. The number of ranks is also smaller, usually six to seven.

Another area that provides the scope for an interesting analysis is the political and administrative control over the police. The autonomy of the typical Indian police forces is greatly diluted by two external influences—the political executive and the administrative authority that functions directly under that executive. While the former used to be a source of remote control till a few decades ago, recent events suggest a more intimate and direct intervention in the day-to-day police functioning. The other influence is that of the administrative apparatus headed by the Chief Secretary in every state and one of his deputies, the Home Secretary, who handles all the logistics required by the police in the field. The impact of these two external agencies on the style of policing can only be felt and not explained in substantive terms.

One does not see a parallel situation in the US. There is no doubt a measurable influence of an elected official in the form of the Mayor—an office that exists in a number of large and smaller cities—who has a say on who his Police Chief will be. Literature on the Mayor-Police Chief relationship does not suggest the kind of a nexus between the political executive and the Director-General of Police that exists in a typical state in India.

There is yet another difference. The Managing Director/City Manager (who are career civil servants chosen for their expertise to assist the Mayor and elected Councils) does not have the vastness of authority over the Police Chief that a Chief Secretary/ Home Secretary in a state in India exercises over the police. This accounts for the thinking within the Indian Police that they should be autonomous from the rest of the civil service and that they should be accountable only to the judiciary. (The demand for the replacement of the 1861 Police Act with a new Act mentioned earlier in the chapter is relevant here.)

The marked growth of Central Police Organizations (CPOs) is a major development in the Indian Police since the British left Indian soil. More noticeable is the close relationship between them and the State Police in areas such as maintenance of law and order, investigation of sensational crime, and training. All pointers are that this collaboration will only grow in the years to come and not diminish. This is particularly in the context of the growing terrorist menace.

An identical development is noticeable in the US. One would necessarily have to consider the FBI, which, apart from investigating federal crime, also looks after domestic intelligence, a function that is performed in India by the Intelligence Bureau of the Central Government. More than before, the FBI may, therefore, be expected to work closer with local police departments.

In one respect, India has done better in the area of resources for tackling large-scale civil disorders. The constitution of the Central Reserve Police Force (CRPF) has been sagacious. With its enormous resources, the CRPF is a great ally of the state governments in tackling civil disturbances. Even states which are run by political parties different from the one controlling the central government have found the CRPF acceptable and highly effective. The US police departments do not have such a fall-back arrangement, because the National Guard, a near equivalent of the CRPF, is only a body of volunteers that does not enjoy the kind of cohesion, formal training and resources which the CRPF can extend to its personnel.

NOTES

1. The Police Act of 1861 remains the bedrock of policing in the country, although many states and cities have additionally their own enactments to supplement it.
2. In view of its vital nature, the Home portfolio is normally held by the Chief Minister himself in many states.

3. It is usual in each state to have four officers of the rank of Director-General. While one of them, normally the seniormost, heads the Police Department, the others hold jobs outside the police.
4. Perhaps Tamil Nadu is the only state where 'crime' in police parlance has the narrow connotation of offences against property such as theft, burglary, robbery, dacoity and murder for gaining the victim's property.
5. The Special Armed Police goes by different names in the various states: Provincial Armed Constabulary (PAC) (in Uttar Pradesh), Punjab Armed Police (PAP), and Tamil Nadu Special Police (TSP).
6. The State Intelligence is normally divided into a Special Branch that deals with matters affecting public order and a Security Branch that deals with VIP security. In many states, there is a third branch that almost exclusively handles anti-terrorist operations.

3

Maintaining Law and Order

> What we need are alert officers, quick movement, reliable communications, a free hand to the men on the spot. In actual fact, all disturbances turn out to be test of administrative morale. If there is a strong political will and proper administrative direction, it should be possible to deal with any type of disturbances.
>
> *Eighth Report of National Police Commission*, India, 1981

THE CRUCIAL test of police effectiveness is how sensitive the police are to matters affecting the preservation of public peace. This area of responsibility—popularly referred to in India as 'law and order'—is discussed almost on a daily basis by the media, and reputations are either made or marred by the ability with which the police handle group violence in the streets. The US scene is different, not in terms of the intensity of violence unleashed by anti-social elements, but only because the frequency of mob violence is much less.

A failure to act quickly for the purpose of neutralizing anti-social elements who tinker with the day-to-day peace in society, reflects poorly on police professionalism. In India, inter-religious riots, especially those between Hindus and Muslims, often lead to a colossal loss of lives and property at the hands of criminals masquerading as protectors of religion. Similarly, the incapacity and, sometimes, a reluctance to step in to prevent wanton destruction of public property committed by political groups and sectarian organizations for the flimsiest of grievances, is another phenomenon that makes a few cynical of police competence. These in particular raise several issues revolving round police preparedness and ability. The US Police also suffers from a credibility problem. For instance, the Los Angeles riots of 1992 highlighted how a police force which did not take immediate control of a situation could become an object of public ridicule and wrath. The impact of such unfortunate occurrences on the police image is extremely negative.

We know that a marked improvement in the quality of criminal investigation by specialized police agencies has been made possible through the use of sophisticated scientific and technological tools. While this is so, an equally sharp police performance on the public order front has been elusive. Adding merely to the numbers of policemen does not *per se* guarantee swift action against anti-social elements. Why is this so? Is it possible to formulate a strategy or a set of ideas that would enable the police to give a better account of themselves in this vital area? These are some of the basic questions which agitate enlightened police reformers, the world over, who constantly monitor standards of policing.

THE INDIAN EXPERIENCE

The Pre-Independence Scene

A staggeringly populous nation, with a low literacy rate (52.2 per cent) and a high unemployment level, both of which are compounded by sharp religious, political and regional differences, India offers a fertile ground for social conflict that frequently manifests itself in the form of riots in public places. But this scenario will have to be viewed against the history of foreign invasions and the long drawn-out struggle for freedom from the British that began during the middle of the nineteenth century and concluded nearly one hundred years later. The nature of political evolution has understandably had a palpable impact on the quality of policing, and the happenings in the political arena continue to strongly determine police perceptions at all levels.

In the eight decades following the promulgation of the Police Act in 1861, till India became free from British rule in 1947, the police were subjected to myriad influences. More than crime, it was in the area of preservation of law and order that they were under tremendous pressure from different sources. There was the ferment in the political arena flowing from enhanced political awareness and a desire to break away from the shackles of the foreign power. This was exacerbated by pronounced bitterness between religious groups, a development traceable to the deliberate British policy of 'divide and rule'. Altogether, it was an important phase of evolution of the Indian Police as a vital arm of government for establishing stability in society. This was again a period in which certain traditions, which even now characterize police attitudes, were established.

A long-winded account of the freedom movement is not warranted here. Suffice it to say that this prolonged struggle posed many problems to the policeman in the field. Different strategies were required to tackle three aspects of the native fight against the British.

First, there was a non-cooperation movement which took the form of abstention from all obligatory responses to government activity, such as attendance at courts, participation in military service, etc. This was followed by a phase of civil disobedience, which essentially took the form of massive public demonstrations when such large congregations in public were prohibited by law. While non-cooperation, by its nature, was passive and therefore non-violent, civil disobedience led to violence against public property and public servants. There were mob attacks on police stations in Bihar, Bengal and United Provinces. In one such instance (February 1922), 22 policemen were killed at Chauri Chaura Police Station in the United Provinces.

Police reaction to such impulsive mob violence was uniformly restrained. Griffiths (1971: 255) wonders whether 'anywhere else in the world, so widespread and dangerous a movement, either could or would have been controlled with so little display of force'.

An unfortunate off-shoot of the civil disobedience movement was the terrorism that was employed by misdirected and overzealous nationalist elements, some of whom had gained more than a foothold in the Congress Party that was spearheading the freedom struggle (Curry 1932). This posed a problem which called for qualities different from those needed to counter an open movement, such as civil disobedience.

There were several instances of terrorist violence directed against the British officials, such as the 1897 murder of two officials of Poona (Bombay Province) and the 1909 murder of District Magistrate Jackson of Nasik. The raid on the Chittagong (now in Bangladesh) Armoury and two attempts on the life of Calcutta's Police Commissioner in eastern India and a series of bomb explosions in Uttar Pradesh (central India) were all indicative of the terrorist might. During 1907-17, in Bengal Province alone, the Revolutionary Party was responsible for more than 200 outrages and the murder of 20 police officers (Curry 1932).

While the initial police response was defensive and tardy, a degree of professionalism was acquired in course of time. This was clear from the number of prosecutions launched and convictions obtained, particularly in the Punjab (Griffiths 1971).

Another area in which the police found themselves in a tight corner was the delicate state of Hindu-Muslim relations. Antagonism between the communities was historically deep-rooted, traceable to the Muslim invasion of India, centuries before the British came in. There was, however, only a limited opportunity for it to explode into an ugly day-to-day confrontation. This was partly explainable by the fact that there were well-defined pockets of influence for each of the two religions, where the weaker group had to necessarily assume a low profile (Griffiths 1971).

To begin with, the British adopted a neutral stance. In course of time this yielded place to a sly support to Muslims. Some historians believe that this was not deliberate, a perception common to some former British civil servants like Griffiths (1971). There is, however, a strong body of opposite opinion that the British were in fact prone to mischief and had evolved a 'divide and rule' policy. It is beyond the scope of this volume to scrutinize the merits of the rival viewpoints. It is enough to observe that there was a marked rancour between the religionists, to which the district administration had to be sensitive. Even a trivial incident could degenerate into mindless violence.

One of the first major riots under British India was in the western city of Bombay in August 1893, when a large Muslim mob coming out of a mosque attacked a Hindu temple. (This was in reaction to incidents that had occurred in Kathiawaar earlier during the Muharram celebrations.) In the violent exchanges, about 50,000 people fled the city, 100 were killed and 800 injured (Curry 1932 and Gupta 1979).

Tension during the annual Muharram festival of Muslims and the Ganapati festival of Hindus was to become a regular feature. It was only some 'firm but judicious action' by the police that helped to check violence (Griffiths 1971).

Two riots in the Madras Presidency (now the state of Tamil Nadu) of southern India in 1912, at Tirupattur and Berhampur, saw an orgy of violence that required the use of force by the police (Griffiths 1971). The 1916 Lucknow Pact brought some temporary peace. This received a setback following the Moplah (a Muslim farming community) rebellion of August 1921 in the Malabar district of Madras Presidency.

The period 1921-40 may especially be looked upon as an era of communal discord that posed major difficulties to the police. The year 1926 was a particularly bad one. Almost the whole of India was affected by Hindu-Muslim conflict. The disharmony was most visible in Bengal, Bihar, the Punjab and United Provinces. In July that year, Muharram celebrations in Calcutta led to 28 deaths and injuries to 226. There were 71 communal riots during 1926 in Bihar and Orissa (Griffiths 1971). The next marked phase of communal violence was in 1929, when, in the Bombay Province alone, 149 people lost their lives and property worth half a million rupees was stolen. Discussing the police role around this period, Curry (1932:304-5) says: 'It was only the staunchness of the Indian Police which prevented India from falling into a bottomless pit of disaster and chaos.'

The completeness of the communal divide was obvious from the unprecedented violence that one saw during 1946-7 on the eve of the transfer of power from the British to India and to the newly carved out Muslim nation of Pakistan. There was senseless violence in Bengal, Bihar and the Punjab, which took the form of mass killing, abduction and rape. Police forces were totally stretched, and it was a measure of their discipline and determination that they did not break down totally.

India's Post-Independence Scenario

Since attaining freedom, India has gone through several traumas on the law and order front. The first problem that faced the infant nation was one of political consolidation. This called for establishing control over some of the Princely States whose rulers were anxious to retain their autonomy even after the British departed. Kashmir and Hyderabad were two such states.

While the Indian Army tackled the problem in Kashmir by throwing out the raiders (a group comprising armed tribals and members of the Pakistan Army) sent by Pakistan to pressure the ruler (Maharajah) into opting for Pakistan, it was the police that was employed in Hyderabad. The Muslim ruler of Hyderabad, the Nizam, in total disregard of all logic and geography, wanted to accede to Pakistan. Responding to popular sentiment which favoured India, the central government sent a police force which swiftly brought about a surrender of the Nizam forces. This remarkable operation, remembered even today as the 'Hyderabad Police Action', highlighted the professional skills and discipline of the Indian Police.

The next test of police efficiency came during 1947-51 from the same area in the south in a cluster of districts called Telengana. Uneven distribution of land and gross ill-treatment of farm workers by landlords had generated a strong leftist movement here. The peasants, under the aegis of the Communist Party, indulged in large-scale violence against land-holders. Since the police from Hyderabad were unequal to the task, large contingents were requisitioned from the neighbouring Madras State (now Tamil Nadu). The movement was contained in course of time, although the methods employed by the police were denounced by some as brutal and illegal.

Developments in India since 1950

Generally speaking, democracy, in its most liberal sense, has survived in India, notwithstanding the few phases of authoritarian rule at the centre and in some states. These phases have, however, been short, thanks to the sensitivity of the fundamental organs such as the judiciary, legislature and press. An undisputed fact also is the stability lent by a well-oiled civil service machinery. The police remains a vital segment of this mechanism and the mainstay of successive governments in their endeavour to maintain law and order.

The use of the police has been frequent and extensive, and the force has been criticized widely for functioning as the handmaiden of the political party in power. This impression has unfortunately become stronger over the years, because the campaign to promote the non-partisan character of the police has remained feeble.

The problems faced by the police on the law and order front since 1950 fall into the following broad categories:

(i) Violent agitations by linguistic groups for re-drawing the political map so as to earmark one state for each language;
(ii) Similar tactics of tribal groups, particularly those in the north-east region;
(iii) The demand for the re-distribution of land ownership, voiced initially by the Communist Party, and subsequently by extremist groups born out of the Indian communist movement, leading to the liquidation of 'class enemies' and police informants;
(iv) Violent agitations engineered by political parties, ostensibly in support of some live economic or social issue, but mainly to bring down lawfully elected governments;

(v) Terrorism by groups wanting to secede from the Indian Union, such as in the Punjab and in Kashmir;

(vi) Violent clashes arising out of the unconcealed fundamentalism espoused by some staunch groups among Hindus and Muslims, a few of the latter aided and abetted by Pakistan from across the border;

(vii) Endemic caste clashes in the rural hinterland, often centering round antagonistic land and related problems between the landlord and agricultural workers; and

(viii) The emergence of a sharp division between the 'forward' and 'backward' classes following introduction of a quota system for distribution of seats in educational institutions and for government staff selections, leading to public violence.

The Police Response in India

A catalogue of some major incidents reported from various parts of the country during 1995-6 is given in Appendix I. It provides the setting against which a few general observations may be made:

(a) Substantial sections of the country suffer from attempts by various groups to tinker with public order. Violence varies only quantitatively. As a result, police forces have to be in a perpetual state of readiness.

(b) Almost every state, at sometime or the other, seeks the central government's help to provide police forces, such as the Central Reserve Police Force or Border Security Force, to bring a disturbed situation under control. Requisitioning the police of a neighbouring state is also common.

(c) Police resort to firearms to quell riots is the order of the day. Very often, this is followed by a popular demand, backed by political parties in the opposition, for a judicial inquiry to find out whether such use was justified by the circumstances of an incident. Except in a very few cases, such an inquiry always ends in favour of the police.

(d) Police intervention in clashes involving rival religious or caste groups is assailed frequently as biased. This is particularly true of a Hindu-Muslim confrontation in communally sensitive states, such as Uttar Pradesh and Bihar, where a division of the constabulary into Hindus and Muslims is often alleged.

(e) In clashes pitting the ruling political party against the opposition, the police invariably tends to side with the former, particularly in the matter of arrests.

The following three areas are of contemporary relevance to police operations:

(a) terrorism;
(b) inter-religious riots; and
(c) physical protection of dignitaries (VIP Security).

Rise of Terrorism in India

Terrorism is no recent arrival to India. As already seen, a section of nationalist elements, impatient with the slow progress towards freedom from the British, and also incensed by the latter's use of repressive methods to put down political dissent, found it appropriate to use violence against British targets. Thus were sown the seeds of terrorism on the Indian soil in the late nineteenth and early twentieth centuries. In post-Independence India, sustained and unmitigated violence in the Telengana region of the then Hyderabad (present Andhra Pradesh) State against land-owners reflected a sea change in militant attitudes, but still stopped short of terrorism. Firm handling by the police proved effective in this case.

In the years that followed, there were similar displays of violence in many other parts of the country over a variety of issues, but none of these could be regarded as terrorism in its classical form.

In the late 1960s, in the Naxalbari region of West Bengal, a breakaway group of the Communist Party of India, led by Charu Mazumdar and owing allegiance to the Chinese Communist Party, unleashed unprecedented violence to prop up the demand for an early re-distribution of farm land. The group's rapport with the poorest of the poor and the traditional support of public opinion in the state for leftist causes proved a great impediment to the police and the rest of the government in taking decisive action. In many encounters with the Mazumdar group, the police lost heavily. Prolonged police action and the break-up of the group into many splinters ensured a return to normalcy in the early 1970s.

The Communist extremist movement launched by Charu Mazumdar in West Bengal, and the subsequent growth of many splinter groups which differed ideologically with him, triggered a similar development in many other states, particularly in neighbouring Bihar and the three southern states of Tamil Nadu, Andhra Pradesh and Kerala. In the latter two states, there was already a strong communist movement which provided a fertile ground for the quick consolidation of those drawing inspiration from Charu Mazumdar. This had its implications for the police who had to tackle murderous attacks on rich land-owners, bank hold-ups, raids on police stations and the kidnapping and assault of civil servants, including policemen. Access to firearms, mainly crude improvised weapons and to explosives, made dealing with the extremists a difficult proposition.

Violence has been contained substantially in West Bengal, Kerala and Tamil Nadu. But the movement is still strong in Andhra Pradesh and Bihar. In the former, the People's War Group (PWG) has been responsible for repeated murders of influential political leaders and their immediate relatives belonging to the land-owning class. In Bihar, the Maoist Communist Centre and the two groups of CPI(M) have pursued a similar policy of mindless violence. Several police personnel have been killed in landmine explosions in both states. (According to *Times of India*, 22 September 1997, in Bihar alone, extremist violence has resulted in more than 750 killings since 1994.) Various police strategies have been of no avail. The movement has now degenerated into a form of terrorism that lacks direction.

Sikh Militancy in the Punjab

Secessionist movements in the northern states of Punjab and Jammu & Kashmir—both border Pakistan—have caused great instability in a geographically vital region. In Punjab, Sikh fundamentalism had propped up the demand for a new nation of Khalistan. It received uninhibited support from the Pakistan Government, although the latter had consistently denied this.

Initially aimed at securing maximum autonomy for the Punjab within Indian Union, the movement acquired a strident secessionist tone around 1983, thanks to the leadership of a religious fundamentalist, Sant Bhindranwale. Taking shelter inside the Golden Temple, Amritsar, the holiest of Sikh shrines, Bhindranwale and a host of militant groups unleashed unprecedented terror on innocent civilians and law enforcement agencies. Finding all efforts to solve the tangle futile, with a view to putting an end to the violence sponsored by the pro-Khalistan elements, the central government organized a major offensive (Operation Bluestar) on 3-6 June 1984, to flush the sacred shrine of the militants who had built up an arsenal inside the complex.

The army and several para-military forces took part in the operation which led to the death of Sant Bhindranwale and a large number of militants.

The projected peace in the state, however, did not come about immediately. There was then a decade of ups and downs in the battle against Sikh terrorism. The assassination of Prime Minister Indira Gandhi by her Sikh police guards in New Delhi on 31 October 1984 as a reprisal for Operation Bluestar, and the nationwide retaliation against the Sikh community that followed, were a painful sequel to the Punjab terrorism. The impact of all these on the Punjab Police was incalculable. (The number of policemen killed during 1983-94 in terrorist action was 1777. This included 8 IPS officers.)

The strife saw terrorists resorting freely to the use of firearms and explosives. Apart from masterminding major assassinations, such as those of Prime Minister Indira Gandhi and prominent Sikh leader H.S. Longowal, they chose soft targets like unwary groups of the public in religious places, shopping centres and cinema houses and those travelling by public transport. Besides direct encounters with the police, as a novel tactic, militants launched many murderous attacks on police families with a view to demoralizing an already battered police force.

Punjab was under President's rule from 6 October 1983 to 29 September 1985, and again from 11 May 1987 to 25 February 1992. During these seven years, considerable operational freedom was given to the army and police in their combing operations and other modes of offensive. Among the many heroes who displayed valour and gave a high quality of leadership during this painful phase of Punjab's history, two names which will be mentioned in history books are those of J.F. Ribeiro and K.P.S. Gill—Directors-General of Police—who belonged respectively to the 1953 and 1957 batches of the IPS. Bringing their impressive physical frames to their position and displaying mental toughness to good effect, they welded the Punjab Police into a highly motivated brigade, that annihilated many dreaded terrorists and made others lay down arms.

Elections to the Punjab State Assembly were held in February 1992 after a lapse of several years. A popularly elected government has been in position since 25 February 1992. The state has gone through another round of democratic elections to the Assembly. This amazing achievement of how an internationally supported and a heavily armed terrorist movement was neutralized through a painstakingly devised multi-pronged strategy deserves a study by itself. The central government's role in giving shape to such strategy and following it up with enormous logistic support is again an example of how an effective and enlightened federal authority could react to an extraordinary situation in one of its states.

The heartening return of peace to the Punjab was not easily secured. The assassination in Chandigarh on 31 August 1995 of its Chief Minister Sardar Beant Singh in an explosion at the State Civil Secretariat, in which 18 persons were killed, was a blow. Also, during 1997, there were slight indications of a resurgence of violence in the state in the form of a series of explosions, including a blast in a railway train that killed several passengers. These fluctuations on the law and order front are a cause for concern.

Terrorism in Kashmir

More than the Punjab, it is the difficult law and order situation in the Kashmir Valley, a part of the northern state of Jammu & Kashmir, which borders Punjab on the south and Pakistan on the west, that engages the central government's close attention. The militant violence here will have to be viewed against the backdrop of the state's accession to India after the latter attained independence from the British, and the illegal occupation of a portion of the state by Pakistan, officially referred to as Pak-Occupied Kashmir (POK).

Article 370 of the Constitution of India accords a special status to Jammu & Kashmir, giving it a certain autonomy from the central government's authority to make laws affecting states. Some segments of the state's population consider this inadequate, and they openly campaign for a greater freedom from New Delhi rule. A few others, aided and abetted by Pakistan, go to the extent of asking for total secession of the state from India. It is the activities of a number of militant groups, ostensibly to prop up the demand for a secession of the territory from the Indian Union, which have disturbed peace in the Kashmir Valley. These groups derive inspiration and material aid from Pakistan's Inter-Services Intelligence (ISI) and support from sections of the local population.

The present phase of unrest over this demand may be said to have begun in mid-1989, but it was later that year, when Rubaiya Sayeed, the daughter of the then Home Minister of the central government, was abducted by the militants, that it gained strength. Since then, there have been more than 1700 such abductions (*India Today*, 15 September 1995).

Apart from bringing the whole state under direct central government rule in 1990, militant violence required large-scale stationing of the army and various central forces such as BSF, CRPF and the ITBP. The magnitude of the problem may be clear from the fact that, while in 1989, the Jammu & Kashmir Liberation Front (JKLF) was about the only group known for indulging in terrorism, now nearly thirty are in action. A few of these are Allah Tigers and Al-Umar Mujahideen, Hizb-ul-Mujahideen [reportedly the largest of groups and said to be controlled by the fundamentalist religious organization called Jamaat-i-Islami (Kashmir)], and Harkat-ul-Ansar (suspected to be controlled by the ISI of Pakistan). One recent group to surface is Al-Faran, a foreign-dominated outfit, said to have a link with Harkat-ul-Ansar (*The Week*, 8 October 1995 and *Sunday*, 5-11 November 1995).

Two major terrorist tactics are the occupation of sanctified Islamic places of worship, followed by a threat to blow them up and abduction of civilians, government officials and foreign tourists. These actions are invariably to back up the demand for the release of militants or their sympathizers held in prison by state authorities.

Perhaps most illustrative of the militant might was the take-over of the Hazratbal Mosque in October 1993 by elements belonging to the JKLF. It required tremendous ingenuity and patience on the part of the authorities to talk them out of the mosque. But there was no such success in the case of another shrine, Charar-e-Sharief, which was burnt down in May 1995. The high quality of training received by the militants in Pakistan, Afghanistan and Pak-Occupied Kashmir was in evidence here, in the ability with which those holed up in the shrine gave the slip to security forces after setting fire to the mosque. It is relevant here to mention that, among the weaponry given by the ISI to the militants, are 107 mm rockets, 60 mm mortars, automatic grenade launchers and Stinger SAMs (*The Week*, 8 October 1995).

Of the several abductions by the militants, the most daring were in July 1995. In three separate incidents, six foreigners—two Britons, two Americans, one German and one Norwegian—were whisked away into the mountains of Kashmir. While one of the Americans escaped, four are still being held hostage. The fifth, Hans Christian Ostro, a Norwegian national, was murdered and his beheaded body was recovered by the authorities on 13 August 1995. Al-Faran is suspected to be responsible for this dastardly crime, committed ostensibly to securing the release of 21 detained militants (*India Today*, 15 September 1995).[1]

President's Rule in J&K has been withdrawn. A popularly elected government headed by Farooq Abdullah is in office. It has been fairly successful in tackling the militants who remain a threat to peace.

Countering Terrorism in India

Police response to terrorism in the two states has been extremely commendable. Very high qualities of leadership and courage have been displayed. Two aspects of the scene compel attention.

Militant tactics have demanded a great degree of professionalism on the part of the State Police, a requirement that calls for new standards of recruitment and training, almost on par with those of the army and central police forces, such as Border Security Force and the Central Reserve Police Force. Secondly, police retaliation of terrorist violence has occasionally been assailed as amounting to over-reaction, giving rise to complaints of excesses. This has generated a public debate of issues associated with human rights, exerting tremendous pressure on the police at ground level.

Handling of India's inter-religious Riots

One major criticism of the Indian Police during the past three decades has been its inability to handle clashes between members of different religions, popularly referred to as 'communal riots', especially of the Hindu-Muslim variety, in a professional manner. A bias in favour of the Hindu rioters, and the delayed and excessive use of force are two specific complaints. The complexity of police tasks in the area is illustrated by a newspaper account of a Hindu procession taken out in Madras in September 1995 (Appendix II).

Commissions of Inquiry in different parts of the country have gone into the causes of many riots, apart from fixing responsibility for failures of civil servants, especially the police. Reports of these commissions are valuable for their observations on police performance. This is notwithstanding the fact that commissions are seldom appointed in quick time, and the evidence placed before them is very often garbled, leading to certain untenable conclusions (Rajgopal 1987).

The gravamen of the charge by many commissions is the initial lack of police firmness against rioters. The Jaganmohan Reddy

Commission—which went into the September 1969 riots in Ahmedabad and other Gujarat towns in which 524 lost their lives—said:

> The Police lost the initiative and, once the situation got out of control at the very commencement of the riot, they were overwhelmed by the situation which confronted them.
>
> A lack of judgement of a developing situation is another shortcoming. The District authorities, police and the magistracy, very often ignored evidence in the form of isolated incidents that could ignite religious feelings. As a result, in a short time, they were faced with a situation that required action which was beyond their capacity.

There have also been occasions marked by an utter lack of co-ordination between the police and army units called to assist them in grave disturbances. This pointed to mutual suspicion, rivalry and an inability to overcome ego considerations when dealing with major religious conflagrations. One of the commissions also referred to an unwarranted interference from the higher echelons of government. This greatly cramped the style and autonomy of field officers and thereby affected their ability to contain riots (Rajgopal 1987).

Possibly the most serious complaint is the alleged police failure to project a neutral image. The Justice Jitendra Narayan Commission—which went into the 1979 Jamshedpur (Bihar) riots—was carping on the pro-Hindu action of the Bihar Military Police. In the Aligarh (1979) and Moradabad (1980) riots in Uttar Pradesh, a similar impression of police bias against the minority community was dominant among the public (Rajgopal 1987). An article (*Times of India*, 25 April 1995) by Julio Ribeiro illustrates the point eloquently (Appendix III).

Deeply concerned over the impact of repeated clashes between religious groups on the social fabric, the central government maintains an active dialogue with state governments. One significant move is the identification of trouble-prone 'communally sensitive districts' in every state which require special attention, so that there is a continuous monitoring of inter-religious relations. Another is the move to pin down responsibility, for swift action to contain trouble, on the District Magistrate (Collector) and the Superintendent of Police. In cases of failure on their part, governments have initiated disciplinary action, such as suspension from service.

Perhaps the most positive of the moves initiated so far to tackle communal riots is the creation of a Rapid Action Force (RAF) within the Central Reserve Police Force. The RAF is a crack force that is normally airlifted to scenes of trouble so that quick action is initiated to contain explosive situations. The RAF performance till now has been satisfactory, though no serious study of its effectiveness is available to facilitate a meaningful public debate.[2]

Physical Protection of India's Dignitaries

The scourge of terrorist violence has added another dimension to police work: the task of physical protection of leading dignitaries, both past and those currently in office, threatened by extremist organizations. Designated as Very Important Persons (VIPs), these include the President, prime minister, ministers in the central and state governments, top career civil servants and leaders of political parties determined to fight terrorism.

Police responsibility here will have to be viewed against the several assassinations since Independence. The first of these, and perhaps the most traumatic, was the killing (30 January 1948) of Mahatma Gandhi, by a Hindu fundamentalist organization. The assassination of Prime Minister Indira Gandhi by her own Sikh police security personnel on 31 October 1984, of her son Rajiv Gandhi, a former prime minister, by Sri Lanka Tamil militants on 21 May 1991 and of Sardar Beant Singh, the Chief Minister of Punjab on 31 August 1995, as well as the murders of several senior police officers operating in the Punjab by Sikh extremists, highlight the importance of VIP security. The problem gets complicated by the compulsively populist style of Indian politicians who are extremely sensitive to the need to be in physical proximity to party grassroots.

Responsibility for protection rests with the police of the state in which a VIP happens to be at a particular point of time. Naturally, the heaviest burden is on the Delhi Police, which has to look after several hundred dignitaries living in the nation's capital. Constant tours of the prime minister and state chief ministers cause great stress on the police. Inadequacies in the system became glaring when Prime Minister Indira Gandhi was brutally murdered by her own Sikh police guards acting in concert with Sikh extremists. This set off a re-examination of security arrangements and the formation (1985) of an elitist Special Protection Group (SPG) which now takes care of the proximate security of the prime ministers, past and present, and their families.

All other arrangements at a place visited by a VIP however remain within the charter of the local police.

The SPG is a crack force headed by a director (of the rank of Additional DGP). It comprises young officers picked for their physical fitness and quick reflexes who are given state-of-the-art training at home and abroad. Supervision is by officers with rich field experience. A few state police forces have also begun raising units similar to the SPG to protect state government dignitaries, such as the chief minister.

Drill for Handling Public Disorder in India

It is the police station, as the basic unit of administration, that first receives a complaint/information of apprehended breach of peace or about an incident that has already taken place. In the rural areas, this is often handed in personally by an interested party. In the semi-urban and urban police stations, there is a telephone—other than the dedicated internal radio telephone—accessible to the citizen and by means of which, news of an incident is very often received from the public. There are also instances of patrolmen alerting a police station. In the larger towns and metropolises, police control rooms receive calls from the public and activise police stations or patrol vehicles.

Police stations respond by despatching small parties of policemen who may not always carry any arms with them. This is normally adequate in a majority of cases. In more serious incidents, where rival parties have employed weapons, police stations invariably indent on the Armed Reserve, which consists of personnel trained to disperse mobs through the use of tear-gas shells or firearms (usually .303 rifles). Police stations do have similar firearms which are, however, used only in extreme emergencies, such as a mob attack on the station premises. In graver situations, when even the Armed Reserve is unequal to the task of restoring order, the State Special Armed Police steps in on the DGP's specific order.

Preventive Action by the Indian Police

There is a reasonably sensitive and focussed machinery down to the level of a police station or a group of stations (called the Circle), which is responsible for keeping track of trends on the ground, so as to facilitate timely preventive action whenever a breach of peace is anticipated. This takes the form of an Intelligence Branch, both at the

State Police and the District Police Headquarters. The former is supervised immediately by an Inspector-General/Additional DGP. It has staff up to the level of a district. In addition, every District Superintendent of Police (SP) has an Intelligence or Special Branch Inspector (in some states, of the rank of Deputy Superintendent) who acts as his 'eyes and ears'.

The task of the Intelligence staff is to keep track of trends which point to dissatisfaction over any act of commission or omission by the government, or that of any individual/group, and is likely to inflame public opinion and affect public peace. Issues as disparate as the non-availability or short supply of essential articles of daily consumption, such as food, water or fuel, misconduct of a civil servant towards the public, show of dishonour to religious symbols, or a wage dispute between the management and labour in an industry, are all capable of snowballing into major conflicts which need close monitoring.

Information on a developing situation, of the kind described, is promptly passed on by Intelligence to the civil authorities. The latter initiate appropriate steps to redress a grievance through negotiation or administrative measures. When such action fails to assuage feelings, and there are individuals determined to embarrass the government by resorting to unlawful modes of agitation, the civil administration normally draws on the authority conferred on it by statutes and sets in motion swift preventive action.

Two important provisions of the Criminal Procedure Code (CrPC) are relevant. First, under Section 144, the administration may direct an individual or persons living in a particular area or the public in general to desist from an act that is likely to disturb public tranquillity. This enables the administration to ban a public gathering of five or more persons for a specified period. Section 145 gives similar authority in respect of a dispute over land or water that threatens public peace. Orders under the two sections are promulgated by the Executive Magistrate on a recommendation from the police or otherwise.[3]

Some provisions of the Police Act 1861 also come in handy to the police. One of these is Section 30, whereby a District Superintendent of Police or his Assistant/Deputy may regulate public assemblies and processions by insisting on their organizers to obtain a prior licence which imposes certain conditions, such as the specific route along which a procession may be taken. Violation of licence conditions invites penal action.

Additionally, the police can make preventive arrests under Section

151 of the CrPC. It has been the police experience that such arrests sometimes lead to further trouble, and hence these could be only the last alternative. Section 107 permits a Magistrate to bind over rival parties, locked up in a dispute, to good behaviour for a specified period. This has also been found useful in maintaining peace.

THE US EXPERIENCE

Developments during 1850s-1980s

Three distinct periods of violent strife in American society are identifiable from the middle of the nineteenth century (Gurr 1989b). The first (1850-76) coincided with the Civil War and the Presidential Reconstruction, namely, the military administration, in southern cities and towns. The dominant issues which led to tension were abolitionism and the revival of southern white hegemony. About 80 riots by whites against the freed slaves and their northern supporters were reported from the south during the first decade after the Civil War (ibid.).

The second period (1880-1920) was marked by 'industrial conflict and violent social regulation'. Prominent characteristics were large-scale immigration, sizeable expansion of industry and the growth of urban centres. There were also bloody clashes between workers and employers. Violent white antipathy to the black continued to be in evidence. Lynching of blacks was a frequent occurrence. Between 1891 and 1901, there was an average of 100 black victims each year (Gurr 1989b).

Perhaps the worst incident of the decade was the East St. Louis massacre of 1917. In reaction to the heavy influx of blacks into the city and the growing competition for work from them, the whites started applying pressure tactics to coerce them into leaving the place. In May that year, after a labour dispute, many whites roamed the streets attacking blacks. Peace returned following the intervention of the National Guard and the exodus of sizeable sections of the black community. The lull was only temporary, as there was again violence following the black attack on a police vehicle. 9 whites and 39 blacks were killed in the police action that ensued (Berry 1994).

The most prominent features of the third period—mid-1950s to the 1980s—were the collective protest actions to press the government for social reforms and the strident reaction from the 'small and relatively powerless groups who felt threatened by change'(Gurr 1989b:20). In this comparative study, we are more immediately concerned with this phase.

Enormous social strife rocked the US in the early 1960s. Great expectations of 'abundance, freedom and justice' had been aroused by President Kennedy's civil rights agenda and these were never realized (Samaha 1988 and Trojanowicz and Bucqueroux 1990). There was a persistent feeling of economic injustice and discrimination. Frustration and anger triggered large-scale riots in many cities, and the Black Power movement launched by groups such as the Black Panthers resulted in bloodshed between rioters and the police. During this decade, there were more than 500 riots.

Perhaps the worst racial riot after the 1917 East St. Louis massacre was the happening in Watts, a predominantly black locality of Los Angeles, in August 1965. Here again, a black arrest led to looting and burning of stores and assault on police officers and citizens. The National Guard had to be called in. Before they restored peace, 34 had been killed and 1000 injured. There was heavy loss to public property. Nearly 4000 were arrested (Pate 1994).

The peak of racial strife was seen in 1966 and 1967. Widespread rioting was reported from Los Angeles, Chicago and Cleveland in June 1966. This was followed by incidents in more than 20 cities—such as Omaha, Dayton, San Francisco and Atlanta—during July and August. According to Pate (1994), the Detroit riots were the worst since the Civil War draft riots in New York City: 43 were killed and 1000 injured. More than 7000 were arrested and property worth $ 50 million damaged.

Efforts to improve the lot of the race were initiated by the administration. Violence nevertheless continued. Simultaneously, there was an upsurge of street crime. The police came under critical scrutiny. Public opinion, instead of probing the sociological causes which contributed to the upheaval, was carping on police performance. 'Law and Order' became the frequently heard slogan and became expectedly a major issue of the Presidential campaign (Samaha 1988 and Trojanowicz and Bucqueroux 1990).

On being voted to office, President Johnson, determined to implement President Kennedy's resolve to push through a regular civil rights legislation, appointed an influential Commission on Law Enforcement and the Administration of Justice. Its 1967 reports suggested far-reaching fundamental changes in police organization and methods. The commission exhorted the police to establish closer ties with the community (Trojanowicz and Bucqueroux 1990). Even before the commission's reports could be implemented, the situation was compounded, first by Martin Luther King's assassination, and later by campus protests over Vietnam and the draft.

Civil disorder and street violence around this time was of such magnitude that the government thought it necessary to direct two other commissions to examine the issues involved. The National Advisory Commission on Civil Disorders (Kerner Commission) and the National Commission on the Causes and Prevention of Violence (Violence Commission) which went into the riots of 1960s were of the view that the police had failed to accord due priority to organization and deployment strategies, as also to the community needs (Trojanowicz and Bucqueroux 1990).

The impetus for changes in police organization and mechanics outlined by all three commissions came in the form of an Omnibus Crime Control and Safe Streets Act 1968. The Law Enforcement Education Programme (LEEP) and the National Institute for Law Enforcement and Criminal Justice (NILECJ) were a concrete outcome of the 1968 Act. Much later, these were to set the tone for what was to be known as 'community policing' or 'new professionalism', and a whole new set of ideas on how the police should fulfil its role of order maintenance.

President Nixon's election in 1968 halted an expansion of the schemes to improve black conditions, although no cut in existing programmes was imposed. As a sequel, one saw the gradual demoralization of black groups and a pessimism about their future, alongside a marked deceleration of violence by early 1970s (Gurr 1989b).

There was one positive outcome of the riots for the average black, in the form of an increase in 'black pride and racial identity' , and the emergence of new groups, as well as electoral mobilization of blacks. One also saw several cities, especially those hit by riots, electing black Mayors (Gurr 1989b and Button 1989).

The 1970s and 1980s were marked by an escalation of criminal violence, along with intense social violence caused by discontent on many fronts. Brown (1989a) attributes this to a 'stressful assimilation' of changes in race relations and economic affairs.

Besides the protest action against the Vietnam War which lasted until 1975, the 1970s were rocked by violent labour unrest. In particular, 1974 saw a national strike by independent truck drivers who were hit by shortages and high fuel prices. In order to quell the violence that ensued and to keep the main highways open, the National Guard was called out in eight states. Several were killed and injured (Brown 1989a).

The 1980s were significant for the downward trend in agriculture. A depression struck the Midwestern farm belt leading to a decline in the number of agricultural workers and a consequent disruption of life in the rural areas. Two violent incidents of 1983 deserve a mention. One was the murder of two bankers in rural Minnesota by a discontented father and son. The other was the murder of two Federal Marshals by Gordon W. Kahl, a North Dakota farmer, apparently acting under the banner of Posse Comitatus, an ultra-right-wing organization which drew some support from those affected by the farm depression (Brown 1989a).

A striking change during the course of past three decades in the class structure of urban America is relevant here. By 1980s, it could be confidently said that America had become decisively pluralistic, multi-cultural and liberal. From an essentially rural and southern group, the black community had become dispersed substantially from the south into a significant segment of major cities in different parts of the country. Thanks to the civil rights movement they had registered several gains rendering the earlier 'iron-clad segregation', a thing of the past (Brown 1989a).

In spite of all these developments, there was no corresponding social peace. Black-white relationship was still delicate and very often adversarial. A perceptible migration of the more affluent sections to suburban areas rendered cities heavily dominated by the poor. This was essentially a black influx into major cities and the white exodus therefrom. According to one estimate, nearly six million blacks moved out of the south to settle in the north-east, mid-west and the west coast, mainly the Los Angeles area (Gainsburg 1994). This phenomenon will have to be viewed against the undisputed economic inequality between the average white and the other ethnic groups, such as the black and Hispanic, which started widening in the 1970s (Bradsher 1995). Alongside this development was a proved neglect of cities by the government, a trend that became pronounced under the Reagan administration (Rivlin 1992).

An associated feature of the urban setting in the 1980s was the rising graph of violent crime. A simplistic and controversial interpretation—perhaps racist in its overtone—was that the black and

Hispanic domination of cities had accentuated the fear of crime, which, in turn, generated an exodus to the rural and suburban areas. While it was difficult to pinpoint which had been the cause and which the effect, levels of fear of crime became distinctly higher in cities (Moore and Trojanowicz 1988a).

Robberies and street violence involving the two communities were soon becoming frequent, and induced some observers to believe that these were a 'substitute' for protest rioting (Brown 1989a). For instance, 17 people were killed in three days of rioting in May 1980 at Liberty City, Miami. The provocation for this was the acquittal of the white men who were being tried for the murder of a black insurance agent (ibid.). One trend that caused acute concern was the expansion of drug-dealing gangs comprising young inner-city males. More than any other development, this phenomenon highlighted the government's failure to provide 'adequate' and 'socially useful' jobs for the urban ghetto residents (ibid.).

Law and Order in the 1990s: The US Experience

Events since 1989 suggest that law and order problems have become more complex than ever before. Exchanges between the lunatic fringe among both the whites and blacks are frequent causes of disorder. Even trivial happenings, which would normally pass off for common crime, take on a racial hue, a trend akin to that seen in India on the Hindu-Muslim front. But police attention has now to look beyond white-black relations. The growth of Asian groups, in terms of number as well as economic might, has introduced a new dimension that has the potential of being explosive from the law and order viewpoint in major cities, such as New York and Los Angeles.

Two other strands of the scene also deserve to be reckoned. One of these is the continued substantial presence of white supremacist groups whose Fascist propaganda packs enough venom to disturb public peace. The other is the arrival of modern terrorism on American soil as evidenced by what happened at the World Trade Center, New York in 1993, at Oklahoma City in 1995 and at the Olympic Park at Atlanta in August 1996 during the Olympic Games.

The three features of the present-day US scene mentioned above receive some attention in the succeeding paragraphs.

Race Relations

The May 1989 attack on a white woman jogger at New York's Central Park by a gang of black youth highlighted not only the contours of urban crime, but pointed also to the nature of the problem faced by those working toward harmony between the two strongest groups in American society. This was followed by the August 1989 Bensonhurst (Brooklyn) shooting by white youth against a group of blacks in which one of the latter, 16-year-old Yusef Hawkins, was killed. Black demonstrations in the essentially white Bensonhurst led to tension. The fact that none was convicted for the murder led to black criticism of a discriminatory criminal justice system (Berry 1994).

Subsequently, in April-May 1992, the Los Angeles riots—triggered directly by the acquittal of four Los Angeles policemen in shocking disregard of the video-tape evidence of their brutal assault of a black motorist—accounted for 58 casualties. Again, in early July 1992, there was mob violence in the Washington Heights area of New York, following the death of an immigrant from the Dominican Republic in a police shooting. Rioters ransacked buildings and indulged in arson and bottle-throwing.

The acquittal (October 1995) of former black football star O.J. Simpson, charged with the murder of his ex-wife and her friend (both white), by a predominantly black jury, provoked countrywide reactions which took predictably racial lines. While the black community displayed unconcealed jubilation, white opinion was unanimous that a 'guilty' person had been let off the hook solely on colour and that the distortion in the criminal justice system needed immediate correction. Media analysts were positive that America unmistakably stood divided racially, something that did not augur well for future social peace.

The racial tension that has come to characterize American urban life has taken on a new complexion with the shrinking economic opportunities pitting the black not merely against the white, but against other groups such as Hispanics as well. A further dimension to these social cross-currents is lent by the black dislike for Asians, mainly Chinese and Koreans, who have taken substantially to small trade in major cities. Also discernible is the Hispanic antipathy to the Korean trading class. This was in evidence during the LA riots of 1992, when the Hispanics indulged in large-scale looting of Korean shops (Oliver *et al.*, 1993). These factors pack the urban scene with a complex set of interactions that directly impinge on city policing.

THE MILITIAS AND WHITE SUPREMACIST GROUPS IN THE US

Racially-motivated violence between whites and blacks dates back to 1712, when the first slave uprising was put down ruthlessly. The Stono rebellion (South Carolina) of 1739 and the New York City rampage of 1741, in which white fury resulted in the burning and hanging of several blacks, again demonstrated the intensity of hatred.

Several slave uprisings of the next century also produced great violence. Not reconciled to the end of slavery, whites of the south formed the Ku Klux Klan (KKK) in 1866, a body intended to intimidate Radical Republicans of the Reconstruction era and to re-establish the whites' right over slaves. While the KKK faded thereafter around 1871-2, it re-appeared in Atlanta in 1915. Unlike earlier, when it was confined to the south, this time, the new KKK managed to gain support in several other parts as well. While it was the strongest in Indiana, its presence was felt also in Oregon and Colorado. Further, there was a departure from the past, in that the Klan now unleashed its strong-arm tactics more at those who did not conform to the 'Bible Belt morality'. Blacks, along with Jews and Catholics, were only secondary targets. A third-time revival of the KKK was in the 1950s, when it played a major part in the violence against the civil rights movement (Gurr 1989b and Brown 1989b).

The 1980s saw the emergence of a variety of white supremacist and far-right groups, who were the perpetrators of violence in some parts of the country. Among several reasons cited for this development, one was the stress resulting from a need to assimilate changes in race relations and economic affairs. Around this time, there was a perceptible drop in the numbers engaged in agriculture and the simultaneous depression that was obvious in the mid-western farm belt (Brown 1989b).

Two violent episodes of the period—the 1983 murder of two Minnesota bankers and of two Federal Marshals by a North Dakota farmer, already mentioned above—brought to light the existence of an organization, Posse Comitatus. Although the Comitatus claimed itself to be a farmers' body spearheading the tax-resistance movement, the murder of Marshals indicated that it was more a part of the fanatic rightist fringe (Brown 1989a). (According to *Time,* 19 December 1994, the Comitatus is now moribund.) Other organizations similar to the Comitatus which have come to notice, include the Aryan Nations (Idaho), Survivalists (Idaho, California and Montana),

Christian Identity and Wise Use (*Time*, 8 May 1995). These groups generally look upon themselves as the defenders and upholders of the Constitution and are uniformly violence-prone and anti-federal control in their approach and philosophy.

Somewhat akin to the above bodies are militias which have sprung up in nearly 30 US states. Most active in the mid-west and the west, these are also armed groups which seriously believe that the US Constitution is in peril and that it needs their armed protection. The better organized of these are the Michigan Militia and the Militia of Montana (reckoned as the most belligerent). Militias are white-dominated. They however claim to be non-racial. There is growing evidence of their links with hate-mongering groups (*Time*, 19 December 1994).

Many of the militias involve their members in military-like endurance-building hardship exercises in rugged territory, so as to prepare them for, what they consider, a prospective 'insurgency' by the Federal Government or external foes, such as the Russians. The communication systems of some militias are highly sophisticated. Publicity and propaganda are quite often through radio talk shows and the Internet.

The explosion (19 April 1995) at a large federal government building in Oklahoma City which caused enormous destruction and loss of 168 lives, shook the whole nation. More shocking was the revelation that the prime suspect, Timothy McVeigh, had possible links with the Michigan Militia. This strengthened the fears that, while a majority of militia members might not subscribe to violence, the basic philosophy of such militias attracted and permitted infiltration by rabid elements who were driven by extremist impulses and grievances over actions of police agencies.

Two incidents of recent years are known to have excited many militia members. One was the 1992 violent encounter between law enforcement officials and white separatist Randy Weaver in rural Idaho. Two members of Weaver's family (including his wife) were killed in the exchange of fire. Next was the AFT/FBI attack on the Branch Davidian headquarters in Waco (Texas) on 19 April 1993, in which cult leader David Koresh and 82 followers were killed. The Oklahoma explosion was possibly intended to synchronize with Waco's second anniversary.

THE TERRORIST MENACE

FBI reports of 1980s pointed to terrorist activities by several US Jewish groups engaged in publicity to alleged injustice meted out to their community. The FBI attributed 18 terrorist incidents during 1981-5 to these groups, most important of which was the Jewish Defence League (JDL) (Sullivan and Victor 1988).

During the 1980s, US citizens and property became repeated terrorist targets. According to a State Department estimate (1994), more than 400 Americans were killed in action since 1987 by Middle Eastern terrorist groups. (Most gruesome was the 1988 explosion on board a Pan Am flight over Ireland.) Significantly, these attacks took place outside the US.

The 1990s have thrown up evidence of the presence of international terrorists inside the US and their resolve to disrupt life within the country. Two major incidents heralded the arrival of terrorism, as it is understood internationally, on US soil.

The first was the 26 February 1993 explosion in the basement of the World Trade Centre in New York in which six people were killed and more than one thousand injured. Sustained investigation unearthed the hand of Arab terrorists. The second was the 1995 Oklahoma City explosion. This was the work of a US national with white militia links who nursed a grievance against the Federal Government. According to Brian M. Jenkins, an authority on terrorism, the Oklahoma explosion was significant not only for its unprecedented scale of attack, but also for its roots in the 'lunatic fringe of the extreme right' (Copper 1995).

A third incident (August 1996) on American soil was the Olympic Park explosion in Atlanta during the Olympic Games. International terrorist groups were originally suspected. Subsequent investigations explored whether white supremacists were involved. Till early 1998, investigation had not come to any definite conclusion.

Apart from the above, according to FBI and State Department reports, there were 32 incidents in the US during 1989-94 involving domestic and international terrorists. Included in these were nine firebombings of fur stores by the Animal Liberation Front (FBI 1993 and US Department of State 1995).

Parcel bombs are also not unknown to the US. A mysterious individual, the Unabomber—so-called because many of the victims have been associated with universities—has been responsible for a number of bombings during the past 17 years in which three people were killed and 23 injured (*Congressional Quarterly Researcher*, 21 July 1995). The April 1996 FBI arrest of Ted Kaczynski, a Harvard-educated maths professor who taught at Berkeley, near Lincoln (Montana), was believed to have solved the mystery of the Unabomber.

The Response of US Police

The arrival of city police departments during the middle of the nineteenth century with a clear-cut charter did not necessarily lead immediately to any functional specialization. Forces continued to be multi-activity bodies although patrolling dominated their routine (Samaha 1988). There was a certain vagueness in the public thinking on police role. Not many knew as to what the police should do besides order maintenance. As a result, a wide variety of chores were imposed on them. These included cleaning the streets, distributing supplies to the poor and operating emergency ambulances. Naturally, the focus shifted from peace preservation to reactive attention required by a spectrum of community needs (Fogelson 1977).

The police at this time operated against heavy odds, chief of which was the general public distrust of any agency 'that imposed obligations on a free citizenry' (Philadelphia Police Task Force 1987). The only way they could gain acceptance in the society was to establish close rapport with the politicians, who, around this time, began to dominate the urban life. Police intervention was naturally biased in favour of the local politician.

The same lack of objectivity was seen in the police attitude to strikes, pickets and other demonstrations. Steeped in conservatism and displaying a preference for the *status quo* that gave them several privileges, policemen were hostile to labour unions, radical groups and racial minorities. Only on select occasions—in situations threatening to go out of control or bring discredit to the political bosses—did the police rise above petty considerations to act objectively and decisively (Fogelson 1977).

Also, police operations were precinct-oriented. It was only during major happenings, such as the draft riots of 1860s, the railroad strikes of 1870s and the great industrial disputes of 1880s, that the police headquarters took control (Fogelson 1977).

A significant move of the reformers, who attempted extensive professionalization of the departments in early twentieth century, was the reorganization of departments along functional lines. Perhaps the first to do so was LAPD in mid-1920s, followed by Chicago in the early 1930s, and later by New Orleans and San Francisco. Equally noteworthy was the creation of many special squads in each department, by divesting the patrolman of many functions.

By the late 1950s and early 1960s, police image as professional crime fighters had no doubt been fairly well established. With the introduction of the telephone and automobile, 'the neighbourhood cop had been replaced by the motor patrol officer' (Langworthy 1994:86). One now heard public complaints of a lack of response to day-to-day concerns which did not satisfy the narrow definition of 'crime' (Trojanowicz and Bucqueroux 1990). It was believed that the focus on serious crimes such as murder, rape and robbery had led to a de-emphasis of emergency services and maintenance of order (Philadelphia Police Task Force 1987).

The anti-Vietnam protests and the civil rights agitation of the 1960s posed serious problems to the police in many parts of the country. Strong-arm methods had to be employed to quell the violent riots. Naturally, complaints of police excesses were frequently voiced in public forums. Simultaneously, one heard the demand for a tough law and order policy. The dilemma here was that, since a majority of departments were small and inexperienced to handle major riots, the traditional attitude of looking upon law enforcement as a purely local function had to be given up (Button 1989).

The turning-point was the Detroit riot of July 1967, which highlighted police incompetence in countering grave disorder. The stage was, therefore, set for a greater federal intervention. As a result, requisitioning the National Guard and US Army became an acceptable practice. Apart from stockpiling anti-riot equipment in different parts of the country and training nearly 15,000 men in civil disorder service, army intelligence collection on potential rioters was greatly stepped up. The 1968 election of Nixon to the Presidency also saw the authorization of FBI to do electronic surveillance as a means of countering ghetto violence (Button 1989).

Administrative response at state and local levels to the civil disturbances of 1960s did not lag far behind the Federal Government. Most of the Law Enforcement Assistance Administration (LEAA) funds provided by the Federal Government for criminal justice research and training were diverted to police-oriented programmes. These were used mainly for buying anti-riot hardware. Drawing up contingency plans, forming special police riot squads and training personnel to react quickly and decisively during riots were the other measures initiated (Button 1989).

In the history of American Police, the 1970s were marked by two prominent activities: community problem solving and research on traditional police practices. The race riots and their repressive handling by the police during the previous decade highlighted the chasm that existed between the community, especially the minorities, and the law enforcement agencies, and the need, therefore, for forging friendly ties between the two groups.

Thus were sown the seeds for what was to become a major area of present-day concern, namely, community policing. Maintenance of law and order was to become the prime beneficiary, although crime control was also sought to be promoted through a larger allocation of resources and deployment of personnel. The concept of community policing and the several programmes tried out in large cities will be dealt with in great detail in Chapter 5. What is of greater relevance here are the many experiments in patrolling, both motor and foot, conducted at various centres, which examined the wisdom of traditional practices and came out with some interesting conclusions.

Drill for Handling Public Disorder in the US

Riots, provoked either by alleged police brutality or incidents impinging on race relations, keep occurring in different parts of the country. These place the police in a tight corner, and stretch its resources. Most of the big-city police departments have each a manual for tackling major riots so as to provide a ready guide for field operations.

The NYPD has, for instance, a booklet (1993) entitled *Disorder Control Guidelines* which prescribes two levels—local and citywide—of mobilization of police personnel to meet such a contingency. The booklet lays down the objectives of the operations as one of containment and isolation of the disorder, while simultaneously securing critical and sensitive establishments. The tactics suggested provide for both stationary and moving crowd situations. The booklet also explains how to counter fire bombs and Molotov cocktails and sniper attacks.

Under extraordinary circumstances, the municipal police turns to federal help. For instance, during the Los Angeles riots (1992), President Bush sent 1000 Federal law enforcement officers and

4000 Army troops and Marines to a beleaguered LAPD. The federal units included a 200-strong FBI SWAT team trained in crowd control and 150 Alcohol Tobacco and Firearms Bureau (ATFB) personnel, who normally investigate cases of bombing and arson, but are trained in security as well. Also deployed were 1400 personnel from the California National Guard trained in riot control.

The wide spectrum of forces sent to Los Angeles was indicative of the array of resources that a municipal police department could command in a real crisis affecting public order. Prior to Los Angeles, such federal assistance to the municipal police was given to Washington (1972) to contain anti-Vietnam demonstrations, and to Virgin Islands (1989) for ending the looting that followed Hurricane Hugo.

Comparative Analysis

An average law-abiding citizen undeniably expects the government to protect his daily routine and avocation from elements who deliberately violate law and cause annoyance to others. It is in this context that the preamble to this chapter begins with a general statement that police credibility is almost wholly determined by the sense of security that prevails in the mind of the public and the police capacity to promote such a feeling of comfort. Judged by this standard, the record of US and Indian police forces is a mixed bag.

A few crises in the two countries—the World Trade Centre and Oklahoma explosions and the Bombay blasts—were handled reasonably well. As against this, police inadequacy came to the fore in responding to situations arising out of the Rodney King trial verdict in Los Angeles and the assassination of Mrs. Gandhi, both of which led to large-scale riots and avoidable loss of life and property. In a sense, the LAPD was slightly more culpable because it had to merely anticipate the fall-out from a scheduled event, namely, the trial of LAPD officers, whereas the Indian police were reacting to a sudden national calamity. (It is an entirely different matter that, even several days after Mrs. Gandhi's assassination, sections of the Indian Police, allegedly, did not act objectively and swiftly to prevent the situation from turning into an anti-Sikh holocaust.)

The problems faced by the police in the two countries on the law and order front are most meaningfully compared under the following broad heads:

(i) handling of riots;
(ii) countering terrorist violence;
(iii) protection of dignitaries;
(iv) utilization of resources.

RIOTS

There is a striking similarity with regard to the backdrop against which riots are handled in the two countries. Black antipathy to the US Police and the Muslim distrust of the Indian Police (though obvious only in some parts of the country) weigh heavily in the minds of many objective and enlightened police leaders. Interestingly, the blacks in the US and the Muslims in India constitute almost the same percentage (11-12 per cent) of the respective population. They do not also get a proportionate share in police employment. There is, therefore, a widespread impression that the American Police is white-dominated and the Indian Police a Hindu-preserve, that is apathetic, if not downright hostile, to minority needs. The Indian Police will have to be additionally conscious of the widespread feeling among the Scheduled Castes (popularly referred as the Dalits) and Tribes that they are discriminated against by the upper castes in society and administration. There is a strong grievance among them that the police generally display a bias and are inclined to side with those who oppress and commit atrocities against Dalits, especially in rural India. The frequent strident and credible allegations of police excesses against them have posed a problem of some magnitude to the police leadership.

After the large-scale protest against the Vietnam War of the late 1960s, which was accompanied by violence, especially in the nation's capital, major riots in the US have turned on the racial factor. An overwhelming number of them have involved the black community, provoked either by the slight of white hate groups or by thoughtless police action.

Black resentment of their perceived low status in society has taken two forms, viz., protest actions and violent ghetto riots. Basically, both constitute an 'unconventional political expression'. While the former carries merely an implicit threat of violence, the latter is explicit in its practice of violence (Button 1989).

Racial harassment, primarily at the hands of whites, and police brutality have been two major factors which have caused black violence.

In the 1960s, 84 of the 136 major riots were precipitated by police action (Pate 1994). The Kerner Commission found this to be true in a half of the 24 disturbances of 1967.

In the major riots, the provocation was routine arrests of blacks by white police officers for minor offences. Nevertheless, in the opinion of Gainsburg (1994), Executive Director to the Kerner Commission on Civil Disorders (1967), it was difficult to conclude that the sole cause was thoughtless police conduct.

'Just below the surface there was a snake pit of often justifiable grievances, arising from widespread white attitudes and reflected in police action.' It is also the experience that, from an initial wrath and attack against the police, such riots sometimes take on a racist colour, with whites becoming the target of mob fury.

In India, riots involving a direct Muslim confrontation with the police and those pitting the former against the majority community of Hindus have no doubt been many, especially in the pre-Independence period. It is, however, reasonable to estimate that these now constitute much less than 50 per cent of the total number of riots, even in the most sensitive geographic area. Riots arising from political demonstrations, labour disputes, and linguistic and inter-state controversies outnumber those arising from religious differences (otherwise known as communal clashes). This accounts for a significant difference in the nature of operational tasks incumbent on the part of the Indian and US Police.

There is the further distinction that, in the Indian setting, incidents involving the minority group of Muslims are almost invariably a confrontation with the majority Hindu community. The attack on the police is only a sequel. But once police-Muslim exchanges begin, there is a strident propaganda that the police are biased and are acting at the behest of Hindus. This is analogous to the black belief of a racist slant in the American Police, except that, there is no charge that this is the result of a link-up with any organized white group. In India, the strong presence of well-organized and active Hindu fundamentalist bodies almost always lends basis to an allegation of police nexus with Hindu bigots.

At the operational level, this feeling of a prejudice in the law enforcement machinery props up the demand, in both countries, for an enlargement of the minority content in police forces. The nature of administrative response to this clamour is discussed in Chapter 7.

Terrorism

Terrorist violence is of great concern to both countries. But, dimensions-wise, there is no comparison whatsoever. Terrorism in India is much more widespread and has affected a sizeable number of the 25 states, sometime or the other. The casualties it has claimed are therefore enormous. The variety of its mechanics—kidnapping, direct firing at innocent groups of people in public places, attacks on families of policemen, sabotage of trains and other public transport, laying of landmines and the use of a human bomb—is mindboggling.

Before the 1993 World Trade Centre explosion in New York, the dimensions of the problem in the US were limited. Terrorist activities were confined mainly to the few Jewish groups aggrieved over what they considered to be injustice perpetrated on the community. The acts of violence committed by them were not directed against the American government. It was only after the New York explosion and the more recent Oklahoma disaster that one could assert that 'terrorism' in its modern connotation had arrived on US soil.

India has a much longer history of terrorism. The numerous attacks on British officials serving in pre-Independence India by freedom-fighters, even during the nineteenth century, may be said to have ushered in terrorism in the country. The left extremist violence, initially by the Charu Mazumdar group in West Bengal in the late 1960s and thereafter by its breakaway groups in many other parts of the country, the Sikh militant atrocities on an unprecedented scale in the Punjab since 1983, the Pakistan-inspired freedom campaign by militants in Jammu & Kashmir and the terror struck by the ULFA in Assam, all represent an uninterrupted and unremitting challenge to authority, aimed at diluting public order in India. The spectrum of terrorist groups operating against the constitutional authority in India is, therefore, very much wider than in the US, a country nearly paranoid over Arab terrorism.

Again, while terrorist activity in the US is an essentially urban phenomenon, the Indian version has different contours. The villages of Punjab, J&K, Andhra Pradesh and Assam tell horror stories of the terrorist savagery. At the same time, metropolises like Bombay and New Delhi have had their own share of the agony. This extensive spread of terrorist operations in India makes the police task much more complex than in the US, because the availability of specialist crack forces belonging to the central government is correspondingly depleted.

PROTECTION OF DIGNITARIES

The US has lost four Presidents at the assassin's hands. As against this, India, apart from losing Mahatma Gandhi immediately after attaining freedom from the alien ruler, has suffered the trauma of the brutal assassination of one serving and one former prime minister, one incumbent chief minister of a state, besides several important public personalities.

From all accounts, the threat to the lives of the President of the US and the prime minister of India is real. While there have been two recent direct attacks on the White House, the continued high level of activity of militant groups in India, especially those inspired from across the border, point to the belief that the *de facto* chief executive, the prime minister—the President being only a titular head of state in India—could be a high priority target. Hence, in both countries, security agencies need to constantly update their techniques of protection to match the ingenuity of terrorist groups. This is an assessment bolstered by the manner in which former Prime Minister Rajiv Gandhi was assassinated in 1991 with the help of a woman suicide bomber. It gets reinforced by the ease with which the Punjab Chief Minister Sardar Beant Singh was assassinated in August 1995, again, possibly through a 'human bomb'.

Notwithstanding the parallels, the task of protecting the chief executive in the two countries is qualitatively different. This is traceable to the need in India, more than in the US, for him to project a national and secular image to neutralize the pulls of competing strong regional and religious pressures.

The Indian prime minister is an intensely political person, being invariably a high-level functionary of the ruling party as well. This imposes on him the direct responsibility of nursing his party's electoral fortunes with great care, sometimes almost on a day-to-day basis. This requires intimate contact with the partymen, even at the grassroots level, through frequent touring of several parts of the country. During such travel, he has to speak at purely party gatherings, besides transacting official business. The contact between the prime minister and the public becomes particularly frequent and close at the time of elections. This has definite hazards from the point of view of his physical security. (It may be recalled that former Prime Minister Rajiv Gandhi was killed at an election propaganda meeting in Tamil Nadu in 1991.) While the US President has also a similar obligation, which is normally scheduled well in advance, the Indian prime minister's commitments are numerous, fulfilled very often at short notice.

At political party meetings in which the Indian prime minister participates, the police role becomes diffused. The imposition of basic security requirements, especially of controlling access to the VIP, is found difficult. This is a delicate task of balancing the desired politically expedient exposure to the public at large, with the rigours of rules of protection. Any laxity in the former and overzealousness in the latter almost always lands the police in trouble. Instances of overbearing functionaries, belonging to the prime minister's political party, clashing with the security staff regarding access to the dignitary, occur almost at every function organized by the ruling party.

Although India is a secular State which does not patronize any particular religion or caste, the prime minister is required frequently to take part in religious functions. The object is to strengthen the constitutional guarantee of freedom to practise any religion. Also relevant is the strong nexus between religion and politics in the country, which affects the electoral fortunes of some of the political parties. In view of the multiplicity of religions—Hinduism, Islam, Sikhism, Buddhism, Jainism and Zoroastrianism—and the State's obligation to project the impression that minorities are not being discriminated against, the prime minister will have to make his symbolic appearance at meets organized by different non-Hindu religious groups. This casts a further burden on India's security agencies. In this respect, the American president is advantageously positioned because, unlike in India, the interaction between religion and politics in America, though present, is somewhat muted.

I believe that the Indian prime minister's exposure to risk is somewhat greater than the American President. Religious and political compulsions of the former dictate his public appearances throughout the length and breadth of the country almost every week. His involvement in political propaganda for his party is so intense that it adds a large dimension to concerns of his security. To this extent, the responsibility of the Indian Police is much more complex and burdensome than that of its American counterpart.[4]

The arrangements for the protection of the two dignitaries have a parallel. Two elitist units—the Secret Service in the US and the Special Protection Group (SPG) in India—are responsible for their proximate security. While they manage the access control, rest of the chores, such as regulation of crowds, effectiveness of the illumination and public address system at the venue of the function, etc., are overseen by the police of the area. While SPG protection was initially available only to serving prime ministers, an amendment to the SPG Act, following the assassination of Rajiv Gandhi, extended this facility to past prime ministers and their families as well.

Utilizing Resources

Both countries have a wide array of forces at their command to tackle grave law and order situations. These belong either to the federal/central or state governments. In both, the basic task of preserving public peace rests with the local police which may, when it chooses, seek external assistance to quell any disorder. The decision to summon such help is wholly that of the state administration. There is this difference that, in India, when a state administration is replaced by central rule—under certain circumstances laid down by the Constitution—the central government itself takes the decision to despatch its forces to maintain peace in that state.

The Central Reserve Police Force (CRPF) of India is unique in its conception. It is raised and managed wholly by the central government, but is almost fully occupied with law and order matters in the various states. Patrolling a troubled area under the command and direction of the State Police is one of its foremost duties. The CRPF is no doubt used to protect the central government property and officials. But the proportion of the force used for this purpose is modest. It is always sent to a state at the request of the latter who also pays for its use. In addition to the CRPF, a few other central para-military forces, such as the BSF and ITBP, are also available to the states to meet any contingency.

The Federal Government in the US does not have at its command a full-fledged police force like the CRPF or other para-military forces which the central government in India can boast of. None of its more than sixty agencies, which enjoy police powers, has a general mandate with regard to preserving order or to undertake patrolling for this purpose. With a few exceptions, they concentrate on investigation and control of crime defined by federal statutes. Only some of them wear uniform and their ranks go by the general nomenclature of *Agents* as against *Officers* known to the municipal police (Langworthy and Travis 1994).

Notwithstanding these practices, as we have already seen, there is a growing trend in the US of drawing on federal agencies during disturbances affecting public peace which would normally have to be tackled by the municipal police in the states, utilizing their own resources. Instances of such assistance by the federal government in the US are much fewer than in India.

The feeling of security and confidence derived by police chiefs in Indian States from the fact that the CRPF is available to meet major situations cannot be exaggerated. This confidence is so even when the central government and a state government summoning the CRPF are run by rival political parties.

In the US, the creation of a corps called the National Guard, comprising wholly of volunteers, perhaps partly satisfies the need for an agency that will provide auxiliary support to a department that is under extreme pressure following large-scale riots. (To some extent, it resembles the CRPF in India, although the latter is a recognizable permanent body with defined hierarchy and sizeable resources of its own.) It is available to the states in times of national calamities, as well as emergencies caused by lawlessness, like the one witnessed in Los Angeles in 1992.

The central government in India does not have a nationwide voluntary organization similar to the National Guard. The nearest parallel is the Home Guards raised at the city/district level in each state, a half of whose cost is met by the central government. Apart from being used for assistance in relief operations during natural calamities, they are called to discharge routine functions, such as traffic regulation and crowd control at religious festivals or a sports gathering. The supervision of Home Guards rests wholly with the local municipal police, and the organization at the state level is headed by a senior police officer of the rank of Inspector-General or Director-General called the Commandant-General.

NOTES

1. For an easy understanding of the militant movements in Punjab and Jammu & Kashmir, I would strongly recommend *The Uncivil Wars* (New Delhi: Harper Collins, 1995) by former Delhi Police and National Security Guard Chief, Ved Marwah. Another recent work in the area is *War by Stealth: Terrorism in India* (New Delhi: Viking Penguin, India 1996) by Vijay Karan, a former Delhi Police Chief.
2. I would commend a field study of the RAF's performance till now to

researchers. This is an unexplored subject of great significance for the future.

3. Commissioners of Police of important cities such as Bombay, Calcutta and Madras, to mention only a few, themselves exercise such magisterial powers.
4. Here, David Bayley differs with me. In his view, the US President is equally weighed down by all the obligations cast on the Indian prime minister, and therefore his protection is as much problem-ridden. I concede that this is an area where qualitative inexactitudes could colour impressions and there are bound to be conflicting perceptions.

4

Perspectives of Crime

Crime does more than express the weakness in social relationships; it undermines the social order itself, by destroying the assumptions on which it is based.

Charles E. Silberman, *Criminal Violence, Criminal Justice*, New York: Random House, 1978

SINCE CRIME is a malaise that afflicts all societies and nations to varying degrees, there is a commonality of interest in trying to find out better ways of coping with it. A comparative study, apart from being fascinating, could be meaningful. It is therefore difficult to explain why, until recently, there were no sophisticated and systematic comparative studies of different criminal justice systems (Bayley 1985). This is especially true of the area of crime, its nature, prevention and detection. One outcome of this drought of literature is the absence of a possible cross-cultural theory of criminal justice (Cole *et al.*, 1987).

THE CAUSES OF CRIME

Patterns of crime and dimensions of criminal activity vary between countries. Regardless of this, there is now a consensus among criminal justice theorists and practitioners that crime is the product of a multiplicity of factors, and that, any strategy for its control needs to draw from many social science disciplines and the expertise of an array of public service agencies (Wilson 1985a, Sherman 1993, and Bayley 1994c). This perception is a sharp departure from the once tunnel-vision approach which treated crime as the concern solely of law enforcement officials and believed that all that was required was a tough and uncompromising application of the criminal law to offenders.

It is now generally acknowledged that we can comprehend the nuances of crime only against a personality, family and social backdrop (Friedman 1993). Relevant here is the widely-held view in the US, one that is possibly acceptable to many other countries as well, that the trend of rising violent crime could be traced to 'social disarray, lack of economic opportunity and racial inequality' (Gurr 1989a:19). (This is in tune with the stand of many criminologists in India as well.) It is further believed that, more than any other factor, it is the size of the crime-prone age group at any point of time that determines the volume of crime (Guyot 1991).

The Third United Nations Survey of Crime Trends, which covered the period 1980-6 (whose findings were made available only in 1993), is one of the few reliable reports available for a global assessment of the crime scene. Its conclusions are of great interest to all of us. The survey stated:

> Over the past ten years, there has been a considerable increase in crime in most parts of the world. The total amount of reported crime has been growing on a worldwide average of 5 per cent every year, well beyond a rise attributable to population growth. At this rate, crime is rapidly outstripping the capacity of many governments to keep pace with it and has already outpaced their capacity to reduce it. (p. 4)

India and the US figure among the many high-crime nations. Although overall crime (13.9 million cases) in the US during 1995 showed a marginal one per cent decline over 1994 and violent crime came down by 3 per cent, the rate of violent crime (crime per 100,000 of the population)—685—was by itself high enough to cause alarm (UCR 1995). In India, during 1995, although cognizable offences and violent crimes rose only by a modest 3.7 per cent and 4.3 per cent respectively, and property crime actually declined by 3.4 per cent, the overall crime rate—654.3—was substantial to demand official attention (*Crime in India*, 1995). A study therefore of how the two police systems have tackled the problem of a high volume of crime is of interest. This chapter will first provide a historical focus, and thereafter highlight the points of similarity and contrast.

THE CRIME SCENE IN INDIA

Crime Statistics

The effort to study crime in terms of numbers began with the Police Commission of 1860 prescribing a set of forms. This was in reaction to the criticism of the Secretary of State for India in England that crime information from India was lacking in details (Venugopala Rao 1981).The 1902 Police Commission examined the problem afresh and introduced a few new forms as part of an exercise to fuse the police and crime statistics with the annual administration report of each state (ibid.). Except for a few changes in 1908 and 1930, these forms continued well into post-Independence India.

In 1953, after the Princely States were integrated into the Indian Union, the central government commenced the annual publication of *Crime in India*. Initially compiled by the Bureau of Police Research and Development (BPR&D), in 1988, it became the responsibility of the National Crime Records Bureau (NCRB), which came into being on the specific recommendation of the National Police Commission in its Second Report.

The NCRB publishes its annual *Crime in India* on the basis of statistics received from each State Police Headquarters. The latter are dependent on statistics furnished by the District Superintendents of Police, who compile their reports on the basis of police station figures. The process, except at its final stages, is manual, greatly susceptible to human error. Wide variations between the figures communicated by districts to the CID, the nodal point, at the end of each month and the consolidated statement given at the year end are not unusual, even in respect of the more serious offences.

A very important fact that dilutes the impact of crime statistics—apart from a tendency of the police to suppress crime—is the reluctance of many victims to approach the police. This is particularly true of rape victims. In a tradition-bound society such as in India, many women and their families are willing to suffer in silence rather than go to the police with a complaint, and risk an irretrievable loss of reputation that could jeopardize a victim's future prospects of matrimony or ruin an existing marriage.[1]

The Nature of Indian Criminal Law

Under the East India Company rule, there were two systems of law administered by two sets of courts. The Supreme Court, which handled serious criminal cases, applied the English law, except in matters of contract, and succession or inheritance, where litigant parties were Hindus or Muslims. There were then the Company Courts which dealt with the Company's Regulations (Griffiths 1971).

Added confusion was from the wide differences in the laws in vogue in the three Presidencies of Bombay, Calcutta and Madras.

To end this unsatisfactory state of affairs, and in pursuance of a stipulation of the Charter Act of 1833, a Law Commission was established in 1834 under Lord Macaulay, an eminent Legal Member of the Governor-General's Council. An outcome of the commission's labours was the Indian Penal Code (IPC) passed in 1860, followed by the Criminal Procedure Code (CrPC) (1861) and the Indian Evidence Act (1873). Together, these three codes constitute the pillars of criminal law in India.

The IPC has been subjected to several amendments since the 1860s.[2] It has 23 chapters dealing with subjects such as punishments, general exceptions, criminal conspiracy and the attempt to commit offences, besides a chapter each on offences against the State, human body, and property and those relating to documents.

The CrPC was subjected to many changes by the British so as to incorporate the provisions in two allied acts, as also to clarify some issues raised in a series of High Court rulings which had led to a degree of confusion (Griffiths 1971). Taking into account the several reorganization measures affecting the judiciary, the CrPC was replaced in 1973 by a new code.[3] Its provisions are manifest in their intention to safeguard the average citizen against police excesses.

The Indian Evidence Act, often viewed as 'an intellectual masterpiece', is an eloquent tribute to the drafting ability of the Englishmen (Griffiths 1971). Drawing liberally from the English Law of Evidence, it is an effective aid to the trial court. Here again, as in the case of the CrPC, police officers are sore about an obvious lack of trust of the law-makers in police objectivity. Their main grievance is against the act's stipulation that no confession made to a police officer shall be admissible in evidence, except when such confession leads directly to the discovery of a material fact—such as the recovery of a murder weapon—when that part of the confession becomes admissible.

PRINCIPAL FEATURES OF THE CRIME SCENE IN INDIA

Pre-Independence India

The earliest reference to crime is in the account of the justice administration under the Mauryas (fourth century BC) by Megasthenes, the Greek emissary to the court of Emperor Chandra-gupta (Griffiths

1971). Thefts were common, and house owners were required to keep a watch on the movements of strangers as a measure of crime control.

Although gang robbery and murder by strangling—otherwise called *thuggee*—were known forms of crime even prior to the arrival (eighth century AD) of the Muslims, they gained menacing proportions only during the Muslim rule and remained unchecked in spite of the harsh treatment meted out to offenders.

The successor administration of the East India Company realized that the problem called for a high degree of coordination between various geographical regions, because gangs, such as the *phansigars* of the Madras Presidency, were extremely migrant (Griffiths 1971). There is evidence that certain measures to combat the evil had in fact been initiated under Warren Hastings, the first Governor-General. But, it was much later, under Governor-General William Bentinck, that the exercise was stepped up through the nomination of a senior official, Agent-General Smith, to proceed against all *thugs*, wherever they were. This step, followed by the setting up in 1835 of a separate Department of *thuggee* and dacoity headed by Capt. Sleeman, imparted to the task a new seriousness and direction (ibid.).

After successfully tackling *thuggee*, the Department's time in the 1850s and 1860s was taken up mostly by the problem posed by poisoners and dacoits. Poisoning of unwitting strangers for robbery was widely prevalent. For instance, in a single fortnight of December 1866, 18 victims—mostly traders from the North-West Province—were admitted to a Bombay hospital (Griffiths 1971). Another class of victims were bullock-cart drivers who were relieved of their vehicles after being poisoned.

The dacoity menace called for a greater perseverance and research. The fact that this crime was hereditary enabled the successful identification of dacoits and prospective offenders, and the building up of comprehensive dossiers. This strategy appeared to have brought about a fair degree of control over dacoits and their associates.

Sensational murders and inter-religious conflict took up most of police time in the first two or three decades of the twentieth century. A masterly work, *Crime in British India* (1924), by S.M. Edwardes describes the crime scene admirably. In 1921, murders were as many as 735 in the United Provinces and 697 in the Punjab. These flowed mainly from agrarian disputes or sexual jealousy. A few cases of human sacrifice and infanticide were also reported from some parts of the country.

Robberies and burglaries fluctuated with the success or otherwise of the harvest and associated economic conditions. Burglaries were particularly difficult to solve, even though, in the rural areas, offenders were far from skilled.

Here and there, individual criminals who had become part of the folklore were also known. Some of them specialized in offences on the highways (History of Madras Police 1959). Kidnapping of minor girls for prostitution was reported from Madras. In one such instance, two Hindu girls, after being converted to Islam, were taken away to a northern city more than 1300 miles away (ibid.). 'Parcel murder cases', in which bodies of victims were packed and booked as rail consignments, were reported in Madras State (now Tamil Nadu) in 1934. Thefts of money from banks by their own employees were also known (ibid.).

Difficult economic conditions immediately after Independence in 1947 led to a spurt in crime. For instance, the increase in the Madras Presidency was about 16 per cent. Migration of criminal gangs, even to the remote areas where they were not conversant with the local language, was another phenomenon which influenced crime (History of Madras Police 1959).

While routine crime was handled by District Police, the more complicated ones required the expertise of a specialized agency. This role was performed by the Criminal Investigation Department (CID) born at the beginning of the twentieth century and was located at the State Police Headquarters. Apart from investigating important cases, a few of which involved inter-district and inter-state criminals, the CID functioned as a storehouse of information and a channel for disseminating criminal intelligence (History of Madras Police 1959). In course of time, it was bifurcated into a Crime Branch and a Special Branch (which looked into sensitive matters in the political arena that impinged on public order and national security matters). Each had a Superintendent of Police who reported to a single Deputy Inspector-General. This arrangement continued well after Independence.[4]

Crime Scene in India since Independence (1947-95)

A distinguished member of the Indian Police Service till the 1970s and an eminent criminologist, Venugopala Rao, identifies (1981) distinct trends of crime during the first three decades of India's Independence.

The first half of the 1950s saw an inexplicable fall. Specifically, the crime rate was down by 24.5 per cent during 1948-55. It started rising thereafter, only to drop in 1976 and go up again the next year. These ups and downs were seen at a time when the population was rising continuously.

Venugopala Rao (1981) describes the drop in crime during 1950-5, even as the population went up by 10.30 per cent, as enigmatic. He does not subscribe to the central government's theory (*Crime in India*, 1955) that it was the improved economic situation that had been responsible for this. In his view, the economic indicators were not all that strong to account for this phenomenon. For the same reason, he discounts sociologist Baldev Raj Nayar's thesis (1975) that the 1952-5 drop in crime was the result of a relative political and economic stability and its subsequent rise was caused by a deterioration in the two spheres.[5]

Venugopala Rao makes three propositions for the post-Independence period. First, since the figures for 1952-5 were questionable, they could be ignored in any longitudinal study. Secondly, the growth in crime seen in the 1960s was consistent with the growth in population. Finally, the annual fluctuations seen are attributable to transient local factors and variations in practices with regard to registration of crime between regions.[6] (See Figure 4.1 for an idea of the fluctuations in crime rate during 1948-77).

Former CRPF Director-General and Member, National Police Commission (1977), Saksena's analysis (1978) of the Uttar Pradesh crime scene is in harmony with Venugopala Rao's. According to Saksena, crime concealment assumed alarming proportions between 1949 and 1960. (For instance, the crime rate which was 115.1 during 1945-54 dipped to 86.9 during 1955-60!) An enlightened leadership

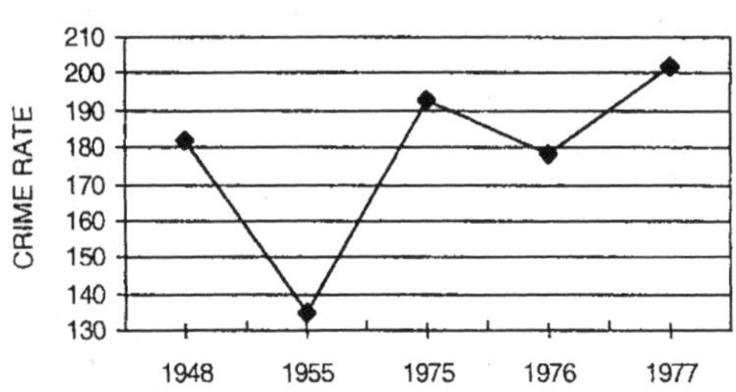

FIG. 4.1: FLUCTUATIONS IN CRIME RATE (1948-77).

in the state launched a movement to promote correct registration of crime, once in 1961 and again in 1970. This led to a spurt in figures. The benefits were only temporary. Actually, such drives in favour of free registration of crime only placed a premium on further concealment of crime in the state, a fact that was confirmed by the conclusions of a 1971 commission headed by a former High Court Judge. According to this commission, crime concealment worsened after Independence in 1947 and reached its peak in 1960. This is being mentioned here only to bring home the point that official crime statistics do not always convey the correct picture.

Population v. Crime

During 1951-91, which in essence represented the first four decades of India as a sovereign nation, the population went up by 135.3 per cent. During this period, crime rose by 158.2 per cent and the crime rate by 9.8 per cent. From a total of about 650,000 offences under the Indian Penal Code (IPC) and a crime rate of 179.9 in 1951, one saw these rising to 1696,000 and 185.1 respectively in 1995 (Figure 4.2).

Violent Crime in India

The rise since 1953—the first year for which official figures are available—has been significant. In particular, during the period 1986-95, this was an unbroken trend, except in 1987 and 1993, when there was a marginal drop. Again, in terms of a share of such crime in total

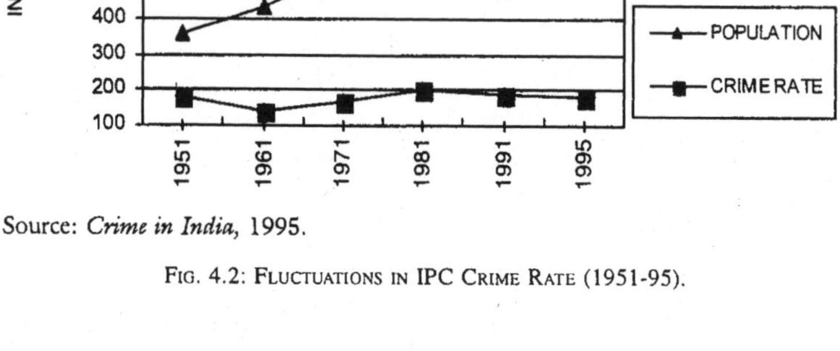

Source: *Crime in India*, 1995.

Fig. 4.2: Fluctuations in IPC Crime Rate (1951-95).

cognizable crime, 1986 and 1993 registered a small fall (*Crime in India*, 1995, and Joshi and Arora 1994). From nearly 50,000 in 1953, violent crime went up to 245,000 in 1995, an almost 500 per cent rise (Figures 4.3 to 4.6).

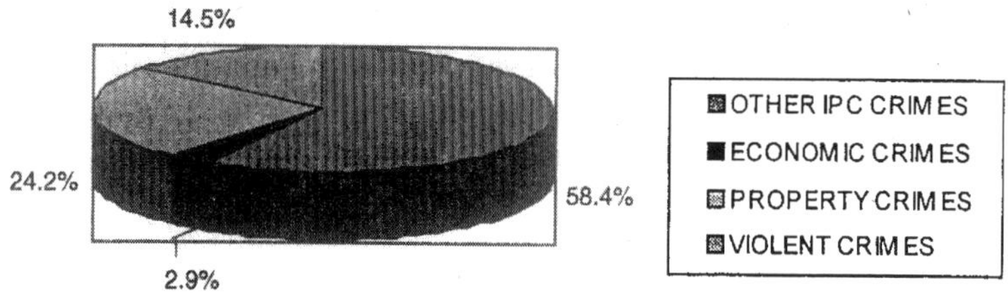

Source: *Crime in India*, 1995, by National Crime Records Bureau, New Delhi.

FIG. 4.3: CRIME IN INDIA (1995).

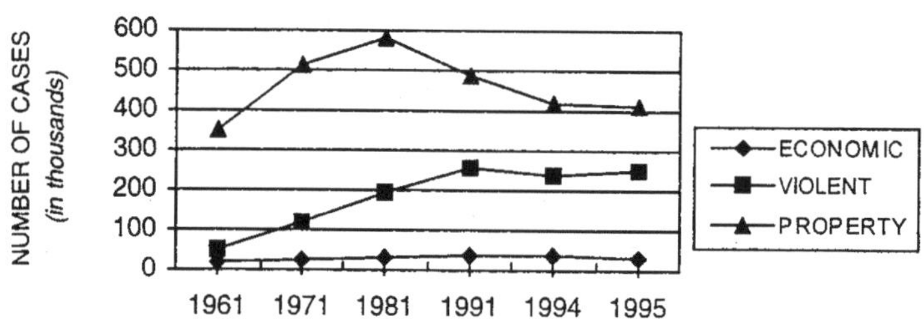

FIG. 4.4: CRIME IN INDIA (1961-95).

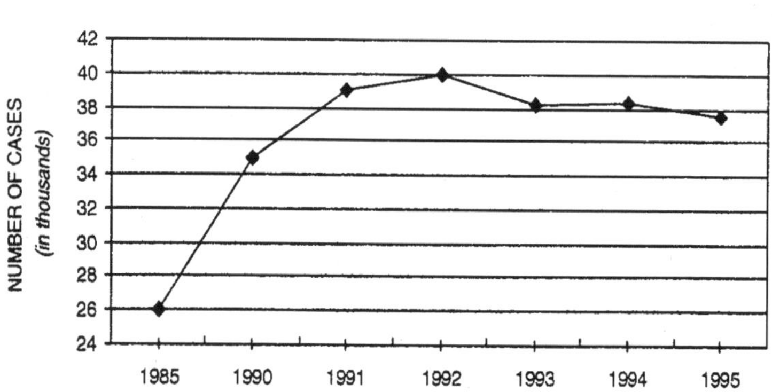

FIG. 4.5: HOMICIDES IN INDIA (1985-95).

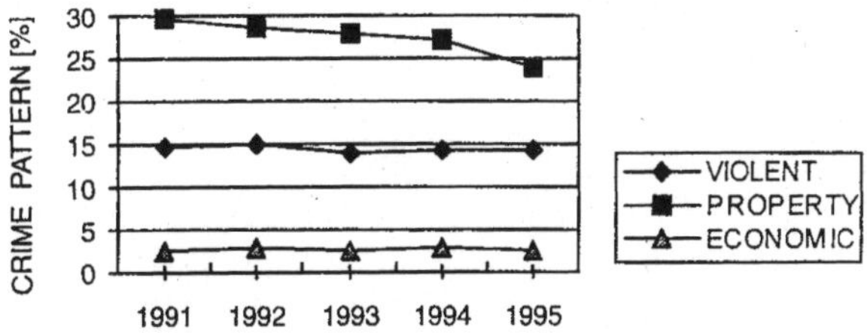

Source: *Crime in India*, 1995.

FIG. 4.6: PERCENTAGE CONTRIBUTION TO TOTAL IPC CRIME (1991-5).

PROPERTY CRIME IN INDIA

There have been many fluctuations since 1953. The current trend is one of a declining share in all IPC crime. From 404,000 in 1953, property crime went up to only 411,000 in 1995 (Table 4.1 and Figures 4.3, 4.4 and 4.6) (Joshi and Arora 1994 and *Crime in India*, 1995).

During 1995, thefts declined by 3 per cent and burglaries by 4.1 per cent. The value of property stolen during the year rose by 22.9 per cent, and the value of recovered property by 22.7 per cent. The percentage of recovery of lost property remained, as in the previous year, at 24.2.

FACETS OF VIOLENT CRIME IN INDIA

Crime in India defines 'violent crime' to include murder and its attempt, culpable homicide not amounting to murder, rape, kidnapping, abduction, dacoity (including assembly and preparation for it), robbery and riots.

TABLE 4.1: PROPERTY CRIME (1953-95)

Year	Total Property Offences	Percentage of all cognizable IPC crime
1953	403946	67.1
1961	355473	56.8
1971	501011	52.6
1981	579599	41.8
1991	495015	29.5
1995	410813	24.2

Homicides have been rising continuously except in 1993 (– 4.7 per cent) and 1995 (–2.9 per cent) (Figure 4.5). Five states (Uttar Pradesh, Andhra Pradesh, Madhya Pradesh, Maharashtra and Bihar) collectively accounted for 60.4 per cent of the homicides in 1995.

Rapes are on the increase. During 1971-95, there was a more than fivefold spurt. (Note: 1971 is the first year from which national figures for rape are available.) The 1995 figure was a 19.4 per cent rise over the quinquennial (1990-4) average and 4.1 per cent over 1994.

Frequent group violence arising from inter-religious animosity is a prominent characteristic of the current scene (Figure 4.7). From less than 100 in the 1960s, the number of incidents per year has gone up well beyond the 1000 mark in the 1990s. (In 1991, there were as many as 1727.) Also, the pattern of violence reveals new levels of brutality and human insensitivity. Attacks on women and children, arson, destruction of places of worship and the uninhibited use of explosives have become marked features of communal frenzy (Joshi and Arora 1994).

Analysis of Arrests by the Indian Police

The year 1995 recorded a 3.4 and a 2.0 per cent rise respectively in the number of arrests under the IPC and under the local and special laws, such as the Arms Act, Prohibition Act, Narcotic Drugs and Psychotropic Substances Act, etc. Of the 2.6 million arrests under the IPC, one-third were for major offences such as murder, rape, robbery, burglary, etc.[7] Only 4.1 per cent of the arrestees in IPC cases were women (*Crime in India*, 1995).

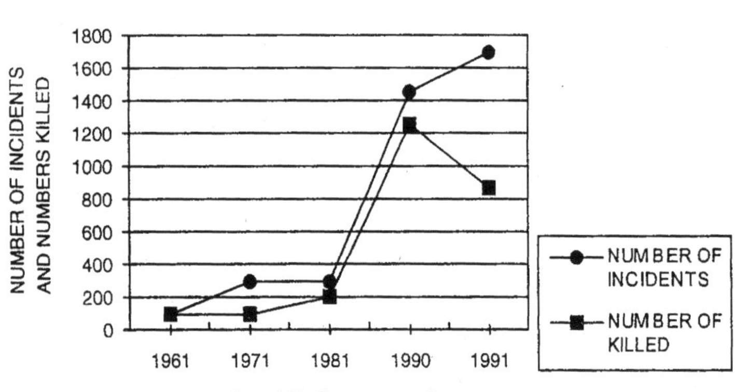

Fig. 4.7: Communal Clashes.

Analysis in terms of age confirms the universally held belief that it is the 16-30 age group which is most active on the crime front. During 1995, it accounted for 53 per cent of all arrests. An interesting fact— one that runs contrary to popular belief—is that only 0.3 per cent of all arrestees were juveniles (*Crime in India*, 1995).

Organized Crime in India

Organized crime in India has both national and international ramifications. Two forms of organized crime—drug trafficking and criminal intimidation—pose a major problem. India does not have any special legislation like the Racketeering Influenced and Corrupt Organizations (RICO) of the US to deal effectively with the invisible hand behind organized crime. Only the ordinary criminal law of the land and some special law to deal with specific problems such as drugs, prostitution, etc., which apply rigid standards of evidence are used most of the time. The quantum of proof required to be let in during the trial being therefore very high, the prosecution is invariably at a great disadvantage.

The Indian Drug Scene

Cannabis (from which hashish is derived) found its way into India several thousand years ago. It is now grown in the Western Ghats (a stretch of hills) and certain parts of the southern state of Andhra Pradesh. The poppy plant (whose products are opium, morphine and heroin) are grown in the three northern states of Uttar Pradesh, Madhya Pradesh and Rajasthan. (India is perhaps the only country where cultivation for the extraction of opium directly from the plant is known.) Sandwiched between the Golden Triangle of Laos, Thailand and Mynmar and the Golden Crescent of Iran, Afghanistan and Pakistan, both of which grow enormous quantities of poppy, India is highly vulnerable to the influence of drugs. Apart from acting as a conduit, it has become a major drug-producing nation. The share of Indian-made heroin in the world market has soared to two million dollars (Reddy 1992).

The Opium Acts of 1857 and 1878 and the Dangerous Drugs Act of 1930 were the backbone of the anti-drug drive until 1985, when the Narcotic Drugs and Psychotropic Substances Act (NDPS) came into being. All offences are cognizable, i.e. the police can arrest without a warrant, and they invite a maximum penalty of ten years of rigorous imprisonment which is extendable to twenty years. Responsibility for enforcing this law is shared by the police in every state with several central government agencies, such as the Border Security Force, Customs and the Narcotics Control Bureau (NCB). (NCB statistics reveal that almost 90 per cent of the seizures every year goes to the credit of the State Police.)

Opium, heroin, ganja, hashish and methaqualone are the major drugs which are seized. While heroin seizures yielded more than 1000 kg annually during 1992-4, hashish accounted for 8238 kg in 1993, only to drop to 6992 in 1994. The enormity of the problem can be understood from the fact that 22,222 persons were arrested in 1995 for possession/transport of drugs. Acquittals by court are very high, pointing to the heavy odds against which drug law enforcement agencies function (*Crime in India*, 1995 and NCB).

Criminal Intimidation

Intimidation by organized criminal gangs, often loosely referred to as the 'mafia' by the media, acting at the behest of influential members of the society for wresting political or pecuniary gains, is present in several parts of the country. The four metropolitan cities of Bombay, Calcutta, Delhi and Chennai (Madras) report this evil in different forms, the most important of which is the demand of 'protection money'.

Bombay (now Mumbai) has perhaps the most fearsome underworld with a stranglehold over prostitution, smuggling, gambling, and drug sale and transport. Dawood Ibrahim, Amar Naik and Arun Gawli are said to head three rival gangs responsible for many violent incidents. For instance, in March 1993, Bombay was rocked by a series of violent bomb explosions which resulted in widespread destruction of property and the death of 257 persons. 713 individuals were injured. Sustained investigation revealed the involvement of Pakistan's Inter-Services Intelligence (ISI) which had manipulated the city's underworld gang of Dawood Ibrahim to organize the blasts.

Use of the underworld's muscle power by industrialists to shape the outcome of trade union elections and whittle down opposition to any management decision is widely suspected. The May 1994 murder of a leading Bombay textile mill owner, Sunit Khatau, which revealed gang influence over textile labour is an instance in point. The murder was believed to have been triggered by the rivalry between two powerful gangs over a real estate transaction. According to the police, the gangs were shifting focus from drugs and gold smuggling to intervention in land deals which were generating enormous unaccounted liquid cash (*The Week,* 22 and 29 May 1994).

A recent development is the nexus between the underworld and the high-profile movie industry in Bombay. It is widely known that some producers are financed by the former. Disputes arising over such transactions have led to physical attacks and murders. Another feature of the scene is the extortion of affluent film personalities by criminal gangs. Perhaps the most sensational incident of 1997 was the murder (August) of music cassette producer Gulshan Kumar. A sense of fear now grips the leading members of the film industry.

Among the states, Bihar in eastern India is the most notorious for gangs known as 'private armies' whose clout and resources very often deter the police from taking strong and decisive action, even in a proved crime. (According to *Times of India,* 23 September 1997, there are 11 private armies in Bihar helping landlords to protect their holdings from the depredations of extremist groups. Since 1995, these have been responsible for more than 120 incidents, in which more than 150 persons were killed.)

The Dhanbad coal belt in Bihar is traditionally controlled by a mafia that indulges in terror through murders and abductions. The mafia is a well known collector of *rangdari* (a form of tax) and the recipient of a cut in coal deals from companies and individual traders. A stranglehold over trade unions, such as the Janata Shramik Sangh and the Janata Mazdoor Sangh, is very often mentioned. In April-May 1994, the murder of two Janata Dal activists in the Lodna fire area was attributed to mafia rivalry. The half-burnt bodies of these two individuals were recovered by the police (*Hindu,* 23 May 1994).

Jamshedpur, again in Bihar and also the home of the reputed Tata Steel Limited (TISCO), is also a mafia-dominated area. According to one estimate, Jamshedpur has eight gangs.

This is the appropriate place to refer to the strong evidence available in many parts of the country of the growing nexus between political parties and individuals with proved criminal record. This is no new phenomenon, but the relationship has come more into the open during the past few decades, with muscle power and money starting to determine the outcome of elections at all levels, especially those fought in villages.

Two frequent crimes committed by *thugs* on the eve of elections to Parliament and State Assemblies, at the instigation of some political elements, are murder and kidnapping. On the day of polling, intimidation of citizens to vote for a particular party or to stay away from the poll, a tactic for which political parties use anti-social elements, is widely known.

It was against this background that the central government appointed (July 1993) a committee headed by N.N. Vohra, then Home Secretary, to go into the growing politician-criminal nexus. The committee's 1993 report was placed in Parliament on 1 August 1995.

The report concluded:

> It is apparent that crime syndicates and mafia organizations have established themselves in various parts of the country . . . (and) have developed significant muscle and money power and established linkages with governmental functionaries, political leaders and others to be able to operate with impunity.

The report referred to the observation of the Intelligence Bureau (IB) Director that 'warning signals of sinister linkages between the underworld politicians and bureaucracy have been evident with disturbing regularity'. The Director was reported to have added that criminal gangs in certain states like Bihar, Haryana and Uttar Pradesh enjoyed the patronage of local politicians and the protection of government functionaries. The dependence of politicians on crime syndicates for money support to fight elections enhanced the latter's clout in dealing with the official machinery. As a sequel to the Vora Report, a nodal agency has been set up in the central government for exchange of information among central agencies for effective follow-up action (*Hindu*, 2 August 1995).

The Role of Firearms in Indian Crime

Crime in India does not provide the number of offences committed with the help of firearms. What is available is only information on prosecutions under the Arms Act 1959, the basic gun law of the country. For instance, during 1995, 64,331 cases were registered under this Act. The number of arrests was 66,747.

The NPC, in its Fifth Report (1980), referred to the popular belief that weapons lawfully held were very often loaned to dacoits and other anti-social elements. In view of this, the commission declared:

> Holding of firearms by individuals, if not eliminated altogether, should be reduced drastically and maintained at a much lower level than now. (p. 29)

It proceeded to recommend the promulgation of a new Arms Act to replace the 1959 Act. This has however not been done.

Licensing practices vary from state to state, although the same act is applicable nationwide. While in some, there is a certain laxity and casualness, in a few others, one is able to perceive some seriousness. There are reports from several parts of the country of the existence of illicit arms factories. According to one West Bengal study for 1970-9, 56 per cent of the 1801 weapons examined by the State Forensic Laboratory were improvised countrymade crude firearms (Nag 1983).

A major incident of December 1995 brought to light the laxity of arrangements available for preventing the influx of arms into the country. On 17 December, an AN-26 aircraft (with Latvian crew) originating from Karachi (Pakistan) and flying over Indian territory after a brief halt at Varanasi (central India), was known to have dropped a consignment of arms (240 AK-type assault rifles, 10 rocket launchers and 81 anti-tank grenades) over Purulia in West Bengal before proceeding to Phuket in Thailand. It was intercepted on its return journey from Thailand on 21 December and forced to land in Bombay (*India Today*, 31 March 1996). The incident set off a major controversy because of its national security implications. The CBI, which is investigating the matter, has made several arrests. The air-drop effected with the assistance of a foreigner, Kim Paulgrave Davy, is suspected to have been at the request of either a religious fundamentalist group or a leftist militant organization operating in India.

Problems in Crime Investigation by the Indian Police

Public discontent over the quality of crime investigation is perennial. The average citizen strongly believes that the police indulge in extremely corrupt practices at every stage, beginning with the registration of a complaint. The 1902 Police Commission said:

> The complainant has often to pay a fee for having his complaint recorded. . . . More money is extorted as the investigation proceeds. When the officer goes down to the spot . . . he is a burden . . . often to the whole village.

Lamenting this, the NPC (1977) observed in its Third Report:

> What the Police Commission said in 1903 would more or less fully apply even to the present situation. If any thing, the position has worsened. (1980:25)

The commission identified several areas and stages of investigation—registration of a complaint, arrest/non-arrest and release/ non-release of accused on bail, and recording of statements of witnesses—as vitiated by corruption. It recommended 'a system of surprise checks and inspections and effective supervision by honest and well motivated officers at the different levels of command within the hierarchy itself' (p. 26).

Complaints voiced through the media, court pronouncements at all levels and periodic reviews of vigilance agencies in the states and the central government reinforce the impression that there has been no perceptible change in integrity levels of police investigators. This is despite the fact that criminal investigation, notwithstanding the excessive attention to public order matters, gets a high priority in the police training curriculum. The recruit, at all three levels—Constable, Sub-Inspector and Assistant/Deputy Superintendent—is exposed substantially to the fundamentals of crime work. Once he or she is assigned to the field, the focus gets distorted and it becomes one of an obsession with the maintenance of law and order. This is because of the high political stakes involved here for the government.

An eternal complaint is the police disinclination to bring crime on record. There is a widely known tendency of police stations to suppress complaints so as to cover up any spurt in crime that could be unfavourably viewed by supervisory officers. The collusion of the latter themselves is not unknown. This unwholesome practice has been brought to light by several public opinion surveys.

Sloth in recording crime is no doubt traceable mainly to the unwillingness of officers to take on the burden of too many investigations. In the opinion of the NPC (Fourth Report, 1980:1) there is an even more important factor:

> the anxiety of the political executive . . . to keep the crime figures low so as to claim . . . that crime is well controlled and is even going down as a result of 'efficient' police administration under their charge. The Chiefs of Police and other senior police officers also find it easy and convenient to toe the line . . . this attitude permeates the entire hierarchy down the line and is reflected at the police stations.

Saksena (1978-9), who was an important member of the NPC, had this to say:

> This evil practice got an official stamp (in Uttar Pradesh) in July 1976 when the then Chief Secretary issued his notorious crime prevention order to District Magistrates (DMs). DMs and SPs were to make a list of all criminals in the districts. . . . In order to reduce crime figures by 50 per cent . . . all these criminals were to be arrested . . . in some crime, real or bogus. The police lost all public confidence in the implementation of this order. Concealment of crime became, in effect, an official policy.

Perhaps the most serious allegation that is often heard against investigating officers is their tendency to use force or, what is commonly referred to as 'third degree methods', in dealing with suspects of crime. The charge gains some credence from the frequent deaths in police custody. Both the central and state governments are highly sensitive to the issue and have conveyed several instructions to curb police misconduct.

Legal Restraints on Police Investigation in India

The most important restraint on police investigators is the Constitutional mandate that no person arrested without a warrant shall be held in police custody for longer than 24 hours before which time he has to be produced before a magistrate. The time allowed is however exclusive of the journey from the place of arrest to the magistrate's court. Many investigating officers find this restriction irksome and impractical. They therefore make incorrect entries with regard to the time of arrest so as to gain the extra time in which to question the arrestee.

The Supreme Court of India and several High Courts have imposed many restrictions on the power of arrest vested in police officers and have prescribed certain guidelines.

In *Joginder Singh* v. *State of Uttar Pradesh* (1994), the Supreme Court stated that an arrest should not be made merely because it was lawful to do so. The officer concerned should actually be able to justify such action. The arrested person should be told that he had the right to have any friend, relative or other person informed about the arrest and the place where he is held. Further, a contemporaneous record of the name of person so informed should be made in the police station diary. The Supreme Court further instructed police chiefs to direct investigating officers to record, in their case diaries, reasons for effecting a particular arrest.

In *Charan Das Chawla* v. *Commissioner of Police, Delhi* (1994), the Delhi High Court laid down that, when information was demanded by a magistrate about a person alleged to be held in illegal custody, the police officer concerned must file an affidavit within a day or two and also produce the arrestee before that magistrate. A refusal to file such an affidavit would amount to contempt of court.

The CrPC permits examination of witnesses during investigation at the police station itself. However, no male below the age of fifteen or a woman can be summoned to a police station. Section 160 of the CrPC is emphatic that these persons shall be examined at their place of residence.

Another area in which police discretion has been greatly curtailed relates to handcuffing of arrested persons. The CrPC does not prohibit this. Section 49 merely states: 'The person arrested shall not be subjected to more restraint than is necessary to prevent his escape.' The discretion that this section permits a police officer has led to abuses. A threat is hurled sometimes at the arrested person that he will be handcuffed. This is motivated by a desire either to humiliate him or to extort money. Taking into account such malpractices, Police Manuals in several states impose many restrictions. Apart from saying that handcuffing shall be resorted to only when a prisoner is a dangerous criminal or where there is information that he is likely to escape from custody, some states insist on the police officer concerned obtaining court permission to handcuff a prisoner. There is also a stipulation that, whenever a prisoner is handcuffed, such fact should be recorded in writing. The NPC (Third Report 1980) commended the adoption of these guidelines uniformly by all state police forces.

This section will be incomplete if it does not refer a momentous January 1996 Supreme Court order. In this case—*Vineet Narain and others* v. *The Union of India*—the court was disposing of a petition which alleged that the CBI and revenue authorities had failed to perform their duty to bring certain offenders to book because the latter were highly placed in society and were influential. The court declared that, in cases where an investigating agency filed a final report stating that there was no material to proceed further against an accused person and the case had therefore to be closed, the court had the right to satisfy itself that this conclusion had been arrived at on reasonable grounds.[8] This is a landmark pronouncement that establishes the judiciary's role in monitoring an investigation and in ensuring that it is fair and fearless, without being influenced by those in authority who may have a vested interest in shaping an investigation on the lines desired by them. This is a significant development that no doubt fetters police discretion, but ensures that such discretion is not used to favour offenders because of their high position in society. In a sense, the Supreme Court stand promotes a major objective of the National Police Commission recommendations, namely, insulate the police from the manipulations of the political machinery.

Crime Control Measures in India

A time-honoured tactic is to keep a watch over past offenders. History-sheets are maintained at police stations with the approval of supervisory officers. A periodic physical check by beat constables or collection of information through sources is the usual practice adopted. This is not a foolproof system. Yet, the knowledge that the police are keeping a tab on him, places the criminal with a record under a modicum of pressure against lapsing again into crime. Apart from raising issues of a right to privacy and allied fundamental rights guaranteed under the Constitution, this practice is liable to abuses, including extortion by the police.

Section of 151 CrPC empowers the police to make arrests for the prevention of a cognizable offence. This is invariably used to frustrate the designs of groups or individuals to disturb public peace.[9]

Two other provisions are also of great help. Under Section 107, persons likely to cause a breach of the peace can be bound over by a magistrate to keep the peace for a year. Any violation of the conditions imposed invites a term of imprisonment. This is invoked frequently by the police to defuse situations in which individuals or groups are locked in a local dispute—usually over ownership of land or right of worship in a religious place—that threatens to disturb peace.

Section 109 helps to bind over to good behaviour—for a maximum period of one year—a person concealing his presence with a view to committing a cognizable offence. This is very often employed against property criminals who display signs of recidivism. Perhaps, more useful is Section 110 that is directed against habitual offenders. A wide range of offences, including the receiving of stolen property and harbouring of criminals, and hoarding, profiteering or adulteration of food or drugs, come under the purview of this section. Also, unlike Sections 107 and 109, the bond executed by an accused under Section 110 is valid for three years.[10]

The beat system known to the Indian Police was conceived more than a century ago as an essentially anti-crime measure. Under this, the geographical area of each police station is divided into a few convenient beats. One or two constables are sent to each beat with specific instructions to collect information from the local population on the movements of strangers and on the occurrence of any crime. Performed with dedication, this could be a very useful source of information for keeping track of and controlling crime-prone individuals. [11]

THE CRIME SCENE IN THE US

A distinctive feature of the average American citizen's life today is the 'fear of crime'. Reported crime figures no doubt show a declining trend, and victimization data since 1978 point to the same. This, however, is a picture which is not endorsed by the common man (Bayley 1994a). All across the country, especially in big cities, there is a fear psychosis that is too pronounced to be ignored. Research indicates that the level of fear is higher among groups which are less likely to be victims of crime (BJS 1988 and Guyot 1991).

The rise in fear of crime was most noticeable during the late 1960s and till the mid-1970s when Gallup polls (1968 and 1977) reported high levels of fear, especially among women. Again in the 1980s, according to the Figgie Report, two-fifths of Americans surveyed were 'highly fearful' that they would become victims of violent crime. The Gallup poll of 1990 reported that 51 per cent of the respondents believed that there was 'more crime' in their area than in the previous year, and 84 per cent said this was true of the country as a whole (Friedman 1993). More recently, 'public fear of crime has reached an apex', according to Joseph D. McNamara (1997), who retired from the NYPD and was later Chief of San Jose Police for 15 years.

Collection of Statistics

There are two sources of data: the Uniform Crime Report (UCR) compiled annually by the FBI from police reports, and the National Crime Survey (NCS) prepared annually by the Bureau of the Census for the Bureau of Justice Statistics (BJS).

The UCR Programme, which began in 1929, relies on monthly

law enforcement reports made directly to the FBI or through centralized agencies. An effort is made to elicit responses from as many law enforcement agencies as possible. For instance, the UCR for 1995 reflected reports from agencies representing about 95 per cent of the country's population. In addition to crime figures and trends, the report gives data on crimes cleared, persons arrested, law enforcement personnel and the characteristics of homicides (UCR 1995).

The UCR's reliability is a matter for continual debate. Its value is nevertheless undiminished because it is the only official nationwide compendium of crime statistics (Weiner and Wolfgang 1985).

The origin of the NCS can be traced to the study of criminal victimization conducted in 1966 by the National Opinion Research Centre for the Law Enforcement Commission. The NCS came into being in 1973 mainly as an exercise to correct some of UCR's infirmities. One of these is that the UCR does not take into account the crime which is not reported to the police. The other shortcomings include the failure of police agencies to register some of the crimes reported or send annual reports to the FBI.

Unlike the UCR, the NCS obtains information on both reported and unreported crime. For this purpose, the latter has compiled a national sample of households. Persons aged 12 and above are interviewed twice a year on their victimization experiences. A major criticism is that NCS depends heavily on the victim's ability to recall victimization, especially as to when it happened, and to describe it clearly so as to help the interviewer assess whether such victimization came under the statutory definition of various offences (Weiner and Woolfgang 1985, and Sullivan and Victor 1988).

Discrepancies between the UCR and the NCS are quite common, as in the case of homicide rates reported during 1973-80. The same phenomenon was evident in respect of burglary also during 1973-81 when the rate showed a 4 per cent drop, whereas the UCR recorded a 34 per cent rise. One explanation could be that different bases were used by the two to calculate offence rates. While the NCS' base was households, that of the UCR was population. It is relevant that, in the 1970s, the number of households increased much faster than the population, thereby accounting for the lower rate of burglaries. If, however, NCS rates for reported burglaries had been linked to the US population and were compared with UCR residential burglary rates, a rise in rates could have been seen in both the series (Sullivan and Victor 1988).

Weiner and Wolfgang (1985) believe that, notwithstanding their differences in approach and their respective limitations, the NCS and UCR could be used to measurable effect, especially for arriving at a profile of criminal violence in the country.

The Nature of US Criminal Law

Unlike India, the US does not have a single penal code for the whole country. There is one for every state, but the codes do have many common features. There is a federal statute which covers a wide variety of criminal offences. Very often, changes made in this statute are adopted by the states. There is a third category of criminal law comprising the ordinances adopted by counties and municipalities which deal with minor crime (Samaha 1988).

Violations are either 'felonies', offences punishable by imprisonment for a year or longer, and 'misdemeanours' which attract a shorter prison term or fine. The latter normally include simple assaults and battery, prostitution and disorderly conduct. There is a third category, 'violation' or 'infractions', such as traffic offences, which invite small fines (Samaha 1988).

A typical crime statute is the New Jersey Code of Criminal Justice. It has 66 chapters dealing with subjects, such as General Principles of Liability, assault, theft, offences against the family, criminal homicide, etc. It has a whole chapter on sentencing and one devoted exclusively to the disposal of stolen property.

Rise and Fall of Crime in the US during the Seventeenth and Eighteenth Centuries

As we saw in the earlier chapters, policing in colonial America was far from proactive. It required a victim's initiative to seek and secure help. More often than not, there was a grudging and inadequate response. The average constable was a non-professional who depended heavily on the victim to give a formal shape to his own case (Samaha 1988). A study of the available court records in New York for the period 1691-1775 revealed that assaults (21.5 per cent), which were rarely fatal, and thefts (13.7 per cent) were the most common crime (Gurr 1981).

The Nineteenth Century

A sea-change came about in the 1830s when urbanization led to riotous behaviour and a crime wave in cities, such as New York, Boston and Philadelphia (Wilson 1985a). For instance, in Boston, there was a notable rise in property offences. This was followed, especially in the 1850s, by a sharp increase in arrests for various infractions. Alongside this, during 1836-55, there was a fourfold increase in committals for crimes against persons for the entire state of Massachusetts (Gurr 1981).

Smaller cities also presented a similar trend. In Buffalo (New York), during 1854-74, arrests for offences against the person jumped from 90 to 1300 per 100,000 of the population (Gurr 1981). This upward trend in many parts of the country was followed by an inexplicable drop in crime during the post-Civil War years. This was contrary to the popular theory that industrialization and new immigrants brought in additional crime.

Towards the end of the nineteenth century, there were minor fluctuations. No spurt in crime that could cause concern to the police or the public was however seen. There was actually evidence of a certain social stability. Life was 'organized around the need for self-control, the delay of personal gratification, and the management of social relations on the basis of mutual restraint' (Wilson 1985a: 234).

The Twentieth Century

In the 1920s, there was an obvious resentment against the efforts of opinion leaders to impose a moral order that amounted to self-abnegation and repression of natural instincts. One heard a demand for the replacement of the values that had been deified for a century. The accent was on 'personality development' rather than 'moral character' (Wilson 1985a).

Against this backdrop, the introduction of a national law on prohibition in 1920 produced adverse reactions. Prohibition was no doubt withdrawn in 1933 in deference to popular pressure and on the assessment that it had failed. Nevertheless, for the short period it was in force, the popular perception was that it had led to a crime wave (Wilson 1985a).

The bootlegging generated by prohibition gave rise to a bitter competition. This led very often to violence (Gurr 1989 and Haller

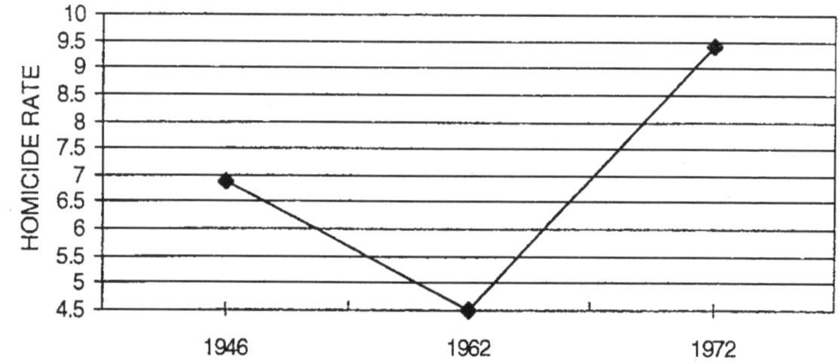

FIG. 4.8: USA—HOMICIDE RATE (PER 1,00,000).

1989). A significant percentage of homicides in Chicago (1926-7) and Detroit (1926-34) were the result of gang warfare that was related to the control of the booze market (Zahn 1989).

Surprisingly, however, the Great Depression of the 1930s and the accompanying economic deprivation did not result in any noticeable rise in crime. There was in fact evidence of a decline in some communities (Gurr 1989b).

Beginning with the end of World War II, until the early 1960s, there was a pronounced downward trend of crime. This got reversed in the 1970s. A murder rate of 6.9 in 1946 came down to 4.5 in 1962, only to go up to 9.4 in 1972 (Figure 4.8). Similarly, robbery suffered a drop of about 14 per cent around 1959. By 1968, it went up, almost doubling the figure for 1946. The rate of auto-thefts, which were understandably less in the 1940s because of a low production priority for civilians during the War, rose from 107.7 to 181.6 in 1960 (Figure 4.9). Thereafter, there was a significant rise each year, sometimes fourfold (Wilson 1985a and Zahn 1989).

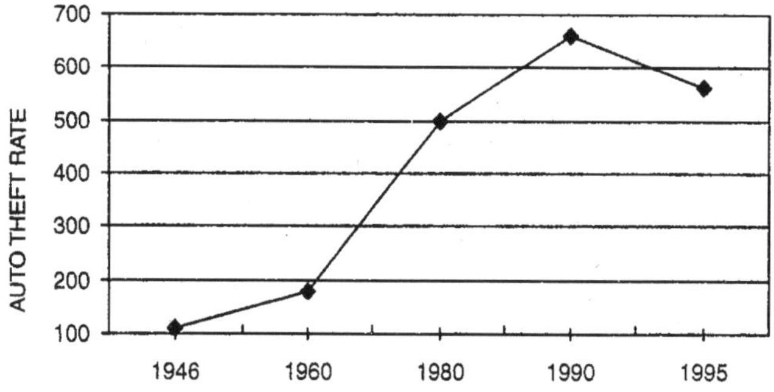

FIG. 4.9: AUTO THEFTS (1946-95).

Certain basic statistics of drug use and levels of unemployment around this time are significant. Particularly relevant is the rise in narcotic-related deaths during 1950-70. There were about 100 deaths in the 1950s. This rose to 200 in 1960, and it crossed 700 in 1967 (Figure 4.10). In one city, Atlanta alone, the number of heroin users went up from 500 in 1963 to 5000 by 1970 (Wilson 1985a).

Growing unemployment among the young was another prominent characteristic of the American scene during 1960-70. While a large number of jobs were created for adults, teenagers did not have the same benefit. Their unemployment grew from two or three times to five times greater than for adults during 1963-8 (Wilson 1985a). Even among this category, the level of unemployment among the non-white youth was greater. In 1963, the latter accounted for 176,000, equivalent to about one-third of the total number of non-whites holding jobs (ibid.).

An equally significant factor was the new age structure of the society. As a sequel to the 'baby boom years' immediately after World War II, the number of youth in the age group 14-24 showed a phenomenal increase during 1960-70. Each year, the number went up by 1.3 million. By 1970, this group was half of the older group of 25-64 as against one-third, ten years earlier (Wilson 1985a and Skogan 1989).

The President's Crime Commission was alive to this phenomenon. It estimated that 40 to 50 per cent of the increase in crime seen during 1960-5 could be attributed to the new age composition of the population (Skogan 1989). Another major finding was that, not only those in the crime-prone age group were numerically larger, they were

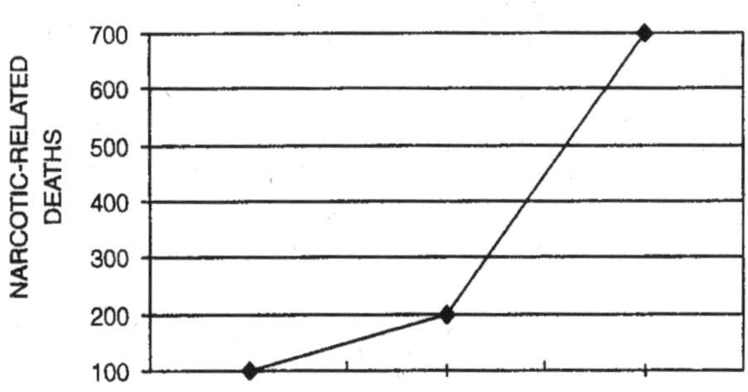

FIG. 4.10: USA—NARCOTIC-RELATED DEATHS.

also offending more frequently and committing more serious crimes than their 1950-60 cohorts. Interestingly, their exit from the crime scene was slower, as revealed by the fact that those in the under-18 age group among violent offenders were less than before (Skogan 1989).

University of Pennsylvania Professor Marvin Woolfgang's study (1972) is relevant. Woolfgang scrutinized the background of all males born in 1945 who lived in Philadelphia between their tenth and eighteenth birthdays. He found that one-third of the 10,000 so identified had at least one recorded contact with the police by 18 and, 50 per cent of these, more than two (Wilson 1985a).

The 1970s registered a nearly 40 per cent increase in the UCR Index Crimes (violent offences, including robbery, and property offences) against a 46 per cent increase in violent crimes alone. For the first time, namely, in 1974, index crimes registered the million mark.

The 1980s were dominated by the follow-up analysis of the results of experiments in patrolling conducted in the 1970s. This helped to clarify certain ambiguities in the police role. While order maintenance was vital, it had to be necessarily supplemented by efforts to combat crime (Wilson 1985).

The early 1980s were noteworthy for a drop in index crimes, a trend specifically in view during the three years of 1982-4. This got reversed thereafter with a marginal increase each year until 1992, when there was again a fall (2.9 per cent).

Two New York City incidents effectively portrayed the 1980s. In the first (22 December 1984), a white electronics expert, Bernhard Goetz, shot and wounded four black youths on a Manhattan subway train and later claimed that his action was purely in self-defence. The episode attracted great media attention, with Goetz being hailed as the 'subway vigilante'.

In the second incident, on the night of 16 December 1986, in the predominantly white Howard Beach area of New York City, four blacks driving through the locality were attacked after their car had broken down. One black was killed and another seriously injured. The enraged black community organized major public demonstrations. The Howard Beach incident and the subsequent racial tension led to the setting up (6 February 1987) of a New York Governor's Task Force on Bias-Related Violence. The Task Force recommended (June 1987) a legislation that made collection of data on hate crimes mandatory, and imposed stiffer penalties for such crime (Berry 1994).

The latest crime figures available are those for 1995 (Table 4.2 and Figures 4.11 and 4.12). The year recorded a 0.9 per cent fall in the number of index offences (13.9 million) and 1.8 per cent in the crime rate. Violent crimes dropped by 3.2 per cent and their rate by 4 per cent. Also, among the eight cities with a million or more population, the decrease in the number of violent crimes was 8 per cent (UCR, 1995).[12]

TABLE 4.2: HIGHLIGHTS OF THE 1995 CRIME SCENE

Violent crimes	13%
Property crimes	87%
(Break-up of property crimes)	
Larceny-theft	57.7%
Motor vehicle theft	10.6%
Property stolen	$ 13.1 billion
Property recovered	35.2 %

Source: UCR, 1995.

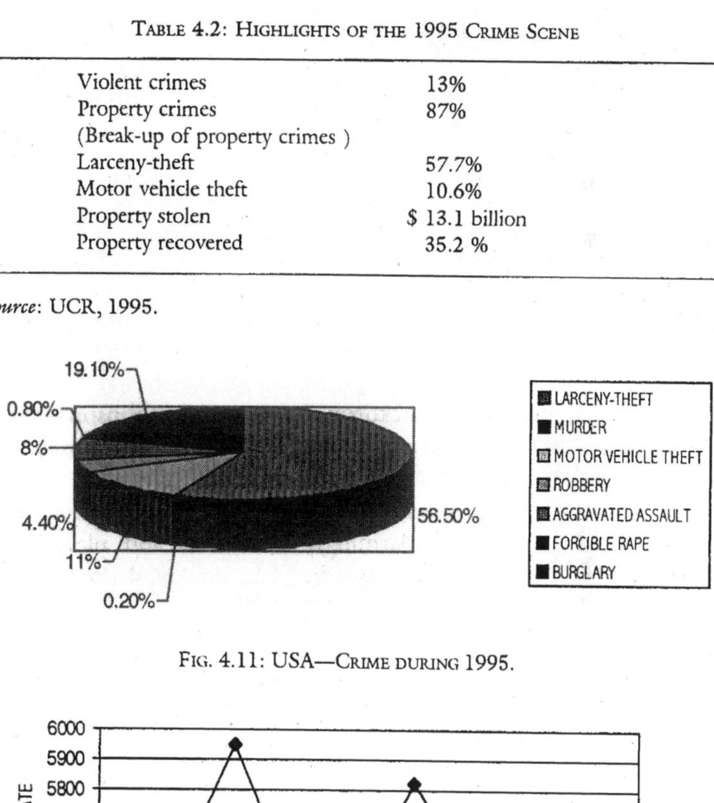

FIG. 4.11: USA—CRIME DURING 1995.

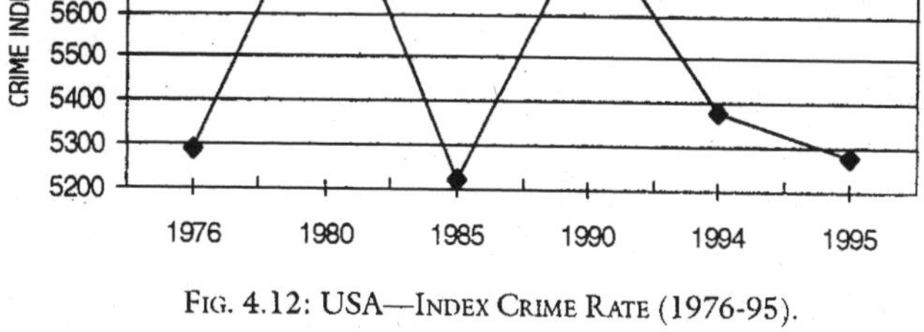

FIG. 4.12: USA—INDEX CRIME RATE (1976-95).

The Rise and Fall of Violent Crime in the US

Violence has always been a part of the American life ('Brutality runs through our history.'—Friedman 1993:454). Even as an infant nation, America had witnessed brutality. This was especially true of the treatment meted out to Native Americans in an effort to push them westward. ('An every-man-for-himself mentality flourished as prospectors, adventurers, and entrepreneurs thrived'—Cronin 1981:5.)

The civil war years (1861-5) saw the homicide arrest rate peaking to 9, from about 3-4 (acknowledged as the homicide indictments in a city, such as Philadelphia known for a high rate for murders). The rate declined to about 5 during the 1880s, only to rise to 13 by 1920 (Figure 4.13).

From about 1929, when the UCR came into being, homicide rates started falling, though not uniformly (Figure 4.14). This was until 1960, when one noticed an increase in collective unrest and a rise in the incidence of all types of violent crime. Apart from the violence triggered by the civil rights movement, there was the protest against America's involvement in the Vietnam War which rocked campus peace and generated a large-scale disorder in many centres all over the country. It was against this backdrop that President Johnson created (10 June 1968) the National Commission on the Causes and Prevention of Violence (Violence Commission).

The Violence Commission concluded (1969: p. xv) that violence in the country had 'risen to alarmingly high levels' and pleaded for a much larger investment of resources to contain violence (Weiner and Woolfgang 1985).

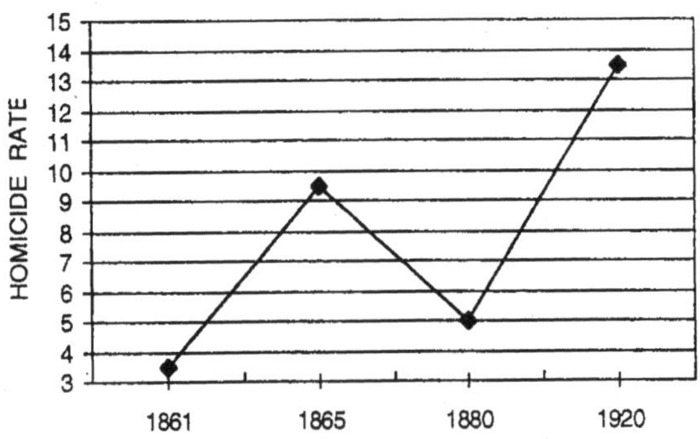

Fig. 4.13: USA—Homicide Rates Civil War Years (1861-65 to 1920).

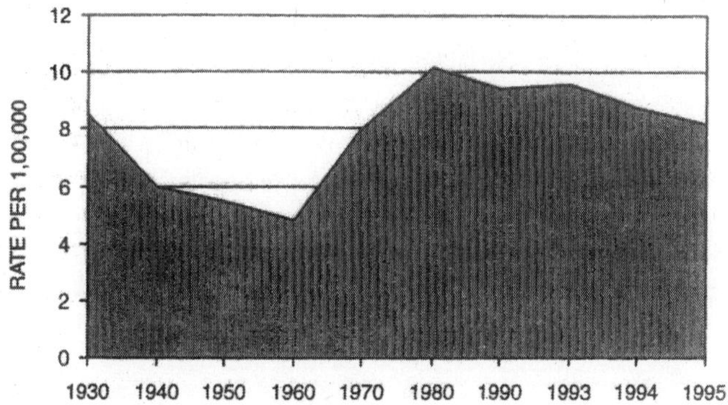

Source: UCR and vital statistics of the US National Centre for Health Homicide.

FIG. 4.14: USA—HOMICIDE RATES (1930-95).

The situation did not show any great change during the 1970s. An analysis of the UCR data for 1969-82 revealed that the combined violent crime rate rose by 69 per cent.

A Bureau of Justice Statistics (BJS) analysis of October 1983 came to two broad conclusions:

> homicides fell sharply during the War years, followed by a short-term rise at the end of the War when most of the soldiers returned home; and the rise in homicides in the 1960s could be associated with the post-War baby boom generation which had reached the crime-prone age of 16 around this time. (Sullivan and Victor 1988)

Ironically, in contrast to the UCR picture, the National Crime Survey (NCS) statistics pointed to stable rates during 1973-80, a discrepancy that we were to observe later also.[13]

The 1980s began with a violent crime rate of 548.9 which went up by 8.56 per cent within a year. This was followed by a drop each year for four years. This trend got reversed in 1985 when the reported rate was 556.6. While it was a rising curve till 1992, the past three years, 1993-5, have successively witnessed a drop. During 1995, the rate of violent crime dropped from 714 to 685 (Figure 4.15 and Table 4.3). Another significant feature of the scene was that a substantial percentage of such crime was still being committed with the help of firearms. It was 30 per cent in 1995 (UCR 1995).

ANALYSIS OF PROPERTY CRIME IN THE US

Property crime constitutes a bulk of the index offences registered by the police. During 1995, the 12 million property cases registered were 87 per cent of all index offences. The property crime rate stood at 4593, a 5.5 per cent drop during the decade (Table 4.4). Most of the crime was contributed by larceny-theft (57.7 per cent) and burglary (18.7 per cent). More than 11 per cent of all arrestees in 1995 were for property offences.

TABLE 4.3: VIOLENT CRIME RATE (1975-95)

Year	Total Violent Crime	Homicide	Rape	Agg. Asslt	Robbery
1975	487.8	9.6	26.3	231.1	220.8
1980	596.6	10.2	36.8	298.5	251.1
1985	556.6	7.9	37.1	302.9	208.5
1990	731.8	9.4	41.2	424.1	257.0
1995	685.0	8.2	37.1	418.3	220.9

Source: UCR, 1995.

TABLE 4.4: PROPERTY CRIME

Year	Number	Rate	Value of property lost
1993	12.2 million	4737.6	$ 14.8 billion
1994	12.1 million	4658.3	$ 15.1 billion
1995	12.06 milion	4593.0	$ 13.1 billion

See also Figure 4.16.

The heavy volume (1.4 million) of motor vehicle thefts is striking. The gravity of the problem is well brought out by the fact that one of every 147 registered motor vehicles was stolen in 1996.

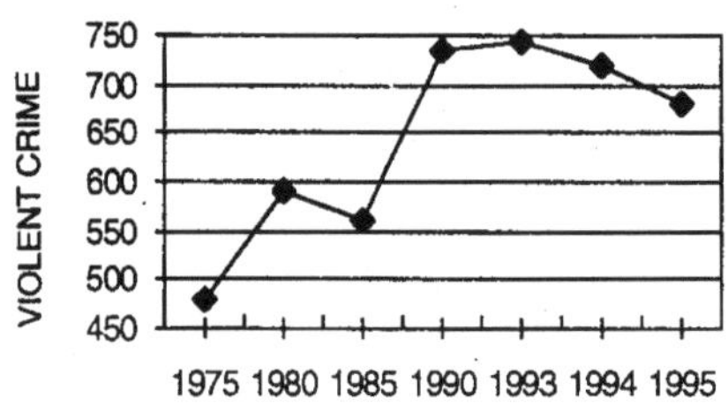

Fig. 4.15: USA—Violent Crime Rate (1975-95).

Analysis of Arrests in the US

An estimated 10.3 million arrests (excluding those for traffic violations) were made during 1995 (Table 4.5).

The generally high volume of arrests maintained the intense pressure on space already seen in federal and state prisons. The number of prisoners reached a record high of 883,593 at the end of 1992 (BJS 1993a). This was a 168 per cent increase during 1980-92. The annual increase was at least 5.5 per cent each year. Aggravated assault and burglary-related arrests accounted for most of the growth, although, between 1970 and 1990, incarceration for serious offences rose by more than 50,000 (BJS 1993a).

As regards inmates of local jails, during mid-1992, overall jail occupancy was 99 per cent of the rated capacity. One of every 428 adult US residents was in jail on 30 June 1992 (BJS 1993b).

Organized Crime in the US

In its nascent form of gambling and prostitution, organized crime was a visible urban phenomenon once the big cities stabilized themselves in the mid-nineteenth century (George 1990). Much later, the opportunity provided by the prohibition years (1920-33) for inter-state and trans-national crime strengthened the base criminal organizations (George 1990 and Cressey 1969). Many bootlegging gangs, active at that time, were essentially of immigrants or their descendants. A mid-1920s study of 72 important bootleggers in thirteen cities revealed that 50 per cent of them were of Eastern European Jewish background, and 25 per cent of Italian descent. The rest were chiefly Irish and Polish (Haller 1989).

Following the repeal of the Prohibition Amendment, the tentacles of criminal organizations extended themselves to fields such as

Table 4.5: Highlights of 1995 Arrests

Driving under the influence	0.9 million
Larceny-theft	1.05 million.
Drug abuse violations	1.04 million
Male arrest	80 %
Arrestees below 25 years	44 %

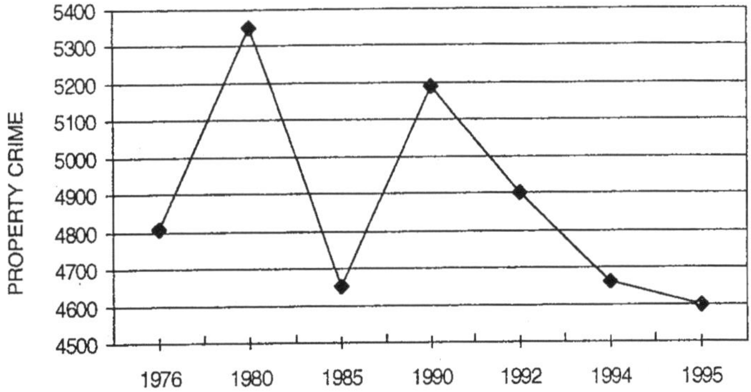

FIG. 4.16: USA—PROPERTY CRIME RATE (1976-95).

prostitution, drug trafficking, labour racketeering, traffic in pornography, illegal gambling (bookmaking and numbers rackets), criminal usury (loan sharking) and extortion (George 1990).

The 1951 pronouncement of the Senator Estes Kefauver's Committee to investigate Organized Crime in Inter-State Commerce that a 'nationwide crime syndicate existed' and the committee's choice of the word '*mafia*' to refer to it caused great excitement. In 1963-4, Joseph Valachi, member of an organized criminal gang 'Family', testified before a Senate Committee on narcotics that several groups engaged in this activity were organized into a *Cosa Nostra* (Our Thing).

The 1967 President's Commission's stand that 24 groups constituted the core of such crime and that their membership was exclusively Italian in descent gave a further sanction to the belief that all organized crime was Italian-Sicilian in nature. This prominence given to the Italian dominance tended to obscure the existence of such crime even during the nineteenth century, much before the massive immigration that was seen later. Many scholars, including Donald Cressey (1969), are not happy with this excessive attention to the Italian involvement.

Conscious of the corrupting influence of organized crime, the US Government has placed several laws on the statute book. Reacting to the grave picture presented by the President's Commission, the Congress approved (1970) the Organized Crime Control Act. An important part of this Act is the RICO (Racketeer Influenced and Corrupt Organizations) Act which has been amended several times over the years to expand the definition of 'racketeering activity' (George 1990). Several states have their own version of the RICO.

Notwithstanding the abundant legislative back-up to efforts to contain organized crime, success on the ground is modest. This is because of the rigid standards of proof required by courts. An instance in point is the acquittal (1990) of John Gotti, a major mafia figure. A questionable move here has been the decision of the Department of Justice to wind up special task forces and place responsibility for tackling organized crime in the hands of Attorney's offices (George 1990).

No account of organized crime in the US will be complete without a detailed reference to the crime generated by the street gangs in Chicago and Los Angeles, two cities notorious for inter-gang rivalry and violence.

An NIJ research of 1993, which studied the problem in Chicago, revealed that gang-related high crime neighbourhoods could be categorized into three: 'turf hot spots' (where territorial disputes are waged); 'drug hot spots' (where there is heavy incidence of drug offences); and 'turf and drug hot spots' (where there is a combination of crimes).

More than 40 major street gangs are active in Chicago, and the four largest of these—Black Gangster Disciples Nation, Latin Disciples, Latin Kings and Vice Lords—with a total membership of about 19,000 accounted for 1000 police-recorded criminal incidents each, during 1987-90. In 1990, 12 per cent of all homicides in Chicago were their handiwork. Most importantly, a gun was the lethal weapon in almost all street gang-motivated homicides. The Chicago Police Department, which contributed most of the data to the NIJ study, has a separate Gang Crime Section which monitors all street gang activity (NIJ December 1993).

In Los Angeles, there are more than 250 active gangs, many of whom are 50 years old. They have a combined membership of nearly 26,000. The most active and violent of these comprise either blacks or the more numerous Hispanics. There are also the non-traditional but well-organized Asian gangs, formed by ethnic groups from countries such as China, Vietnam, Korea and Philippines.

In the early 1970s, sensing the gravity of street gang proclivity to violent crime, the LAPD launched a special programme called Community Resources Against Street Hoodlums (CRASH). There is a CRASH unit for each of the four operational bureaux in the LAPD. Sensitive to the narcotic aspect of black gang activities, a Gang Related Active Trafficker Suppression (GRATS) was also formed in January

1988. Incidentally, 1988 was a landmark year because gangs were responsible for as many as 250 homicides at a time when homicides were generally on the decline.

There is a Gang Activities Section attached to the Detective Support Division of LAPD headquarters which monitors gang activity, and also encourages the public to share information through a special gang hotline telephone (LAPD 1989 and Daryl Gates and Robert Jackson 1989).

Godson and Olson (1993) present a grim picture of the future of organized crime in the US. It is their belief that the US, like most other countries, does not understand the magnitude of the threat. In their estimate, the economic cost—over $ 200 billion per year in health care, lost productivity and revenue—and lives lost (27,000 during 1988-91 from drug overdose alone), equal those of a limited war. The consequences of organized crime include a rise in violent crime, collapse of neighbourhoods, spread of disease, especially AIDS, and strains on the cost and quality of the US judicial system.

The activities of two organizations should in particular cause concern to the US. These are the Colombian cocaine cartels and the Chinese criminal groups organized around Triad secret societies. The former's operations are large and sophisticated, affording them resources which can destabilize governments and enable them to evade even international collaborative exercises directed against them. The Triads have a broader sweep than the Colombian cartels and dominate the import of heroin into the US. In addition, they have a major hand in the smuggling of illegal Chinese aliens—nearly 10,000 per year—into the country. Viewed in conjunction with the increasing activities of groups of Russians in the US with links to the former Soviet Union, Godson and Olson (1993) predict that future organized crime will be dominated by these ethnic-centred groups.

Firearms in US Crime

Most striking is the involvement of firearms—particularly the handgun—in a large volume of crime in the US. The Task Force on Violent Crime (1968) observed that handgun crime was 'perhaps the most serious problem of violence facing our nation today'.

According to one estimate, there are about 60 million handguns and more than 100 million long guns (rifles and shotguns) in private hands (Gurr 1989a). The enormous number of weapons in private hands, lawful or otherwise, points to the citizen's lack of faith in the police. Widespread gun ownership no doubt deters crime. This is a position buttressed by the admission of some convicted robbers and burglars (Gurr 1989b). It is however known that this deterrence applies mainly to property crime, and that gun ownership invariably leads to deadly brawls. While it is difficult to assert that guns produce avoidable crime, there is evidence to suggest that homes with a gun were likely to experience a handgun death, seven to eight times more than those who did not possess a gun (ibid.).

Relevant here is a study of the impact of a major increase in gun ownership seen after 1965. A simultaneous increase in crime was noticed around this time. But, even as crime levels stabilized, gun ownership continued to grow. The study, using computer-assisted statistical techniques, concluded that an ambivalent effect was seen. While violence rose because of a greater use of guns, citizens bought more guns as a reaction (Kleck 1984). Interestingly, while handguns constitute only one-third of all firearms in the country, they account for 80 per cent of all firearm-homicides (Roth 1994). A Rand analysis (1990) of the use of handguns in crime during 1979-87 is highly revealing (Table 4.6). Apart from the presence of the handgun in a wide spectrum of offences, it is significant that a majority of the victims were urban black males in the age group 16-34.

During 1995, firearms came to notice in 30 per cent of violent offences (excluding forcible rapes) (UCR 1995).

The National Rifle Association (NRA), chief spokesman for the gun lobby, is against any tightening of the gun law. In its view, a firearm is the best protection to the law-abiding citizen, and a stricter control over licensing would only embolden the violent criminal. A TIME/CNN poll of December 1993 however found 70 per cent support for gun control and 78 per cent for mandatory registration of

TABLE 4.6: USE OF HANDGUN IN CRIME (1979-87)

Annual average of violent crime with handgun	639000
Killed annually	9200
Injured annually	15000
Handgun involvement (Offence-wise)	
All violent crime	10 %
Rapes	7 %
Robberies	18%
Aggravated assaults	22%

all guns. Nevertheless, 74 per cent were against a ban on handguns (*Time,* 20 December 1993).

An eternal complaint of law enforcement agencies, especially the police, is that the existing law permits free availability of guns and their use, thus contributing to permissiveness. The Brady Bill, which became law in 1993, provided for a five-day waiting period before the sale of a firearm. The expectation was that it could reduce the prospect of a weapon being acquired lawfully by a person with a criminal record. Its impact will be known only after a few years. Similar is the scheme of rewards announced by some states to persons voluntarily turning in weapons. The Crime Bill, passed by Congress in August 1994, incorporated a law that banned assault weapons (AK-47, Uzis and Street Sweepers) and other semi-automatic weapons and detachable magazines with a capacity of more than 10 rounds of ammunition.

While it is difficult to go totally with the NRA or the anti-gun lobby, statistics of gun-related crime do give the feeling that the country deserves a stern gun law that would respect the right of private defence without allowing a weapon to get into the hands of a psychopath or a habitual criminal. In any case, a pragmatic approach is called for here. One is inclined to agree with Kleck (1984) when he says that, ultimately, this becomes a supply-demand paradigm. It is futile to believe that the stock of nearly 185 million guns can be reduced so much as to cause any inconvenience to criminals. What can be done at best is to make the latter understand that the penalty for illegal possession or use of a weapon would be stiff (Kates 1989).

Drugs and Crime in the US

The high volume of arrests and prosecutions for drug offences imposes a tremendous strain on the criminal justice system. For instance, during 1987, about 937,400 arrests were made for drug-law violation. Also, during 1980-7, such arrests increased by 52 per cent, although the arrests for all crime increased only by 11 per cent (Belenko 1990). During 1989, drug abuse arrests were 20 per cent above the previous year. It also represented a 55 per cent rise over 1985 and 126 per cent over 1980 (UCR 1989). During 1995, 1.04 million arrests were made nationally for drug abuse. This represented a nearly 65 per cent rise over the decade (UCR 1995).

A matter for concern is also the substantial number of arrestees in non-drug offences testing positive for drugs. Although some studies of early 1970s did not indicate a clear relationship, by late 1970s and a little later, it was becoming clear that 'violence was a common part of the world of the street drug user'(McBride and Swartz 1990:148).

Interviews (1978-81) of one cohort of 573 Miami narcotics users revealed that 83 per cent of them were active in the streets and had used heroin or illegal methadone once or more during the 90 days prior to the interview. Almost everyone in the cohort had a criminal record, dating possibly back to the age of 15. Their first offence was invariably related to stealing property. The average number of crimes worked out to 375 per head. A similar analysis of 429 non-narcotic drug users revealed a lower criminal activity, namely, 320 crimes per respondent (Inciardi 1989).

Investigating the parallel between bootlegging and illegal drug markets insofar as they lead to violence, Haller (1989) believes that the Miami of the past two decades almost rivals Chicago of the 1920s. The relatively high penalties which are imposed on drug dealers lead to the liberal use of threat or actual violence to protect themselves from criminal justice agencies. Also, the lack of trust and a fear of being cheated, evident among players in this field, generate pronounced violence.

Preliminary results of an NIJ Drug Use Forecasting (DUF) Programme suggested a high probability of the drug-crime nexus. Addressed to arrestees in various cities, the study revealed that, in New York City, 82 per cent of male arrestees tested positive for at least one illegal drug (Trojanowicz and Bucqueroux 1990). Perhaps, more than any other offence, it is in the case of homicides that the nexus with drugs is most pronounced. Of the 1459 homicides reported from New York City in 1984, 23.8 per cent were identified as drug-related (Brownstein and Goldstein 1990).

The above studies do nothing more than heighten the probability of a drug-crime relationship. Any positive assertion of a direct link appears untenable, particularly in the light of known pre-drug criminal activity of many of those arraigned by the criminal justice system. The hint of a link should, nevertheless, continue to agitate the minds of researchers exploring causes of crime.

There is no hope of an immediate decline in drug abuse. Deterrence through various criminal justice sanctions has not worked. In view of its enormous dimensions, police officers tend to ignore street drug-dealing as long as it is unobtrusive and is not accompanied by violence

(Bayley 1994a). The impact of such laxity on the future of general crime in the country needs to be studied.

The Racial Factor in US Crime

In no other country perhaps has the relationship between race and crime been so much felt or discussed. This is because of the pronounced black involvement in crime, principally as the aggressor, and secondarily as victim.

Blacks comprise only 12 to 13 per cent (just about one-eighth) of the population. Taking a typical year—1990—they accounted for 61.2 per cent arrests for robbery. It must be noted that 53.1 per cent of all criminal deaths were attributed to blacks, who also formed 56.4 per cent of the arrests (Hacker 1992). Mention must also be made that 47.0 per cent of those awaiting trial in local jails or incarcerated there for short terms were black. They also accounted for 40.1 per cent of prisoners under sentence of death, and 45.3 per cent of all those lodged in state or federal prisons (ibid.).

During 1995, black arrestees for all offences comprised 31.0 per cent of total arrests. The black share of crime was most pronounced in the case of robbery (59.5 per cent), followed by murder (54.4 per cent).

There is also a disproportionate rise in the black incarceration rate since 1930. From a mere 22.4 per cent in that year, their numbers increased to 45.3 per cent of all those behind bars in 1986. During the same period, the figures for whites dipped from 76.7 to 39.6 per cent (Hacker 1992) (Figure 4.17).

In a forthright estimate, Hacker (1992) finds it difficult to believe that whites had become more honest or law-abiding than they were earlier. According to him, one interpretation could be that, while the whites went up the economic and social ladder, the blacks had been left behind. The fallacy here is apparent when one considers the fact that crime is not as high among the Hispanics whose levels of income were lower than blacks in some cities.

According to one study for 1976-87, 1800 black individuals were killed by law enforcement officials. The whites suffered 3000 casualties. The figures, in relation to their respective populations, highlight the fact that the black has a three times greater chance than the white in falling to a policeman's bullet (Hacker 1992).

The charge of a racist bias in the system however gets somewhat muted by the fact that the black offender's preference, except probably in the case of robbery (where an assault on a white is likely to be more lucrative), is also for a victim from his own class. During 1990, 93 per cent of black victims of homicide were killed by blacks themselves, confirming that this crime in the US was really intraracial. 33.2 per cent of rape victims identified the aggressor to be black (Hacker 1992). (This is only partially explained by the relatively difficult black access to white women.)

Again, the 1992 statistics revealed that, except for theft and simple assault, blacks were more victimized than other groups. For example, the robbery rate was 15.6 for the blacks, while it was only 4.7 for whites and 5.1 for other racial categories (*Congressional Digest*, June-July 1994). Of some significance here is a Wesley G. Skogan finding that black women complained of being raped twice as frequently as their white counterparts (Trojanowicz and Bucqueroux 1990). Also, nearly 75 per cent blacks arrested for rape had black victims (Hacker 1992). In the same manner, a large number of black deaths in encounters with the police have been at the hands of black policemen (ibid.).

Statistics over the years do lend a basis for the feeling that black crime gets disproportionately highlighted under the US criminal justice system, if one considers that blacks account for only one tenth of the population (See Figure 4.18). The question why this is so deserves some reflection.

Charles E. Silberman (1980:161) believes that this is due to the unique position of the black in the country: 'Black crime is rooted in the nature of the black experience . . . an experience that differs from that of other ethnic groups.' Richard Stengel (1985) refers to the view of some experts that the driving force 'is the hopelessness that

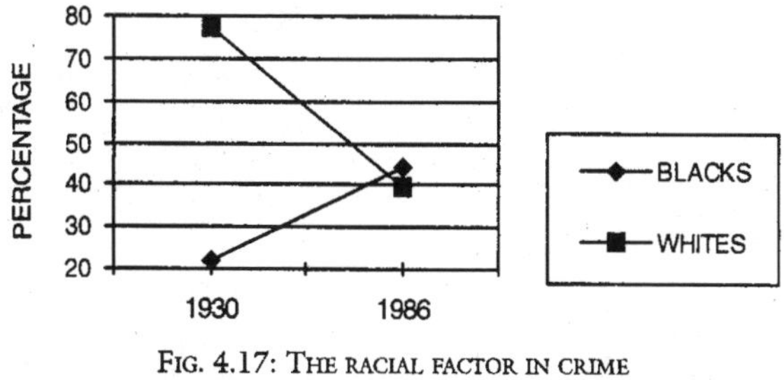

FIG. 4.17: THE RACIAL FACTOR IN CRIME
PERCENTAGE OF BLACKS AND WHITES IN PRISON.

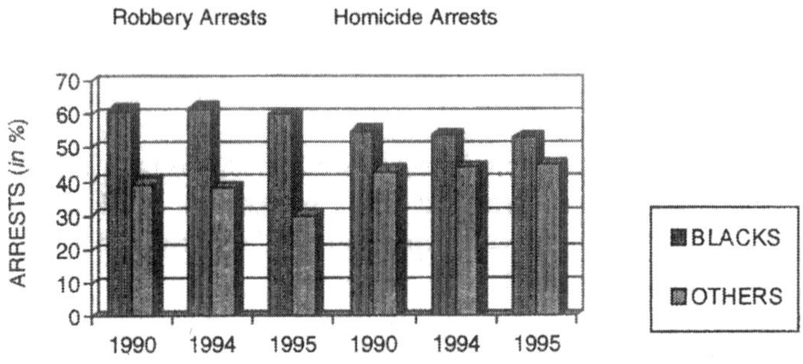

FIG. 4.18: BLACK CONTRIBUTION TO CRIME.

pervades the urban ghetto, which fosters a kind of nihilism, a feeling that nothing is worth anything'.

Trojanowicz and Bucqueroux (1990) identify discrimination as a key factor that explains black alienation and their predilection for crime. Skogan (1989) also draws attention to the fact that, in the aggregate, blacks are younger than whites, and are thereby over-represented in the 15-24 age category, a group that is most crime-prone. There is also the phenomenon of blacks outnumbering other groups in the urban pockets where violent crime is higher than in rural areas.

Wilson (1985b) and Herrnstein sum up the evidence (arrest data, victim surveys and homicide statistics) as indicative of a higher rate of common crimes among blacks as compared to whites and the much higher rate of violent crime.

In sum, since crime and the average black have become so much intertwined, 'discussing crime is often interpreted by blacks as a coded way to talk about race' (Trojanowicz and Bucqueroux 1990: 144). The resultant situation is one dominated by mutual 'mistrust . . . suspicion . . . (and) fear that skin color can become sufficient reason to be stopped, searched, harassed and even harmed' (ibid.:145). It is in this context that protagonists of community policing claim merit in their philosophy. An attempt to remove the impersonalism that marks professional policing and replace it with a proactive style that is sensitive to the needs of large sections of the community, it could help reduce levels of racial fear and tensions. The next chapter will examine how far this theoretical base gets translated into practice.

Problems of Crime Investigation in the US

Documentation of how exactly crime was investigated during the eighteenth and nineteenth centuries is sketchy. The absence, however, of formal police departments till about the middle of nineteenth century raises the presumption that investigation was not structured then. Since policing was essentially proactive, the question of looking for crime and apprehending its perpetrator hardly arose.

In colonial America, there was no equivalent of the modern detective. As a result, the victim played a prominent part in developing his case and identifying or apprehending the offender. The police role was extremely limited (Samaha 1988).

Even after the formation of regular departments around 1850, the scene did not change quickly. Detectives came into the picture only towards the close of the nineteenth century. This too did not bring about any major improvement in the quality of police handling of crime (Samaha 1988).

Accounts relating to the early years of the twentieth century throw up a nexus between detectives and local politicians. Investigation work was naturally individualized, arbitrary and corruption-ridden. Police collaboration with criminals for pecuniary benefits for politicians and themselves was not wholly unknown (Watson and Young 1991).

It was against this background that the professional era of policing arrived. Extending to nearly four decades, reforms during this era aimed at reducing subjectivity and enhancing the use of science and technology in crime control. As time passed by, a certain sophistication became discernible in crime investigation. But, even after three decades of professionalism, no great breakthrough was registered in the area of offender-apprehension.

An Institute of Defence Analysis study—in conjunction with the Los Angeles Police Department—quoted by the President's Commission (1967) found that only 25 per cent of the cases were cleared by arrest or otherwise. The crucial factor here was whether the suspect was identified by the victim or was arrested at the scene of crime. If neither happened, the case almost always went unsolved (Watson and Young 1991). Two later studies—NY City Rand Institute (1970) and Stanford Research Institute (1972)—revealed that detectives were wasting a lot of time on cases which, right from the start, had no prospect of clearance (ibid.).

Perhaps a landmark study (1975) was that of the Rand Corporation which confirmed that clearance depended on information supplied by the victim to the patrol officer immediately after the occurrence. Also, a majority of the serious crimes received only superficial attention. More significantly, the study found that much of detective time was spent on procedural formalities and allied paperwork. A case cleared without the victim's help was invariably an outcome of mechanical procedures 'requiring no imaginative exercise of investigative experience and skill'. A major Rand Institute recommendation was the employment, in serious cases, of a team of investigators, instead of a single officer, and shorter follow-up investigation in minor offences (Watson and Young 1991).

The Stanford and Rand reports led to the drafting of a national programme—Managing the Criminal Investigation (MCI)—for sharpening crime investigation. One of its prominent features was enhancing the responsibility of the patrol officer who filed the incident report and making his initial enquiry more comprehensive. This move was in response to the general complaint of detectives about the poor quality of the preliminary investigation. The MCI did not bring about any distinct upgradation of detective output. On the contrary, moves like these gave detectives a feeling of loss of autonomy and greater accountability. This was the position in the late 1970s (Watson and Young 1991).

The 1980s saw the emergence of a new thinking on crime work, both preventive and investigative. An expansion of the role of an average police officer, the promotion of his interaction with the community in an effort to contain crime and an incisive analysis of crime by field officers as envisaged by Herman Goldstein's 'problem-oriented policing' were all features of a fresh strategy. Meanwhile, research that began towards the latter part of 1970s and continued into the 1980s (such as the Kansas City Police Department Preventive Patrol experiments and the National Institute of Justice study on Differential Police Response (DPR) to citizen calls for service), re-affirmed the earlier belief that patrol officers responded to a call in a mechanical manner, just to document an offence rather than investigate it. A subsequent study (1987) by Rossman revealed that the quality of investigation could be raised through proper selection, assignment and rotation of personnel, reduction of paperwork and improved report preparation (Watson and Young 1991).

Taking into account all available research findings on the subject, Watson and Young (1991) make several suggestions. These include an enlarged role for the community *vis-a-vis* the police and a closer liaison with courts and prosecutors 'as a means of developing training for investigators and to ensure quality control of the investigators work product'. Apart from expanding the investigative role of patrol officers, they plead for their integration with detectives, a move that would cut at the compartmentalized approach that dominated most departments.

Legal Restraints on the US Police

Till about the mid-1950s, legal control over police conduct was minimal and symbolic as, historically speaking, the early restraints on the criminal justice system operated mainly on trial procedure. A series of Supreme Court decisions from about this time clamped several restrictions even at the investigation stage. These brought about a sea-change and ushered in almost a new era in the style of policing (Walker 1993). Many departmental regulations and court rulings now reduce police discretion.

What weighs down the average police officer most is the 'exclusionary rule' which forbids the use of confessions by violating the Fifth Amendment prohibiting self-incrimination and deprivation of life, liberty and property, except under the due process of law. This rule came into being in 1914 (*Weeks* v. *US*), when it was applied to federal prosecutions, and was extended in 1961 (*Mapp* v. *Ohio*) to the local police as well. In 1984 (*U.* v. *Leon*), however, the Supreme Court permitted a 'good faith' exception to the rule (Samaha 1988).

Perhaps the most historic of Supreme Court decisions, *Miranda* v. *US*, came in 1966, when the court ruled that the Fifth Amendment protected suspects against coercive interrogation while in police custody. It ordered that, before being questioned, suspects should be told of their rights, a prescription that has come to be known as the 'Miranda warning'.

Again, in *Terry* v. *Ohio* (1968), the court extended the Fourth Amendment protection against 'unreasonable searches and seizures' to the stopping and frisking of persons encountered by the police on the street. The judges ruled that stops were seizures and frisks were searches, and these were reasonable as long as they were purposeful, such as uncovering concealed weapons and preventing a possible crime (Samaha 1988).

An area of great importance is the right of the police to employ deadly force, especially the use of firearms at suspects. The year 1972 saw the issue of a new and restrictive deadly force policy for the NYPD by Police Commissioner Patrick V. Murphy. This envisaged a review of every shooting by a departmental committee on the basis of a report filed by the officer who used the firearm. Many other large departments followed suit.

Generally speaking, till about the mid-1980s, the law in different states permitted police officers to kill fleeing suspects, if this was necessary to make an arrest. However, many departments began curtailing this authority drastically to allow the use of such force only when it was required to save the lives of citizens or police officers themselves or where the felon had been involved in a violent offence or where he was believed to be armed and therefore dangerous. The Supreme Court clearly ruled (1984) in *Tennessee* v. *Garner* that the use of deadly force to prevent the escape of a felony suspect was unreasonable and struck down a Tennessee statute on the subject. ('Where the suspect poses no immediate threat to the officer and no threat to others, the harm resulting from failing to apprehend him does not justify the use of deadly force to do so'—Samaha 1988:243).

Also important is the question whether the police have the authority to enter private homes to arrest an individual without a warrant. In *Payton* v. *New York*, the Supreme Court ruled (1980) that under 'exigent circumstances', the police could so enter. As per a Federal Court decision (1970) (*Dorman* v. *US*), such circumstances would include violent crimes and a reasonable apprehension that the suspect will otherwise escape (Samaha 1988).

Earlier in the chapter, we saw how confessions made to police officers in India during investigation were inadmissible in evidence, unless they led directly to the discovery of a material fact. In the US, generally speaking, such a confession is admissible, provided it had been obtained after administering the 'Miranda warning'. An excerpt from the Texas Code of Criminal Procedure (Appendix IV) is fairly representative of the position that obtains in many states.

Crime Control Measures in the US

Like anywhere in the world, the US scene is also marked by an animated debate on how to reduce crime. Both theorists and practitioners are its participants.

Bayley (1994a) points to a sharp division between criminologists and the general public on what to do to combat crime. While he believes that the limits of deterrence have been reached, the public and their political representatives place their faith in 'get tough' policies which may not have the desired impact on crime rates. In this context, Bayley (ibid.:27) points to the unpretentious grassroots efforts of communities all over the country in the form of several anti-crime programmes:

> The US has little to teach the world about making deterrence work through criminal justice sanctions, but it has a lot to demonstrate about how communities can help themselves, do what government cannot or will not on its own.

An index of the growing federal involvement is the rise in annual spending under 'administration of justice', from a mere $535 million in 1965 to $11.7 billion during the fiscal year 1992. A plausible explanation for this expanded role for Washington may be the more and more liberal interpretation of the 'commerce clause' (Article 1, Section 8, Clause 2) which gives Congress the power to regulate inter-state and international trade. Also relevant is the belief of Congress and courts that certain categories of crime, apart from their overall impact on the community, pose a threat to commerce (*Congressional Digest*, June-July 1994).

The US Police has great faith in patrolling as a means to control crime in the streets. As a result, patrolling, especially by automobile, is fundamental to the several mechanics in a multi-pronged crime control strategy. The early 1950s saw a marked change in patrol tactics. This was the proposal to replace the two-man patrol cars with one-man cars, a move by some chiefs who believed that this would lead to greater economy and efficiency. Despite the opposition of the rank-and file, the chiefs pushed through with this reform. One of the first to opt for the change was Parker of LAPD. Between 1947 and 1964, a majority—16 out of 20 large cities— switched over to one-man cars (Fogelson 1977).

By the late 1950s and early 1960s, police image as professional crime fighters was well established. With the introduction of telephone and the automobile, 'the neighbourhood cop had been replaced by the motor patrol officer' (Langworthy 1994:86). This led to public complaints of a lack of response to day-to-day concerns which did not satisfy the narrow definition of 'crime' (Trojanowicz and Bucqueroux 1990). It was believed that the focus on serious crimes such as murder, rape and robbery had led to a de-emphasis of emergency services and maintenance of order (Philadelphia Police Task Force 1987).

It was against this background that a Kansas City Preventive Patrol Experiment (1971-2) was conducted. Its objective was to evaluate the impact of three levels of patrolling. For this purpose, the fifteen beats in the city were grouped into three—reactive, proactive and control—of five beats each. While the proactive beats had additional cars, the control ones persisted with the existing level of patrolling. Patrol vehicles entered the last group only on receipt of a call. The study concluded, after a year of experiment, that variations in routine preventive patrol had no impact on the incidence or fear of crime, police response time, traffic accidents and the community's evaluation of the police delivery of service (Kelling *et al.*, 1974, and Langworthy and Travis 1994).

The 1970s also saw two foot patrolling experiments in Flint (Michigan) and Newark (New Jersey). These revealed that citizens were generally positive about the foot patrolman and felt safer with such patrolling. This was notwithstanding a general lack of enthusiasm to foot patrolling among policemen. While no reduction in crime was noticeable in Newark, a small drop in crime and a fall in the number of calls for service were reported from Flint (Police Foundation 1981, Trojanowicz 1982 and 1983, and Langworthy and Travis 1994).

A recent NYPD experiment is of some interest here in the context of the substantial drop in crime in New York for two successive years (1994-5). This coincided with the leadership of Bill Bratton, the NYPD Commissioner, a great votary of the 'Broken Windows' concept enunciated by Wilson and Kelling (described in detail in the next chapter). Promoting what has come to be known as 'zero tolerance policing', Bratton drove his officers into focussing their attention on 'quality of life issues' and 'disorder reduction'. Cleveand, Milwaukee and St. Louis are other cities which are known to be practising this style of policing. In essence, the approach was one of tackling the fear of crime and paying attention to minor offences which were being ignored, instead of merely concentrating on the prevention of serious crime (Sarah Gibson 1997).

Zero tolerance policing has however been discountenanced by many who believe it to be too aggressive to fit into a democratic polity and that it raises many human rights questions. The success in terms of a reduction of crime is also disputed by a few. For instance, Charles Pollard, Chief Constable of Thames Valley Police in the UK says:

> That part of the zero tolerance principle characterized by the aggressive policing, confrontational management, opportunistic short-termism and undue emphasis on the 'number game' poses an enormous threat to the future. If this culture is not tackled, then, on the basis of the British experience, the risk of serious corruption and inner-city disorder in the future is real. (Sarah Gibbons 1997)

Another critic of zero tolerance policing, Joseph McNamara says:

> Cities in free nations will never reflect the orderliness of Berlin under the Nazis or Moscow under the Communists. In America, police methods must comply with the law and community standards. They must not arise from a rigid concept of public order formulated within the police, culture. (1997:23)

Bratton has since left NYPD. His successor Howard Safir's follow-up of Bratton's crime prevention strategy will be watched with great interest.

As for the legislative and administrative support to anti-crime efforts, more than the series of steps taken by several states and big city administrations, it is the federal government's initiative that is laudable. This counters the general perception that the Tenth Amendment to the constitution contemplates a nearly exclusive role for the states in respect of 'police powers' (*Congressional Digest*, June-July 1994).

Since the passage of the Law Enforcement Assistance Act of 1965 which gave birth to the Office of Law Enforcement Assistance in the Department of Justice, there have been a number of enactments covering various classes of crime. The Comprehensive Crime Control Act 1984 created the Office of Justice Programmes meant to coordinate the activities of the Bureau of Justice Assistance, the National Institute of Justice, the Bureau of Justice Statistics, etc. Additionally, the act brought in a lot of changes in sentencing and bail procedures, besides establishing a victim compensation programme in the Department of Justice.

The Anti-Drug Abuse Act of 1986 prescribed mandatory minimum sentences for a few offences. It also made new provisions for preventing money laundering and for a greater authority to seize and forfeit assets bought out of criminal activities. A similar act of 1988 imposed new and increased penalties for drug trafficking and enhanced funds for drug law enforcement. The act also created a new federal agency headed by a cabinet-level director called the Drug Czar.

The Crime Control Act 1990 authorized $220 million in matching federal grants to help states formulate stronger prison programmes. More stringent anti-child abuse measures, especially child pornography, and increased allocation to federal drug enforcement programmes were the other prominent features of the act.

The Crime Bill approved by US Senate on 25 August 1994—passed by the House earlier in the same month—made life imprisonment mandatory for those convicted of three violent felonies and extended the death penalty to 60 federal crimes. The bill banned, for ten years, the manufacture and possession of 19 specific classes of assault weapons. It made registration with state law enforcement agencies mandatory for those on parole after conviction for crimes against children and for violent sexual offences. The bill allotted $30,200 million for anti-crime initiatives. This included $8,800 million for 100,000 extra state and local police officers to patrol the streets. Another $380 million was set aside for local crime prevention block grants which was to replace a number of current prevention programmes.

COMPARATIVE ANALYSIS

The Statistics

Although crime is a universal phenomenon, difficulties arise when crime rates of different countries are sought to be compared. Definitions and interpretation of statistics pose a problem (Fairchild 1993). This is in spite of the Interpol and the United Nations' efforts to bring about a certain standardization in the matter (UNAFEI and AIC 1996). An across-the-board comparison, ignoring cultural and enforcement differences, could be totally misleading. (The temptation to make such comparisons is difficult to resist, notwithstanding its fallacy.) This is particularly in the context of the reputation of many forces for suppressing crime, either on their own, or under political compulsions. It has, therefore, been found that longitudinal, rather than cross-sectional studies, would give a better idea of the crime scenario (Bennet and Lynch 1990). It is also likely that a fair relation between crime rate and societal factors could be reached only if an effort is made to control for criminal justice variables and definitional variables (Fairchild 1993).

Perhaps most relevant here is the substantial variance in procedure for the reporting of crime, as also its entry into police records. There is here a distinct need to control for under-reporting and non-reporting. Further, comparisons become really skewed when one considers the fact that hardly has any country the kind of elaborate victimization survey available in the US. As Bayley (1985) would say :

> efficacy measures such as clearance rates, usually meaning the ratio of arrests to the number of reported crimes, are wholly spurious. Not only are they based on unreliable reported crime figures, but they measure what the police do—making arrests—rather than what police achieve—preventing crime.

As for the reliability of crime figures in the US and India, my impression is that the former carry greater credibility because of the availability of the NCS as a base for cross-checking. Also, the existence of an automated complaint service (911) in a majority of cities and towns, which reduces the scope for suppressing complaints, enhances the accuracy of US figures. This is without prejudice to the fact that a fair percentage of crime does not at all get reported to the police, a phenomenon that explains the wide divergence seen occasionally between UCR figures and NCS projections.

One charge hurled at the police by many in India is the reluctance to register crime. Media perceptions and public opinion surveys endorse this. Supervisory officials are prisoners to a system that links performance to an ability to show a decline in crime. This encourages them, either to connive at this pernicious practice of non-registration of complaints, or not make a serious effort to track down the delinquents in the department responsible for this and punish them. In this situation, the introduction of an NCS in India on the US pattern will alone enable the building of popular pressure on the executive to come down heavily on the evil of suppression of complaints of crime. It will also pave the way for introduction of a 911-Computer-Assisted Dispatch (CAD) facility in at least the major cities. This would ensure that all requests for service in a crime or non-crime situation are recorded in a central registry and acted upon, if not immediately, at least according to a priority classification. The communication revolution that is very much in evidence in the country, and the anxiety of a sizeable section of police leaders to upgrade police technology offers some hopes here.

TABLE 4.7: CRIME SCENARIO

	USA			INDIA		
	1994	1995	Change %	1994	1995	Change %
Total Crime						
(in millions)	13.98	13.86	-0.9	5.51*	6.0**	8.9
Crime rate	5373.5	5277.6	-1.8	612.5	654.3	6.9
Number of offences (in thousands)						
Murder	23.3	21.6	-7.4	38.5	37.5	-2.9
Rape	102.2	97.5	-4.6	13.2	13.8	4.1
Robbery	618.9	580.6	-6.2	23.9	22.4	-6.2
Burglary	2,712.1	2,595.0	-4.3	121.5	116.5	-4.1
Theft	9,419.1	9,473.3	0.6	303.6	294.3	-3.0

Note: *The figure 5.51 for India in 1994 is made up of 1.63 million IPC offences and 3.88 million special and local law offences.

**The figure 6.00 for 1995 is similarly made up of 1.70 and 4.30 respectively.[14]

See also Figures 4.19 to 4.23.

OFFENCE CATEGORIZATION

The UCR and *Crime in India* (CII) provide the basis for comparing the crime scenario in the two countries. While most of the major offences are nearly identically defined, one difference is that, the CII, unlike the UCR, does not make a distinction between 'statutory rape' and 'forcible rape'. It also furnishes a classification of 'dacoity' (robbery committed by five or more persons) in addition to 'robbery'. Yet another divergence is that the CII does not give figures for 'aggravated assault' or motor vehicle thefts (which would be covered by the broad head 'theft').

PATTERNS OF CRIME

A generally stable crime situation in the US and a rising curve in the case of India are indicated by the latest statistics (Table 4.7).

Interestingly, when we compare the share of violent crime in all crime, the 13 per cent of the US compares unfavourably with India's 4.1 per cent. However, in the case of share of property offences, there is a wide divergence; 87 per cent in the US against 6.9 per cent in India.[15]

To make the comparison more easily absorbed, homicide rates

A comparison of total crime figures (1994 and 1995)

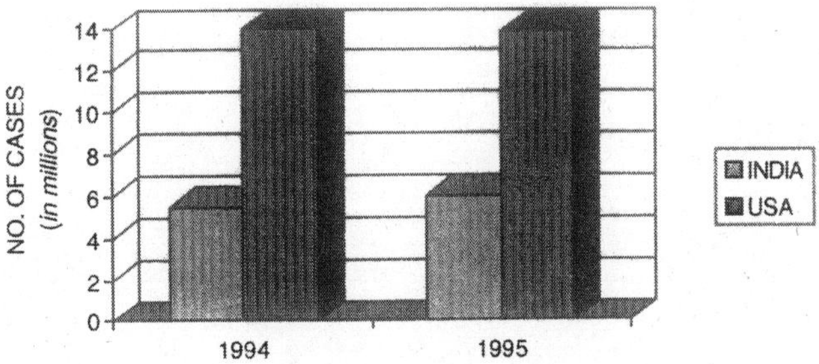

FIGURE 4.19: US/INDIA CRIME SCENE.

Offencewise Comparison

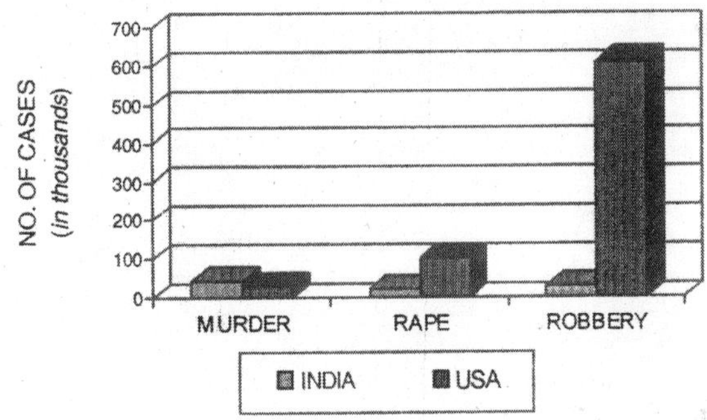

FIG. 4.20: US/INDIA CRIME SCENE (1994).

Offencewise Comparison

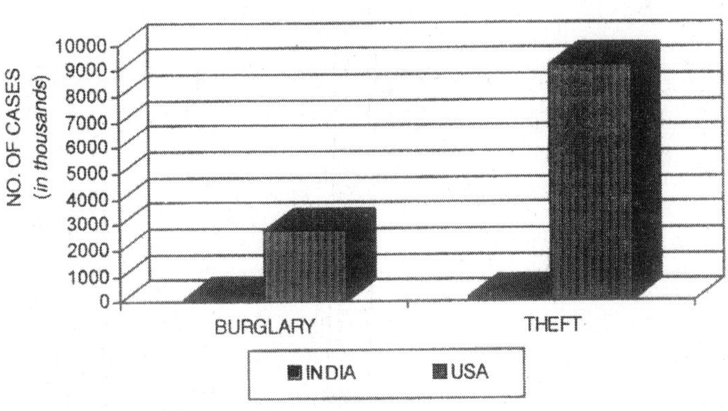

FIG. 4.21: US/INDIA CRIME SCENE (1994).

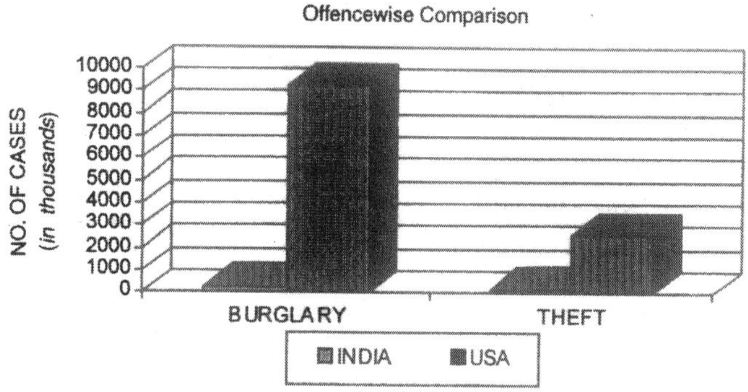

FIG. 4.22: US/INDIA CRIME SCENE (1995).

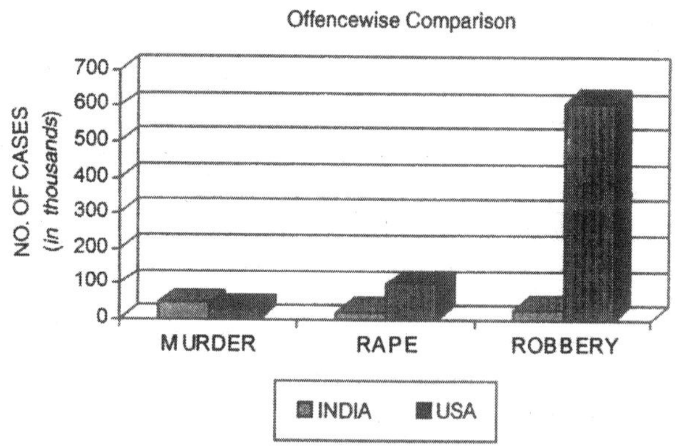

FIG. 4.23: US/INDIA CRIME SCENE (1995).

possibly provide 'the most accurate barometer of actual violence', because they generally escape 'definitional and reporting problems' (Lanier and Carter 1994). Also, homicide is one crime that is best reported, and is generally regarded as difficult to suppress. It is therefore reasonable to assume that, except for a small percentage, all homicides get reported to the police. A comparison of crime in two different countries, therefore, acquires some credibility through a study of homicide figures.

During the past decade, the US reported a 4.8 per cent rise in the number of homicides, against the 44.3 per cent spurt in India. A comparison however of the rate (per 100,000 of population) of homicides gives a slightly more favourable picture of India. The US rate of 8.2 during 1995 was twice that of India (4.1). The high level of fear of violent crime in the US gleaned from a majority of surveys squares with this statistic.

As for property offences, a prominent feature of the US scene is that motor vehicle thefts constitute about 10 per cent of all crime. This is not surprising for a country where almost every other family has at least one vehicle. There are gangs which specialize in such thefts, and there are locations in the country which are notorious for a high volume of this crime. One major handicap in the way of a comparative study with India is the absence of exclusive auto theft figures. Nevertheless, the impression is one of a rising trend, given the phenomenal increase in the number of vehicles on the roads, especially in the major cities. The NCRB will possibly do well in obtaining exclusive auto theft figures so that research and preventive strategies are facilitated.

Offender Background

Crime in the US is very often analysed in terms of the ethnicity of arrestees and victims. For instance, in 1995, 67.0 per cent of the arrestees were white and 31 per cent black, who constitute only 12 per cent of the population. As for victims, the National Victimization Survey for 1991 revealed that, under each age group, blacks were much more likely to be victimized. (While this is 20 per cent more in the group 12-15, it is at least 10 per cent more in the groups 16-19, 20-4 and 25-34.) These figures are often cited to highlight the disproportionate black involvement in criminal justice processes. For the purpose of analysing currents and cross-currents within the American society and initiating rehabilitative measures, they provide some useful indicators.

Official crime statistics in India do not attempt any such analysis. One explanation is the absence of a nationwide racial diversity. The next plausible basis for analysis, religion, cannot be attempted because India is a secular democracy and any break-up of crime in terms of religion could be questioned for its constitutionality, even igniting fundamentalist feelings which already cause a lot of social tension. Also, it is highly unlikely that such a comparison of the criminal proclivities of the various religious groups will yield indicators of any great significance.

The only parallel—though slightly laboured—to the black involvement in US crime is the presence in some pockets of India of certain nomadic groups known for criminal activity marked by a high degree of specialization and dexterity. This phenomenon was quite marked in pre-Independence India and had been studied with great interest by many criminologists who produced classical treatises. The sweep of modernization over many parts of the country, particularly the creation of opportunities for education and full-time employment, coupled with the welfare projects initiated by some enlightened police officers, has absorbed these groups into responsible sections of the society. It is, therefore, difficult any longer to identify these groups in specific locations earlier associated with them.

Crime Facilitators

While several factors contributing to crime offer scope for drawing parallels, I believe that, in the current context, the following alone deserve a special mention. (The others have been dealt with in passing under each section.)

Drugs and Crime

There is a high level of drug-related crime in both countries. While a bulk of the enforcement of drug-law in the US is the outcome of operations by federal agencies, state police departments carry the brunt in India. The latter account for a larger number of seizures every year although, for guidance, they are not averse to seeking the assistance of central government organizations.

Perhaps much more important is the difference in perception of the impact of drugs on crime. In the US, research backs the premise that a substantial portion of general crime is traceable to drug consumption. While the relationship is not totally dependent, all available material suggests a strong nexus. I am not aware of any major reliable research on the subject in India. It is this situation that possibly explains the lack of a serious concern on the part of criminal justice policy-makers and practitioners. The failure to make it mandatory for every arrestee to be subjected to a drug test is, therefore, not surprising. Till this is done, it will not be possible in India to estimate the influence of drugs on crime in the country.

Firearms and Crime

The dominant role played by firearms in the US has been already discussed elaborately. The fear induced by the gun in the mind of the ordinary citizen is difficult to describe. It can only be felt by walking the streets of any major city. I have had this experience in Philadelphia, New York and Newark, and can only say that fear stalks every law-abiding individual. The extent of fear is such that, unless the contrary is proved, you could seriously believe that almost every other person whom you pass by in the streets is armed.

In view of the presence of a large number of unlicensed guns, the estimate of total number of firearms available in the country is very approximate. There is, however, some basis for computing the extent to which firearms are used in the crime that is reported to the police. The UCR provides the information. For instance, we know that, in 1995, some type of firearm or other was used in 30 per cent of violent crimes (UCR 1995).

The general impression in India is that the situation is not as alarming, although there is reason for concern. Traditional weapons of a wide variety (in shape and sharpness), which are manually employed, continue to provide the means for committing a bulk of the crime. The scenario is fast changing.

The manufacture of crude guns is known in many parts of the country. The expanding activities of terrorists in certain regions of the country and their liberal use of firearms invest the situation with a new dimension. This has substantially pushed up the number of firearms available. It is believed that the AK-47 rifle is now fairly easily procured by elements having access to terrorist groups which smuggle them across the border.

There is need for action on a war footing. The lack of a statistical base is a definite shortcoming. Unlike the UCR, *Crime in India* does not give figures of crime committed with the help of firearms, and merely carries the number of prosecutions launched under the Arms and Explosives Acts. This is a major lacuna that contributes to a certain complacence in the drive against unlicensed weapons.

The terrorist menace is also an eye-opener in respect of explosives.

A number of explosions are reported from time to time from various parts of India. Sophisticated explosives, such as the RDX, have come to notice in many such incidents. The assassination of former Prime Minister Rajiv Gandhi and the series of explosions in various parts of the country point to a grave situation. The none too tight control over the manufacture and sale of explosives projects a dangerous future.

NOTES

1. I am not aware of any serious effort to estimate the percentage of rapes that goes unreported. I would commend this area of research to future criminal justice students in India.
2. Although it is an Act of the central government, it can be amended by state governments to suit local requirements, subject to such changes being ratified by the President of India.
3. The main object of amending the Cr.P.C. in 1973 was to give effect to the Constitutional requirement of separating the judiciary from the executive. The concept of Judicial Magistrate was introduced for the first time in the Cr.P.C.1973. At the same time, the concept of Executive Magistrate was also introduced, although it was totally repugnant to the need for completely separating the judiciary from the executive.
4. In recognition of the abnormal increase in the volume of work handled by the two CID branches, each of these now comes under a DGP or Additional DGP/IGP with a support staff of two or three Deputy Inspectors-General and Superintendents. Another important development is the establishment of field offices of Crime and Special Branches at the headquarters of districts in a bold departure from their earlier centralized organization.In addition, every District Police force has a District Crime Branch (DCB) to which are entrusted complicated crime, especially of the white collar variety. This has been found by District SPs to be a useful squad, especially for investigating cases which have been handled unsatisfactorily at the police station level.
5. To reinforce the view that the Indian picture of the times defied any simplistic interpretation, Rao also refers to David Bayley's observation (1969) that, when a rise in crime was a universal phenomenon, the almost static situation reported in India was surprising. Bayley had thrown up a proposition for consideration. It was possible that the figures were suspect. If this was not so, Bayley wondered whether India could be given the benefit of a 'critical uniqueness' to explain why it was out of step with most of the rest of the world .
6. C.V. Narasimhan, a former Director of CBI and Member-Secretary of the National Police Commission (1977), brought to my notice (while reviewing a draft of this chapter) the phenomenon which he noticed during general election time in 1952, 1957 and 1962. Before the conduct of an election, he saw quite a lot of movement of muscle men and money

number of 'floaters', who could otherwise be resorting to crime for their living. Crime figures therefore tended to drop during such times.

7. One has to reckon here the fact that sponsors of political agitations very often seek large numbers of arrests so as to derive political mileage. Many of these do not relate to public order as perceived by the common man. Figures of such arrests may have to be excluded from any analysis of public order and the community's fear of crime.
8. Known as the Jain diary or the Hawala case, this unearthed the alleged money laundering by a private businessman and payment of bribes by him to public officials (both political leaders and civil servants). Several important personalities are facing trial in this case whose investigation has been closely monitored by the Supreme Court.
9. The National Police Commission (1977) suggested amendment of Sec.151 Cr.P.C. with a view to providing for the preventive detention of potential criminals, for a short period, say, of one or two weeks. At present, there is no law that permits such short-term detention. The National Security Act and the Goondas Preventive Detention Act contemplate only longer detention.
10. Police officers employ all three sections in their routine with a view to maintaining peace and containing crime, especially property offences. It is the experience that some officers at the police station level resort to such action mechanically and too frequently to boost statistics and impress supervisors.
11. Over the years, this sound system of collection of criminal intelligence has fallen into disuse in many parts of the country. Absence of manpower and a lack of faith in traditional crime control mechanics account for this.
12. As this book goes to the press, 1996 UCR figures have become available. The broad picture that emerges is that, during 1996, index offences and violent crime registered a 2.8 per cent and 6.5 per cent drop respectively. Homicides alone declined by 9.1 per cent.

    The NCRB has released the 1996 figures also for India. According to these, the IPC crime rate dropped 0.9 per cent, while that of all cognizable crime (IPC plus Special and Local Laws) went up by 3.3 per cent. Significantly, violent crime dipped by 0.7 per cent.
13. Woolfgang and Weiner (1985) plead for a balanced approach in comparing UCR and NCS figures. They recommend that the figures should be compared for a period during which they nearly overlap, and conclude that violent crime did in fact increase during the decade, although not to the extent depicted by the UCR statistics.
14. (i) If IPC offences alone are taken into account, the crime rate in India during 1995 was 185.1—a drop of 3.4 over 1994. This gives a very favourable view of the Indian scene, because the 'index offences' (violent crime and property crime that includes arson) from which the US rate of 5277.6 is worked out, are broadly the same as those covered by the IPC in India.

    (ii) The total crime figure for the US given above covers all index offences. In the case of India, the total figure covers offences, both under the IPC and the local and special laws. Since the incidence of the latter is twice and the local and special laws. Since the incidence of the latter is twice as many as IPC cases, it is difficult to ignore them while studying crime in India, particularly when they cover important legislation, such as drug law, prohibition, and the arms and explosives acts.

15. There is a fallacy here, because, in India, both violent crime and property crime are essentially handled by the IPC and it will be more appropriate to discuss a rise or drop only with reference to the quantum of IPC cases each year. This has however not been attempted here because such an analysis will distort the comparison with the US picture where no distinction is drawn between ordinary crime and specialized crime, such as drug abuses, illegal possession of arms, gambling, etc.

5

Community Policing: Theory and Realities

> Just as physicians now recognize the importance of fostering health rather than simply treating illness, so the police—and the rest of us—ought to recognize the importance of maintaining intact, communities without broken windows.
>
> JAMES Q. WILSON AND GEORGE L. KELLING
> 'Broken Windows', *Atlantic Monthly*, March 1982

IT IS RECOGNIZED the world over that policing is a distinct public service whose focus should be on the consumer, namely, the whole community. We also know that whenever they have been out of tune with consumer needs, the police have been roundly criticized for a lack of perspective and sensitivity. In specific terms, they have been accused of downright brutality and graft in daily delivery of services to the community. For their part, the police charge the former with unreasonable demands for service, sometimes even those beyond their charter and a total denial of cooperation in tackling crime and related public order situations. This police stance flows from the stressful times in which we live, wherein the police find that there is no correlation between the resources available to them and the consumer's expectations.

In this atmosphere of mutual misgivings and recrimination, the main casualty is police credibility. What is worse, inherent in what has unfortunately come to be a bureaucratic relationship, the chasm between the police and the citizen widens. Such a development is unhealthy for a democracy which is nothing but a delicate political arrangement that rests mainly on trust and an understanding between the executive and the community.

It should be obvious against the above backdrop that it is not mere altruism but clear self-interest that should persuade the police to take the initiative for forging intimate ties with their consumers. In practice, however, one finds a certain lack of perception of the issues involved and a latent hostility between the producer and consumer.

Conscious of this apparent lack of harmony, efforts have been made recently in the US and India by a few enlightened elements to bring the two together for mutual benefit. It is gratifying that there is now a willingness on the part of police departments and their leaders to experiment and also permit greater scrutiny of their operations by outsiders, a situation that facilitates research (Goldstein 1990). This is a sign of the changing police perception of their role in the community.

The evolution of 'community policing' and its off-spring, 'problem-oriented policing' is of immense significance. This development has produced abundant literature in the form of both theoretical essays on basic ideas and practical accounts of experience from on-going experiments. The present chapter will examine a few meaningful practices in the two countries for upgrading the quality of police service through exclusive community policing projects and therefore explore whether there could be mutual learning.

Community Policing: The Theory

The term 'community policing' has been used rather loosely by extending the label to almost any programme which seeks to strengthen police ties with the community (Braiden 1990). As a result, it has unfortunately become almost synonymous with police-community relations. The truth is that the community policing strategy has a few distinctive characteristics not found in many existing 'police-community relations' (PCR) programmes. These are:

(i) decentralized operations and decision-making;
(ii) a greater priority to the ends rather than means of policing; and
(iii) an involvement of the public (the client) in decision and policy making.

(Kelling and Moore 1988, and Greene 1989)

The message of community policing is that policing concerns are not merely those of the departments alone, and that 'constructive action by Police and the Community is always better than action by the Police alone' (Wasserman and Moore 1988: 6). Individually and collectively, the community has also every stake in police activities acquiring a focus on substance than mere form. According to Greene (1990: 27), the effort is one of linking ' the consumers of service, the producers of service and the managers of the service in a unitary public safety service delivery system'. This implies that the community has not only a role in crime prevention and fear reduction projects, but that it should be enabled to seize that role. In sum, it is ' proactive servicing, as opposed to emergency response' (Bayley 1988: 226). Also, the exercise in community policing has been one of converting the community into a 'co-producer' of police service (Goldstein 1990). Several innovations have resulted from this process. Studies such as those by Bayley and Skolnick (1986), Trojanowicz (1982), Greene (1981, 1990) *et al.*, have contributed to a wealth of theory.

Though community policing may not be wholly new or radical, it does provide a fresh opportunity to re-orient police priorities and work methods at a time when the police are under pressure from the stark violence that dominates the streets. In this endeavour, the preliminary effort comes from the police who help the community to play their allotted role. The latter subsequently build on this structure, taking advantage of the ambience provided by the police. The rationale is that, being only moderately influential on crime rates, the police can at least make an impact on the environment in which crime takes place (Greene 1989). The community's authorization of police tasks—such as order maintenance, negotiation and resolution of conflicts, even though these may be already authorized by law—and an expansion of the definition of police function (so as to include activities such as order maintenance, resolution of conflicts and provision of services through problem-solving and similar devices) are significant characteristics of this strategy.

It is appropriate here to reflect on what we understand by 'public order' in relation to the police. The concept itself is vague, permitting it be used rather loosely, and in a manner that suggests it to be an area apart from 'crime prevention'.

Wilson (1968:21-2) is most perceptive here: 'The difficulty, of course, is that public order is nowhere defined, and can never be defined unambiguously, because what constitutes order is a matter of opinion and convention, not a state of nature.' However, we can generally make out the difference between 'disorder' (such as riots, drunken behaviour, etc.) and 'order' (such as motorists submitting to a traffic light, pedestrians sticking to the sidewalk, etc.), and say without fear of contradiction that much more than the latter, it is the former that requires pointed police intervention.

Many scholars have laboured to establish the symbiotic relationship between order maintenance and crime control. As early as 1977, Herman Goldstein, without however directly linking order with crime control, talked of the police need to comprehend the difference between controlling the fear of crime and tackling the actual levels of crime. He seemed to suggest that the two required equal attention, although they might call for separate tactics (Langworthy 1994).

The significance of Goldstein's proposition became obvious in March 1982 when Wilson and Kelling wrote their classic essay, 'Broken Windows', for the *Atlantic Monthly*.[1] They discussed at length the 'foot patrol experiment' in Newark (New Jersey) of the early 1970s and the subsequent Police Foundation evaluation which concluded, that foot patrolling hardly had an impact on crime, although, the public in the patrolled area, as compared to those elsewhere, felt more secure and less bothered by crime. According to Wilson and Kelling, this public perception was no illusion, because crime was not the only source of citizen fear. A likely encounter on the streets with disorderly people was an equally important source. What foot patrolling did was to substantially reduce this, through enhancing the level of order.

In Wilson and Kelling's view (1982), equally true was the fact that, unattended, any signs of disorder in a community, such as an unrepaired broken window, tended to exacerbate the situation, thereby widely disseminating the impression that no one was in charge of the area, and that anyone could get away with whatever he wanted to do. Recalling how police preoccupation with crime control in the 1960s had led to a costly neglect of the order maintenance role, Wilson and Kelling stated:

> the link between order maintenance and crime prevention, so obvious to earlier generations, was forgotten. That link is similar to the process whereby one broken window becomes many. The citizen who fears the ill-smelling drunk, the rowdy teenager or the importuning beggar is not merely expressing his distaste for unseemly behaviour, he is also giving voice to a bit of folk wisdom . . . serious street crime flourishes in areas in which disorderly behaviour goes unchecked. (1985:82)

'Broken Windows' may be rightly looked upon as a landmark in criminal justice literature, which helps us in the 1990s to comprehend how order and crime are inextricably linked to each other. A police agency that treats the two as watertight compartments, and believes that the neglect of one does not impact the other is doomed to failure. Langworthy (1994) opines that, by focussing their attention on areas with broken windows, the police help to halt social decay and to tackle public fear of crime. The high level of fear of crime in cities such as Los Angeles, New York, or Delhi amply demonstrates the effect, not only of municipal inattention to basic civic needs, but also of police inability to take stock of all broken windows.

THE INDIAN SCENE

Literature on police relations with the community in the pre-Independence era is sparse. We only know that, in ancient India, there were local bodies (*panchayats*), in which the public participated directly, and these were involved in criminal justice administration. Dispute resolution was their main function. These survived the Muslim rule, which, while tinkering with the system at the district level, left the tiers below untouched. The arrival of the British, and the setting up of their own courts to look into civil and criminal complaints led to a decline in the influence of *panchayats*. Public participation in the administration of justice was reduced almost to nothing (Rana 1993). It was only much after the advent of Independence that the moves to revive the time-worn *panchayat* system gained ground.

Post-Independence writing on the subject deals abundantly with programmes evolved by the police in different parts of the country to bridge the gap with the community. The impression that one gains is that these were born out of an admission of a poor police image, as revealed by some public opinion surveys.

One of the first such surveys was that of David Bayley who was in India on a Ford Foundation grant to study the Indian Police. His study (1965) found the public generally believing that they received shabbily by the police. 'Rude and tricky questioning', intimidation and physical assault of those taken to police stations and demand of a bribe even to perform their legitimate functions were some of the complaints levelled against policemen by samples investigated by Bayley.

These findings received support from a 1978 survey of the Indian Institute of Public Opinion, New Delhi, sponsored by the National Police Commission. It highlighted the charge that the constabulary were threatening and rude in their behaviour. It also referred to the widespread prevalence of corruption which greatly affected police image (Indian Institute of Public Opinion 1979).

My own survey of 1982 came to only slightly different conclusions. While 44 per cent of the respondents expressed the view that police were responsive to the needs of the common man, 31 per cent disagreed. Also, a majority opined that policemen were generally partisan in their conduct (Raghavan 1989).

The National Police Commission (1977), in its Fifth Report (November 1980), expressed its anguish over the poor state of police-pubic relations. It believed (p. 48) that the 1902 Fraser Commission's observation that people 'do all they can to avoid any connection with the police investigation' held true even after a lapse of nearly 80 years. It went on to say: 'People now may not dread the police, but they certainly dread getting involved with it in any capacity.' It acknowledged that some efforts in the form of crime prevention weeks, setting up of boys' clubs, etc., had been made to improve the situation. But these were sporadic, as, for instance, no crime prevention week had been held after 1971. It suggested that the police should not merely highlight the responsibilities of the public, but go beyond this to focus attention on police difficulties and how citizens could help to mitigate them. In this context, it referred to a majority response to its questionnaire that favoured more liberal appointment of Special Officers (permitted by Section 17 of the Police Act 1861) from the community so as to aid the police in specially difficult law and order situations. It endorsed the suggestion that this arrangement should be an on-going process, rather than one invoked on special occasions.

Perhaps most perceptive was the NPC's call (1980) for the utmost care in improving the quality of beat patrolling and traffic duties. Drawing attention to its own finding that those who had 'direct experience of police have a slightly better opinion of police than those who have not had any such experience', it recommended (1980:53), 'exemplary performance of visible activities and better communication with people'. Highlighting the impact of the 'very high visibility profile' of the traffic policeman and the beat constable, the commission strongly pleaded for the revival of beat patrolling and for combining it, in urban areas, with the system of neighbourhood policing. Thereafter, it suggested that policemen could be earmarked to specific localities so that they could get to know what was happening there, besides finding out from residents whether they needed any help.

The NPC also commended the concept of Boys Clubs, which sought to channelize the youth living in poor localities into sports and reading activities so that they were not drawn into delinquency. It sought the creation of more such clubs, as also the expansion of a Road Safety Patrol movement operating in schools. The commission bemoaned the fact that police-public interaction on the sports field initiated several years earlier, had declined. The Second Saturday Sports Meet, which pitted policemen in a police station with the local population every month in a volleyball or football match, a programme launched by IGP Stracey in Tamil Nadu in the late 1970s, is worth recalling here. Unfortunately, this promising device fell by the wayside a few years ago.

The Delhi Police Experiments

Community policing programmes in the recent past have focussed attention on crime prevention. A few experiments conducted by the Delhi Police, an essentially urban police department serving a population of nearly 10 million, deserve a mention.

In 1985, a scheme of Special Police Officers (SPOs) was introduced. These were able-bodied adults without a crime record who were willing to undertake various tasks, such as patrolling, handling de-addiction camps, training young girls in self-defence measures to ward off sexual harassment and helping victims of property crime. The success of this scheme could be gauged by the fact that more than 1500 SPOs are now enrolled with the Delhi Police.

The Neighbourhood Watch Scheme launched by the Delhi Police in 1989 aimed at reducing property crime and juvenile delinquency, and bringing about better ties with the community. Here, the police first identified a suitable community for motivating its residents to be alert in preventing crime. With the help of local Special Police Officers—private citizens earmarked for policing duties in a contingency—and residents' associations, meetings were organized for the purpose of explaining details of the scheme. Thereafter, a Neighbourhood Watch Committee (NWC) was formed for each block of 500 residents which undertook various anti-crime tasks, including the strengthening of physical security arrangements in individual houses, and registration with the police of the names of domestic servants and outsiders such as vendors, who frequent the locality. Nearly 90 residential areas were said to have been brought under the scheme. The kind of motivation that had been aroused was evident from the fact that, in a case of attempted burglary, following the alarm raised by an occupant of the house, almost the whole neighbourhood rushed to her rescue and successfully nabbed the culprit.

Another innovation was the 'adoption' of an area coming to notice for a high volume of crime. Apart from inducting additional policemen, the scheme involved special campaigns for the verification of the antecedents of domestic servants and for building public awareness on home security systems. This is known to have brought down crime appreciably, although exact figures are not available. Juvenile aid camps have also been set up by the Delhi Police to identify willing street children for teaching them trades and later helping them to find suitable jobs.

Finally, as an anti-sexual harassment measure, a team of young policewomen has been formed to teach self-defence measures to girls in schools and colleges.

The 'Mohalla Committees' of Maharashtra

A scheme floated in 1990 by the police in Bhiwandi (Maharashtra State), a town notorious for Hindu-Muslim strife, to promote religious harmony can rightly be regarded as an attempt at community policing. Local bodies called 'Mohalla Committees' have been formed in this town to sort out problems in the community. There are about 30 members in each committee which meets once a week and discusses various issues with the local Sub-Inspector of Police. It has been arranged that the police help the community even in non-police matters, such as supply of electricity, availability of rationed food commodities, etc. The close relationship that the police have forged with the population ensures that the hard ground level intelligence required for monitoring the state of Hindu-Muslim relations is available without any extra effort. Further, thanks to the increased opportunity for Hindus and Muslims to interact among themselves through the Mohalla Committees, violent exchanges have become few and far between.

The Karnataka DGP's Directive

The Karnataka State Police, in the south of the country, have also been making efforts to take the message of community policing down to the police station level. A Standing Order, issued by the DGP in February 1994, directed the formation of a Citizens Committee at this level to meet at least once a month to discuss matters such as deviant behaviour of individuals, patrolling, and distribution of protective duties during outbursts of crime. Further, policemen visting villages on their beat were directed to ascertain citizen grievances, not only with regard to the police, but also in matters such as street lighting, water and power supply, conditions of road, sanction of old age pension, etc. The DGP's order contemplated the grant of incentives to policemen achieving significant results in the area of police-public relations (Standing Order No. 920, February 1994 of DGP, Karnataka: 'Introduction of Community Policing'). No material, is however, available as yet to indicate the measure of implementation of this order and its impact on the average citizen.

The Tamil Nadu Scene

Policing in the southern state of Tamil Nadu has been traditionally known for its emphasis on good relations with the public. A forum in the form of Village Vigilance Committee (VVC) at the police station level is available for promoting this. Viewed mainly as a crime prevention measure, the VVC's effectiveness has depended almost wholly on the enthusiasm displayed by the individual Station House Officer. It is known that, over a course of time, VVC meetings had become a mere ritual intended for the consumption of supervisory officers during their inspection of police stations.

Alongside this distressing apathy of field officers in the essentially rural setting, one, however, sees a new awareness among higher police officers in the larger cities, such as Chennai (Madras), Madurai and Coimbatore, of the need to involve citizens in police chores. This trend is the direct result of growing complexities of urban policing, especially the rise in violent property crime and its extensive reporting by the print media. (Tamil Nadu has a relatively high literacy rate and has a powerful local press that enjoys wide circulation.) There is palpable recognition by the top brass that unless better communication with the public is established and the latter are directly involved in policing tasks, police forces are likely to become swamped and even paralyzed by the staggering demands of order maintenance and crime prevention.

The birth (1993) of a 'Friends of Police' (FOP) movement in different parts of Tamil Nadu that owes itself largely to the dynamism of a young District Superintendent of Police, Prateep Philip, is an encouraging development. The FOP made its appearance first in the coastal district of Ramanathapuram. It has now been adopted by others, including Chennai (Madras) and Madurai Cities. Established as a purely voluntary agency to promote crime awareness and civic responsibilities, the FOP is open to any person, male or female, above the age of 18 who has no police record or involvement in a civil dispute. FOPs carry identity cards and are used mainly in neighbourhood watch schemes. A few prominent members among them are designated as Community Service Officers. The FOP concept has received recognition from the state government and, judging from the initial citizen response, it is likely to gain momentum in the future (Balasubramaniam 1994). Appendix V gives an extract from the blueprint drawn up by Prateep Philip.

A final word on the community policing scene in India. There is awareness that, other than going to the community and seeking their greater involvement in the daily chores of the police, no alternative exists. There are two factors which operate against success in this endeavour. First is the declining attention to local community problems. This is explained by the fire-fighting exercises that are dumped on the police by an escalation of group violence. Perhaps a more important limitation is the fact that the average constable is ill-equipped by training, law and police tradition to interact with the citizen at a level of mutual confidence. These constraints are not likely to disappear for a long time.[2]

The US Experience

Bayley (1994c: 36) refers to the eternal complaint of the police that 'they are understaffed and overworked. In the face of rising crime rates, it is unrealistic, they argue, for the public to expect them to be more effective without additional resources.' The issue in focus in the US, among other countries, is how to enlarge police resources, and at the same time help departments to arrive at the right mechanics for forging a proactive relationship with the community. The proposal to inject 100,000 more police officers into the community, as part of the Crime Bill approved by Congress in 1994, is an index of the all-round anxiety on this score. It is expected that this approach to law enforcement would enhance police effectiveness and public satisfaction.

Community Policing Experiments in US Cities

About 400 US cities are known to have experimented with community policing in some form or the other, with varying degrees of success. In response to a 1990 survey conducted by the NIJ, a majority of the participating departments cited the need for research in the area. They also believed that training in community relations could be beneficial

(*Congressional Quarterly Researcher*, February 1993). A few programmes tried out in different parts of the country in the recent past are described in some detail here.

Santa Ana: The Substation Experiment

Although located more than 30 miles from Los Angeles, Santa Ana is part of the greater metropolitan area. With a population of 310,000 and an area of 27.2 square miles, it is an urban centre with a history of uneasy police-minority relationships. Hispanics (65.2 per cent) constitute the largest segment. 23.1 per cent are white, 9.1 Asian and Pacific Islanders and 2.2 black (SAPD Annual Report, 1994).

The early 1970s were marked by a high crime rate and consequent public dissatisfaction with police performance. Police relations with the community had reached their nadir. It was at this juncture that Police Chief Raymond C. Davis took over (1973) the department. He started with an advantage over his predecessors, namely, the hiring of 100 additional personnel, who included 88 patrol officers. Quickly assessing that the situation needed an unconventional approach, he launched a programme which Skolnick and Bayley (1986:20) would later identify as 'a philosophy of public service policing that sought to combine community responsiveness with professionalism and high technology'.

Davis gave Santa Ana a new system that vastly improved on 'team policing', a concept which came into vogue in the troubled 1960s, and laid emphasis on the continuous functioning of a small team in the same community so as to promote integration and motivation. Calling his project 'community-oriented policing' (COP), he outlined an integrated plan for both crime control and community relations. In accordance with this plan, Santa Ana was divided into four areas, each under a commander—usually a lieutenant—with considerable discretion for day-to-day assignments and drawing up new projects.

Perhaps the most noteworthy of Davis' innovations was the civilianization of the department. Although 25 per cent of the department was already civilian, Davis worked at a significant addition which raised this figure to nearly 40 per cent. These Police Service Officers (PSOs) comprised men and women placed exclusively in charge of service-related work, which accounted for 70-80 per cent of the charter of the Santa Ana Police. Wearing uniforms but no guns, the PSOs moved about in patrol cars to tackle a variety of situations which would normally have been the concern of a patrol officer.

Davis' another bold measure aimed at community mobilization through appointment of a large number of block captains in each of the four community areas. These were responsible for a specified number of citizens signing up to attend meetings convened by block captains for the purpose of disseminating information on crime control.

One more feature of the Santa Ana scheme was the setting up of four substations. These encouraged citizens to file complaints of minor crime which would not otherwise have received any attention because patrol officers were burdened with work relating to more serious crime. Substations also served as community centres where crime education through display of films, posters, etc., was undertaken.

The latest information received by me from Chief Paul M. Walters of the Santa Ana PD indicates that community-oriented policing (COP) continues to be the principal philosophy of the department and one of its 'most effective crime prevention tools'. It 'empowers the police to develop a network of coordinated neighbourhood crime prevention strategies by helping neighbours to get acquainted, identify areas of common concern, and developing lasting solutions to those concerns'. The principal components of COP are Response to Incidents (R2I) and problem-oriented policing (POP). R2I takes care of the need to react to events, both crime and non-crime, that have already taken place. It is also partly proactive in that it studies crime patterns through mechanics such as directed patrol and targeted identification (Walters 1992 and 1993). The SAPD claims that its various strategies were responsible for the 7.46 per cent drop in crime during 1994.

The SAPD has now six sub-stations which provide a variety of services. For instance, the Downtown Substation is committed to maintaining peace in the commercial district through foot, bicycle and electric cart-patrols. The North-east Substation offers its facility for holding community meetings and various activities aimed at crime reduction. In the Westend District, there is a four-member Community Policing Team which tackles persistent neighbourhood problems. During 1994, it launched several problem-oriented policing projects. These included the condemnation and demolition of an abandoned residence, which was responsible for gang, narcotic and prostitution activities (SAPD Annual Report, 1994).

Worthy of mention here is the SAPD Investigation Division's several anti-crime operations. One of these is the Street Terrorist Offender Programme (STOP) that was responsible for a 15 per cent fall in gang-related murders during 1994. The importance of STOP may be gauged from the fact that, in the city of Santa Ana, there are about 50 active gangs, with about 8000 persons identified as members or associates of these gangs. The programme has helped to identify the hard core gang members and thereby reduce gang-related violent crime through the prosecution and sentencing of active gang members or through supervision of those on probation. During the first half of 1994, of the 46 targeted subjects taken into custody, nineteen were sentenced to terms ranging from one year to life plus 11 years. The remaining were awaiting trial.

DETROIT: THE MINI-STATION EXPERIMENT

A crime-prone city with a very poor record of race relations, Detroit reported violent ethnic riots in the 1960s when racism was blatant. A majority of the city's population is black. Poverty is very much in evidence and violent crime, particularly homicides, has been on the increase.

Adopting a positive approach to its task, the Detroit Police department rightly started with the premise that a massive programme was required to mobilize community support (Skolnick and Bayley 1986). The emphasis therefore was on crime prevention through community involvement. A low priority was given to reactive policing and a high priority to 'an intensive community mobilization for self-defense' (ibid.:53).

The Detroit programme consists of two parts. The first is a crime prevention section of 35 officers who are responsible for coordinating prevention activities. Placed under the direct command of the Police Chief—an arrangement that signifies the importance of its function—this section undertakes several activities. It organizes the public into various watch systems oriented to the needs of neighbourhoods, high-rise apartments and the business community. It also conducts special programmes for school children and private security personnel.

Throughout Detroit, 52 mini-stations constitute the second aspect of this new community-oriented policing. Each precinct has three to four such stations, and, as with the crime prevention section, the mini-station represents an independent command reporting directly to the chief. It is from these stations that officers placed on community crime prevention work operate. They do not come under the radio network. They encourage walk-in calls for service from local citizens. Complaints so received are then forwarded to the precincts. Although, initially, they were put on patrol duty (in addition to organizing neighbourhood self-defense), this was changed in 1980, so that their responsibility was solely crime prevention. This change of strategy facilitated the creation of crime prevention associations in a majority of the city's 12000 blocks.

Mini-stations, as reorganized in 1980, play a complementary role to precincts. Officers attached to them act as 'unofficial security advisers' and mobilize the community to bring about an awareness of how to prevent crime. The forum offered by some service associations is utilized for this purpose.

Houston: The DART and Storefront Experiments

A major southern city with considerable racial tensions, Houston has a 60 per cent white population. The white-dominated police department's reputation in the 1970s was one of a corrupt and brutal force. Geographically, the city extends over 655 square miles. Naturally, police resources are rather thinly spread.

In 1982, the white Mayor made a significant change in the police leadership by appointing Houston's first black Police Chief, Lee P. Brown, a police officer with impressive academic credentials and a firm believer in value-based policing and the efficacy of planned action. After studying the problems of his department for nearly a year, Brown came out with a 'Plan of Action 1983'.

With an emphasis on decentralization and community involvement, Brown introduced the DART (Directed Area Responsibility Team) programme for modifying patrol practices. This was initially tried in one district which had both a substantial black population and a high crime rate. Essentially a team policing experiment, DART entrusted all policing tasks to a single group of patrol officers and detectives, and freed this district almost totally from the jurisdiction of centralized units. A further innovation was that the prevailing untargeted and perfunctory patrolling yielded place to deliberate and purposeful patrolling. Under this new scheme, patrol officers were permitted to draw up their own strategies and priorities, taking into account the special needs of their respective areas. In essence, this was an 'explicit attempt to make reactive patrolling more proactive', and was based on 'the expectation that patrolling would become problem-oriented' (Skolnick and Bayley 1986: 95).

Another aspect of the community policing experiment in Houston was the creation of the 'storefront' or the community police station. Five such stations were set up in 1983, one of which was to be part of the Police Foundation's 'fear reduction' project. These stations concentrated on matters which normally rated low in police priority, but were nevertheless important from the community's point of view. Such matters included resolution of conflict between neighbours, building community pressure on disorderly and neglectful people, removing abandoned vehicles, and following up complaints of poor municipal services.

The storefronts made commendable efforts to reach out to the community (Skolnick and Bayley 1986). They encouraged the public to come to them without any inhibition and represent their grievances, even if these did not even remotely pertain to crime. Monthly community meetings proved useful here.

The DART experiment was rated a success, perhaps because it had been the pet project of the chief and everyone in the department was aware that he was personally monitoring its progress (Skolnick and Bayley 1986). A Police Foundation evaluation team studied the Houston innovations as part of its fear-reduction experiments. Among its strategies were the Community Organizing Response Teams (CORT), the creation of a storefront police station, door-to-door visits to citizens to assess their policing needs, and issue of newsletters on the crime situation. The team came to the conclusion that, notwithstanding the success of the Houston experiment, the lower strata of society were relatively unaffected by the programme, and their awareness of the programme was minimal. The situation was better in the area where a door-to-door contact had been established (Skogan 1990).

Lee Brown was succeeded in 1990 by Chief Elizabeth Watson who also shared the former's enthusiasm for community policing. Unfortunately, this was the time when violent crime peaked in Houston and the police came under fire. Specifically, the police was accused of neglecting the fight against crime in favour of theories and studies. A new Mayor, Bob Lanier, lost no time in shaking up the police. Watson gave way to Sam Nuchia, a believer in 'back to basics' law-enforcement style. Although he did not suggest abandonment of all that had been done by Lee Brown and Watson, this was the time when community policing was being subjected to critical scrutiny. For instance, a team of management consultants, who audited Houston Police experiments, stated in their report of August 1991 that, notwithstanding the 'tremendous amount of management attention' to community policing, 'little comprehensive impact on citizens' safety or quality of life can be demonstrated.' The study was critical of the rigidity that had set in with regard to beat policies which did not permit re-deployment and thereby increased response time to calls. There was the added problem of lower levels of the police starting to believe that community policing was more important than achieving 'traditional goals.' The consultants further believed that police salaries, at their existing level, were not attractive enough to people with the complex skills which community policing required (*Congress Quarterly Researcher*, February 1993 and *Telemasp Bulletin*, December 1994).

The challenge to Lee Brown's version of community policing has come from Mayor Bob Lanier's '655 Programme' which highlights crime-specific policing in the place of earlier strategies. (Lanier had promised in his election campaign that, if elected, he would place one police officer in every one of the 655 square miles in the city.) The Houston Police now claim that proactive patrol and investigative methods have led to increased arrests and a sharp 14.8 per cent drop in crime during the 30 months following the introduction of the 655 Programme (*Telemasp Bulletin*, December 1994).

The Newark Experiment

A small and congested city with a predominantly black population, Newark has all the problems of an urban setting: considerable unemployment, run-down housing and a high crime rate. Police response to public calls for assistance had always been known to be tardy in spite of a comfortable manpower position.

The appointment of Hubert Williams as the Police Director in 1974 was a watershed. He set the tone for several reforms aimed at greater responsiveness to the public. His Truancy Task Force, established in collaboration with the School Superintendent, targeted those teenagers who were contributing to a bulk of the crime for removal from the streets and transfer to social workers. Nearly 8000 youths were picked up by the task force leading to some public criticism of police highhandedness (Skolnick and Bayley 1986). This strategy was dovetailed into four other innovations: the sweep (forcing dispersal of loitering crowds under threat of arrest), roadblocks (stopping vehicles to detect drunken driving and stolen vehicles), inspection of buses and subways (as a measure to make them safer for travel), and a storefront (called the Police Community Service Centre), which, incidentally, formed part of the Police Foundation's fear reduction project.

Skolnick and Bayley (1986) believed that the above innovations definitely improved the public's estimate of police ability to tackle disorder. The report of a private consulting firm, Touche-Ross, which went into the management problems of the department also said: 'Few . . . organizations could react as effectively in tailoring the services to meet a continuing workload.' (Skolnick and Bayley 1986:207). A Police Foundation evaluation came to the conclusion that the Newark strategy lent support to the contention that the police could effectively reduce levels of social disorder by using intensive enforcement tactics such as the sweep, roadblocks and inspection of buses and subway. Perhaps greater was the impact of the community service component of the strategy in the form of a storefront and door-to-door visits (Skogan 1990).

The NYPD's Community Patrol Officer Programme

Designed by the Vera Institute of Justice, the Community Patrol Officer Programme was intended to assist the New York Police Department (NYPD) to experiment with community-oriented policing in a limited area. Launched in July 1984, this was tried in a sector covering nine patrol beats, each comprising anywhere between 12 and 30 blocks of residential and light commercial property. The nine Community Patrol Officers (CPOs) assigned to these beats were divested of their routine patrol functions, and directed to engage themselves in foot-patrol in their respective beats. They were permitted to operate to a time-schedule which, in their opinion, best fitted their areas.

The role expected of each CPO comprised planning, problem-solving, organizing the community, and serving as an information-link between the police and the community. Specifically, the officer was first required to identify the major problems of the beat and evolve strategies for solving them. The next task was to implement those strategies and, in doing so, work in concert with the existing community organizations or develop new ones wherever demanded. The final component of the CPO's charter involved keeping the department informed of the nature and content of the community's problems. At the same time, the CPO was to continually apprise the community of ways in which the department could assist them (Weisburd and McElroy 1984). To help CPOs comprehend their role, they were given an initial training of 80 hours.

With regard to problem-identification, two observations were significant. The CPOs found that this task required active community participation. In fact, many of the problems were identified this way. Secondly, these often related to quality-of-life concerns which would normally not have received the attention of the average patrol officer (Weisburd and McElroy 1984). Indeed, many of them (such as clearing up abandoned lots) could not be looked upon as strictly police problems. The process, to start with, was tortuous. In course of time, the CPOs found that their growing familiarity with the neighbourhood helped them greatly in locating more and more of the issues needing police attention (ibid.).

The NYPD's community policing programme received a boost in February 1991 with Mayor Dinkins' announcement of a $1.8 billion dollar anti-crime plan which contemplated recruitment of 5000 more officers, all of whom to be drafted for community policing. The programme, however, suffered a reverse in August 1991 with the sudden resignation of Commissioner Lee Brown. Fortunately, his successor, Raymond W. Kelly, shared his enthusiasm for community policing. However, there are many who still do not believe that this style of policing has had an impact on the city. One of them, Thomas A. Reppetto, President of the Citizens Crime Commission, a watchdog group, was not sanguine about the future of the programme, once Kelly also departed (*Congressional Quarterly Researcher*, February 1993).[3]

THE PHILADELPHIA EXPERIMENT

The City: Its Traditions and Problems

Philadelphia enjoys a unique place in US history. As the venue for drawing up the new nation's Constitution, it had played a major role in fusing a union out of diverse colonies. This tradition of unity out of diversity explains the multi-ethnic character of the city. While this image of tolerance has, by and large, been preserved, the city has undergone basic economic changes. From a burgeoning commercial metropolis linked to the manufacturing industry prior to the 1950s, during the late 1980s it had declined to a low-key and nearly decrepit city with continuing trends of migration to the suburbs. Unemployment and, therefore, poverty became quite marked. The city government was weighed down by its acute financial problem which affected the quality of public services.[4]

The Philadelphia Police: An Overview

The Philadelphia Police Department (PPD) is the country's fourth largest metropolitan police agency. It has a little more than four police officers per 1000 of the population, making the city one of the most intensively policed. The department runs an efficient 911 service which responds to more than two million calls every year. Nevertheless, it has a high crime rate. Discipline in the department is fragile and quite a few scandals have tarnished its image in the past. The PPD has always been known for its high sensitivity to public needs and quick response to citizens in distress. This was why, in spite of a fiscal crisis during mid-1970s, it did not opt for a cut-down of its services. However, the style of policing was mostly reactive, with the available limited resources not permitting a proactive style of operations (Task Force Report 1987).

In 1980, a study programme called COPE (Community-Oriented Police Education) was organized with the help of a Ford Foundation grant. This involved direct interaction between line police officers and community residents/leaders from a number of neighbourhoods. The study highlighted the fact that the attitudes and perceptions of the police and citizens affected the extent to which they were able to co-exist in a crime control or prevention programme. It also brought to focus a number of factors which impinged on the effective implementation of community policing projects. These included the existing organizational structure, command and control assumptions, flexibility or the lack of it in decision-making, rewards and punishments, etc. (Greene and Decker 1989). The study's findings therefore anticipated the recommendations of the Task Force seven years later, and set the stage for a South Division experiment in decentralization.

Beginning May 1986, a Task Force studied PPD's operating practices with a view to bringing about an improvement in the quality of its services. The Task Force report (May 1987: 30) declared that 'the current strategy for policing is flawed . . . not only in its technical features, but also in its overall philosophy.' It, therefore, recommended (p. 153) 'an explicit mission statement . . . that will guide planning and operations toward a strategy of 'community' or 'problem-solving' policing and which 'should be developed in consultation with the citizens.'

As a sequel, the PPD adopted a new Mission Statement which pledged the department to 'work in a true partnership with our fellow citizens.' In accordance with this philosophy, 'community policing' and 'problem-oriented policing' became the new strategies. Mini-stations, Victim Assistance Officers, Crime Prevention Officers, Neighbourhood Advisory Boards, Walk-and-Ride and Foot Patrol Programmes were soon launched as measures to extend community policing to most parts of the city.

In October 1988, the Police Commissioner issued a document 'The Direction for the Future: A Five-Point Plan', which expressed the resolve to 'expand and elaborate on programmes that solve community problems' with a view to 'providing a responsive service to Philadelphia's many and varied communities'. Specifically, it expressed a determination to tackle the drug menace through 'a police-citizen-business leader alliance.'

The South Division Experiment

In December 1987, which was even prior to the Commissioner's formal announcement in favour of strengthening community policing, a decentralization experiment—as part of the community policing project—was launched in the South Police Division in an attempt to implement the major recommendation of the Task Force. The main features of this experiment as observed by me in 1990 were:[5]

(a) A Management Team at the division level, comprising the Inspector, his five Captains and the Administrative Lieutenant attached to the Inspector, met frequently to chalk out the plan of action for strengthening community policing and for monitoring on-going projects. This was looked upon as a means to introduce a participatory style of management in the division. A similar team functioned in each district under the leadership of the Captain.

(b) Each district in the South Division formed a Police District Advisory Council (PDAC). Consisting of about 25 members drawn from the community, each PDAC drew up a State of the Community Report, which identified problems and helped to frame a plan of action to tackle them. The State of the Community Reports generally aimed at improving the quality of life in the districts through the following measures:

(i) tackling sanitation problems by aggressive action against violators of law, organizing weekly neighbourhood clean-ups and establishing an advisory council committee on sanitation;
(ii) combating thefts of and from autos through a public awareness campaign regarding automobile security, distributing 'Stop a Thief' flyers containing common sense tips, organizing a workshop to be addressed by experts, and establishing a committee to monitor court cases of those arrested for auto-related thefts;
(iii) combating burglaries through an action package similar to that against auto-related thefts; and
(iv) providing boys and girls with an opportunity to meet positive role models and participate in constructive activities.

(c) At division level, a South Philadelphia Service Support Group was formed for coordinating city services and neighbourhood resources, and thereby bring about an orderly development of the neighbourhood. Monthly meetings were held and the problems of target areas in each district discussed. The presence of representatives from various service organizations was described to have been of immense benefit.

(d) One or two mini-stations were formed in each district to encourage greater police-community interaction. In addition, the following officers in each district promoted greater integration with the community: Community Relations Officer, Victim Service Officer, Crime Prevention Officer, Sanitation Officer and Abandoned Vehicle Officer. (Similar stations and officers with specific community functions were seen in other divisions also.)

Special Projects in Philadelphia

One project initiated by South Division was the Queen Village: Project DOE. This was a plan to form 'an active partnership' with the village neighbourhood for the purpose of bringing police officers closer together with the community 'to identify and solve drug and crime-related problems in the neighbourhood'. The division claimed success in having

(i) forced the closure of a vacant house which was being used for sale of crack;
(ii) brought about the much-needed physical improvements to the neighbourhood;
(iii) devised effective responses to thefts from vehicles; and
(iv) rendered more than 50 residents drug-free.

(Meeks and Hasson 1989)

The Carr Family Neighbourhood Drug Operation (1989) was another project cited to prove the success of a strategy that brought up a community-oriented solution to clear a drug-infested area (Hasson 1989).

CITIZENS CRIME COMMISSION EVALUATION

On a request from the Police Commissioner, the Citizens Crime Commission of Philadelphia evaluated (1988) the decentralization experiment in South Division. The commission conducted a random telephone survey of South Philadelphia residents and interviews with police commanders and line officers in the division. The commission, in its report of June 1989, came to the following general conclusions:

(i) Community/problem-solving policing had not yet been fully implemented. In the commission's view, decentralization and creation of specialized officers, such as Crime Prevention Officer, Victim Assistance Officer and others, were no doubt important steps. But more was needed to be done in the form of change of 'value objectives and behavioural norms' of officers.
(ii) The project had not produced a favourable impact on overall community attitudes toward the police. In support of this, the commission pointed out the findings of the opinion survey it had conducted. In particular, it referred to the community's view that there was a lack of commitment to community policing which was visible in the department.
(iii) The attitudes of Commanders toward the new style of

policing were positive. The commission formed this impression from the responses to the interviews with Commanders it had held.

(iv) The impact of the project on line officers was slightly positive. The commission observed that most line officers, particularly those on patrol, were, no doubt, 'relatively uninformed and untouched'. But, they did not express any major negative view, and some of them felt that the project had 'created better teamwork and more efficient operations'.

(v) Decentralization had little impact on arrest and offence rates.

Common Themes in Community Policing Programmes

A few of the above programmes are still functional, though not in their original format. The others have faded into memory. Nevertheless, they demonstrate a police willingness and ability to reorient operations. They reflect a capacity to go beyond theory and translate ideas into solid fieldwork.

The emphasis in all the cities is one of rendering field-level police officers proactive so that they are more easily accessible to public. This has been made possible through organizational flexibility and a greater freedom of action to police officers on the street. Hierarchical concerns in these cities appear to have been somewhat pushed to the background so as to permit this measure of autonomy. We shall now turn to some of the ongoing experiments whose emphasis is slightly different from those of the 1970s and 1980s.

SOME RECENT PROJECTS

The Portland (Oregon) Experiment

One of the more recent converts to the philosophy of community policing is the Portland Police Bureau. Although the Portland programme began formally only in 1990, a spadework of two years had preceded. First, Chief Richard D. Walker appointed one of his Captains, Tom Potter, to prepare a blueprint. For this purpose, the latter formed a task force consisting of residents, bureau officials and representatives from the Mayor's office and the Office of Neighbourhood Officials. In February 1989, officials of the Police Bureau were consulted for their views. This was followed by the hiring of two outside planning consultants, who drafted a time-table which contemplated a five-year transition period.

May 1989 saw the creation of a community policing division. Within a space of six months, the City Council passed three resolutions, first, to confirm its commitment to the philosophy and, later, to adopt it officially in January 1990 over a five-year transition period. Since then the programme is being closely monitored and periodically revised in the light of happenings. This clinical approach to community policing should, apart from explaining the success of the Portland experiment, serve as a model to many others wanting to introduce it (*Congressional Quarterly Researcher*, February 1993).

It is believed that, following the introduction of community policing, there is a routine 'pooling of talents' in finding a solution to crime and 'livability' problems. An example that is confidently cited is the unique drug-busting strategy that has been evolved in cooperation with the community. First, the menace of drug sale at public parks was put down by the turning on of sprinklers at nights, a novel solution proposed by citizens. Another strategy was the devising of a landlord training programme which was essentially a five-hour course that dealt with topics such as applicant screening, warning signs of drug activity, eviction options and police-landlord relations. A manual containing relevant laws and a list of support groups is given to course participants. Perhaps the most important aspect of Portland's programme is the creation of Neighbourhood Liaison Officers. Each of these is assigned to a particular neighbourhood with a view to interacting closely with business and civic groups. This has contributed greatly to better understanding.

The New Haven (Connecticut) Programme

Despite its relatively small size, New Haven reported the sixth highest violent crime rate in the country during 1990. In particular, murders were showing an abnormal increase. Robberies and aggravated assaults did not lag behind. It required a new Police Chief, Nicholas Pastore, to find out that the then reactive style had to be replaced with a proactive approach, and this led to the introduction of community policing.

Twelve neighbourhood substations were created, and Sergeants and below assigned long-term to them. As a result, a close relationship has been forged with the community and 'healthy neighbourhoods' created, where 'people live without fear'. Success of the programme has been claimed on the basis of reduced crime—a 10.3 per cent drop during the first half of 1992—as against a national figure of just 2 per cent (*Congressional Quarterly Researcher*, February 1993).

LAPD's Operation Cul-de-sac (OCDS)

Aimed at assessing the potential of community-based policing to 'restore order within the most crime-ridden, inner-city neighbourhoods', the OCDS placed 60 LAPD officers, who worked overtime for two weeks, in a specific locality (RD 1345) with a high incidence of assaults and street robberies. The officers undertook foot, bicycle and horseback-patrolling to maximize citizen contact. After this initiation period, 6 officers were assigned permanently to the area. In conjunction with the community, these six officers sponsored picnics, graffiti clean-up and neighbourhood watch programmes. The impact of this showed up shortly in the form of citizens starting to use public facilities, such as parks which had once been avoided because of gang activity. It was found that Part I crimes had decreased by 20 per cent and drive-by shootings fell by more than 70 per cent. On LAPD's request, a few academicians from the California State University, Fullerton, analysed OCDS impact on citizen attitudes. The study revealed that face-to-face contact was twice as effective as a mere visual contact in terms of citizen attitude to the police. Such contacts made at home had a stronger impact than those in the streets. Most telling was the 80 per cent opinion that officers cared for the respondents 'as a person.' In sum, the OCDS threw up a means by which public attitudes toward the police could be unfrozen (Vernon and Lasley 1992).

An Evaluation of US Community Policing Projects

The concept of community policing has evoked mixed reactions. Does community policing work? This is the oft-raised question.

Some, like Kelling and Moore (1988), believe that this is a new organizational strategy which, properly guided, will help to enhance police effectiveness. In their estimate, it is a panacea for many ills which afflict the police, particularly the chasm that divides the public and the police, and the lack of job satisfaction and the consequent low morale of a majority of police officers who work at the street level.

Traditional police officers are not so effusive. They look upon community policing as merely 'old wine in a new bottle' (Bayley 1988). By implication, their stand is, instead of frittering away their energy in such pointless image-building exercises, the police would do well to concentrate on areas of professional work which would upgrade police output (Skogan 1990:9).

A pioneer in community policing, Lee Brown (1993), believes that this style gives officers 'a chance to be more creative and independent in their approach to police work'. He is, however, of the view that departments will be under tremendous pressure to abandon the programme when 'urban conditions worsen.' He recommends that they should not buckle under this and, rather, strengthen the movement by making community service police officers permanent and highly visible.

Perhaps the most strident criticism against community policing is that it is long drawn out, and requires a lot of patience and perseverance on the part of both sides. The transition period could be painful and disillusioning, sometimes even at the leadership level. An instance in point is the resignation (September 1992) of Isaac Fulwood, Chief of Washington, D.C. Police Department, because of disappointment that his community policing programme did not help to bring down the city's high homicide rate. Change in leadership for unrelated causes, as in the case of Lee Brown, could also affect programme results.

Bayley (1994c:117) no doubt concedes that evaluations done till now have not been positive about the efficacy of community policing and that the latter 'has had a small effect or has produced contradictory results. He is, however, sceptical about these evaluations. They have either been mere 'descriptions of processes of implementation' or 'tend to be impressionistic and anecdotal.' These do not take into account the fact that specific exercises have solved problems like drug-dealing in parks, disorderly behaviour in malls and burglaries and thefts in specified locations.

Comparative Analysis

It is the new orientation that police-community relations has acquired over the years that should strike anyone who reads the above account of community policing as practised in the US and India. What should be obvious is that the accent is no longer merely on the police wanting to establish cordial ties with the public. The police have now reached such a high level of intense activity that there is a clear mismatch between their responsibilities and resources. This has, therefore, driven them to go beyond seeking the community's goodwill. The community is actually being persuaded now to perform some of the police chores. This is a silent revolution whose impact may possibly be felt only after a decade.

The material presented in this chapter would highlight the clear lead that the US has gained over India in the matter of exploiting new opportunities that community policing has thrown up. One obvious explanation for this is the enormous theoretical inputs that have been made available to the US Police by academicians in the country. The latter have either unearthed hidden facets of this style of policing or have critically studied ongoing experiments so that their shortcomings become known for future guidance.

The Indian Police has unfortunately not had this benefit. Excepting for stray articles by field level police officers, which can at best be called experience-sharing, the subject has hardly aroused the curiosity of criminal justice scholars. This is intriguing because many other areas which form part of the discipline, such as the rise and fall of crime, rehabilitation of offenders, juvenile delinquency, victim rights and assistance, etc., have all received more than fair attention in the campuses and a variety of research institutions in India.

The near deification of community policing currently in the US follows a certain disillusionment with the earlier extremely professional approach to policing that laid emphasis on objectivity and extensive application of the tools of science and technology to police routine, regardless of the need for an intimate personal relationship between the average patrol officer and the citizen. The message now transmitted to the police is that a faceless matter-of-fact policing based on the rule book is no longer adequate. It has to mesh with the psychological requirements of a community which places a feeling of security above all creature comforts.

This realization that community policing is more than a slogan and it is of great practical import has come about in the US Police only after the police had acquired the elan of a professional body that relied on science and technology to carry out its tasks. In contrast, many state police forces in India are still struggling to prove their credentials of professionalism. The message commended to them now, day in and day out, is that they should use more and more of science and technology in their work, especially crime investigation. This is based on the hope that their professional skills will help to tone down the penchant for arbitrariness and ad hocism for which the Indian Police has been blamed over decades. If the experience of the US Police is any indication, the demand for extending the basics of community policing—incorporated in the experiments of a few forces—to wider geographical and functional areas may become strident only when police professionalism gains unassailable roots in India. Till then, one may not see the community and the police making any serious concerted efforts in this direction.

One prominent feature of the US experiments is the endeavour to decentralize police operations. The belief is that every effort should be made to bring the police physically close to the community. It is this belief that explains the creation of sub-stations, mini-stations and storefronts, which receive citizen complaints and which are sometime manned at least partly by the citizens themselves. Interestingly, India has, for many decades, this structure of police outposts (OPs) attached to a few regular police stations, with a view to catering to the special requirements of certain areas. These outposts have generally been useful in meeting crisis situations and forging close ties with the communities they serve. Unfortunately, the current trend is one of converting outposts into regular police stations or disbanding outposts altogether for reasons of economy. This move therefore overturns the rationale that had earlier influenced the state governments to create a limited number of outposts in high-tension and high-crime areas.

Community policing in the US is directed mainly against disorderly behaviour and select aspects of crime, such as drug peddling. Cooperation between the community and the police has sought, not only to bring to book those who had already come to adverse notice, but also to reduce the opportunities available for indulging in disorderly behaviour or for committing crime. The experiments done in India no doubt aim at both. Nevertheless, what stands out is the focus on prevention, rather than the systematic tracking down of past offenders with a view to facilitating punitive action. One explanation for this stress on prevention is the need to avoid enormous inconvenience caused by the tortuous processes in courts to those who would like to assist the police in tackling crime and disorder.

All these issues take us to one basic question. How much community policing does each of the two countries need? This effectively reduces itself to an examination of how frequent is the interaction of the average citizen with the Patrol Officer in the US and the Beat Constable in India. Most relevant here is the fact that, in the US, the patrol function has been almost wholly motorized. Almost every Patrol Officer has a car exclusively for himself. At worst, he shares it with another colleague.

The picture is totally different in India. Patrolling by individual constables is still by foot or by bicycle, almost wholly in the rural areas and partly in the cities. Patrol vehicles are an urban phenomenon, and these are supplemented liberally by foot or cycle-patrolling. This provides the setting for a greater day-to-day interaction between the lowest rank in the police and the citizen in India, than is the case in the US. Possibly this makes up, to some extent, for the police failure in India to formalize community policing experiments.

NOTES

1. I cannot exaggerate the importance of this seminal work. I would therefore strongly recommend that India's police training institutions should prescribe this as required reading for its trainees.
2. I must acknowledge that this perceptive analysis of the scene is that of N. Krishnaswamy, retired IGP, who recorded this while reviewing my draft chapter on community policing.
3. The NYPD has since seen two more Commissioners. While an up to date assessment of community policing is not available, information received by me reveals that one ongoing project is the Bicycle Patrol Programme. The NYPD claims that this has shown several benefits, namely, an increased visibility and the ability of officers to respond to calls for service while remaining accessible to the members of the community. In this context, the substantial drop in crime in the city cannot go unnoticed.
4. Very recent reports however speak of a resurgence of the city's commerce, greater financial strength of the city government, and, therefore, better attention to civic needs.
5. As a Graduate Student at Temple University, I had the privilege of working in close collaboration with the South Division. I should thank my Professor at Temple, Jack Greene, for making this possible. (Incidentally, Jack was a Consultant to the Philadelphia Police and was a great source of strength to the then Commissioner, the legendary Willie Williams, who later moved over to head the LAPD after the controversial Daryl Gates.) I recall with nostalgia the many meetings of South Division that I attended and the warmth with which I was looked after by Inspector Edward McLaughlin and his officers.

6

Science and Technology in Policing

> Advances in technology do not inevitably advance the performance of police departments. Police departments must manage technology rather than allow themselves to be managed by it.
>
> Malcolm K. Sparrow, 'Information Systems and the Development of Policing', *Perspectives on Policing*, March 1993, National Institute of Justice, Washington

DURING THE past few decades, the globe around us has been witness to mind-boggling advances in the realms of science and technology. There is hardly a sphere of human activity that has remained untouched by this development. Many organizations, small or big and government or private, have been anxious to take advantage of the several breakthroughs in science and technology, with a view to improving the quality of their products or services. Although organizations have differed with regard to the approach and the extent of their use, there is now a consensus that advances in science and technology should be fully exploited. Unlike private industry, government bureaucracies have been slower to react. Lately, however, there are signs of a desire on their part to make up for lost time.

Among the public service agencies now keen to benefit from science and technology, the criminal justice system—especially the police—is prominent. This is a welcome trend because of the crucial role that the system plays in a world increasingly rocked by crime of growing complexity and sophistication and violence of enormous proportions. In this context, an important consequence of the march forward by technology is that it facilitates not merely the police in their task of preventing and detecting crime, but also unwittingly helps the criminal in committing his act with greater dexterity. Actually, the latter is more ready to adapt himself to new technology and plunder a society that is becoming increasingly dependent on communication and computers. A whole new genre of computer-based crime, which does not recognize national boundaries, now poses a threat of serious dimensions to public security. Police forces across the world are not yet fully aware of the implications and methodologies of these new forms of crime.

The Indian police system and several police departments in the US are no doubt enthusiastic about enlarging their use of science and technology. The latter have a clear advantage over many others because of America's superior resources and proximity to centres of advanced scientific and technological research. This chapter will chronicle, separately, police achievements in the two countries from this perspective and thereafter highlight any commonality or divergence in approach.

The Police Need

Perhaps, more than any other segment of government, the police all over the world are under tremendous pressure from an increasingly sensitive and demanding clientele. This is no matter for surprise because of the escalating political and social tensions that have rendered the task of protecting life and property extremely problematic. Alongside this, is the growing ingenuity of an underworld whose activities now transcend national frontiers. There is, therefore, a case for police agencies to continuously update their knowledge and skill so that criminal deviance is held in check.

For criminal justice in general and the police in particular, there are a few areas of scientific knowledge which are relevant. The first relates to developments in the field of information science. The incredible progress in computer applications provides the opportunity to greatly push up the police capacity to collect and store information for retrieval at any desired point of time. Most helpful here is the facility that is now available for a rapid exchange of information globally between police agencies (Manning 1992). Many of these were till recently introvert and reluctant to share information.

Thanks again to the computer, we now know that the social sciences—previously looked down upon for their essentially qualitative nature and, therefore, for their inexactitude—have now acquired a new elan. The imparting of a quantitative approach to social science studies has brought to them a certain credibility that is difficult to ignore. As a result, a large number of statistical and behavioural models are now available for various purposes, including the prediction of criminal behaviour and the optimum use of the modest and overstretched resources of police forces all over the world. In this process, social sciences resort mainly to computer technology, highlighting the fact that there is a definite scope for linking developments in the different fields of science and technology mentioned earlier.

Finally, while traditionally-organized forensic science laboratories attached to police departments make use of past discoveries in the disciplines of physics, chemistry and biology, the evolution of a new science, 'molecular biology', has raised exciting possibilities. Perhaps the most exciting breakthrough in forensic medicine in the recent past is the DNA testing of samples picked up from a scene of crime or a suspect. DNA technology throws up a new tool for identifying victims and tracking down offenders involved in violent crime and sex offences (*FBI Law Enforcement Bulletin,* July 1991). Also, an analysis of human behaviour and the functioning of the human mind from the point of view of their chemical and genetic basis provides new techniques for identification, testing and screening, using body fluids or tissues (Miller 1991).

THE SCENE IN INDIA

Forensic science institutions came into being under the British to tackle specific problems. In this process, Chemical Examiner's Laboratories were set up during 1849-70 in the three Presidency Towns of Bombay, Calcutta and Madras and at Agra. These were mainly to deal with the investigation of cases of poisoning, a grave problem of the times. A Fingerprint Bureau (FPB) was established at Calcutta in 1897. It is believed that this was the first of its kind anywhere in the world. Such bureaux came into being soon in many other cities. Thereafter, till the advent of Independence (1947), police use of science and technology was quite modest. A Forensic Science Laboratory (FSL) was set up in Calcutta in 1952 and in Bombay in 1958. At present, most of the states have a laboratory of their own. In addition, there are a few under the Ministry of Home Affairs of the central government [Third Report (1980) of the NPC and Bami 1976].

Wireless communication linking state police forces with one another was set up for the first time in 1946. The birth of a Directorate of Coordination (Police Wireless) in 1949 gave an impetus to the strengthening of such communication. In course of time, Delhi was connected to several state headquarters by radio. This was followed by the states themselves linking their capital cities with district headquarters towns. This link was operated on High Frequency (HF) channels, and transmission was through Morse code signals.

The year 1964 saw the inauguration of Very High Frequency (VHF) channels supported by repeater stations. This enabled the introduction of speech communication replacing the cumbersome coded messages. A logical sequel was the establishment of control rooms in principal cities and the use of VHF-fitted mobile patrol vans.

The next stage was the demand for allotment of frequencies in the Ultra High Range (UHF) and the micro-wave channels to set up multi-direct-speech channels between the State Police Headquarters and different units in the districts. The central government's Postal & Telegraphic Department (since bifurcated into Department of Posts and Department of Telecommunication) raised several objections. It was only after the tremendous pressure brought on it that it agreed to provide these channels for a separate dedicated network to a lone state, Tamil Nadu, whose successful experiment triggered the demand for a similar facility by several other states. As a result, at present, a number of states have microwave telephones [Third Report (1980) of NPC].

The Police Modernization Scheme

Conscious of the benefits that science and technology could bring about in the quality of police performance, the Ministry of Home Affairs (MHA) of the central government initiated a scheme in 1969 for providing financial assistance to state governments for modernizing their police forces. For the first few years, 25 per cent of such assistance was treated as grant-in-aid and the rest as a loan. Since 1974-5, the grant portion has been doubled. Under this modernization scheme, state governments are permitted to buy data processing machines, equipment for forensic science laboratories, fingerprint bureaux and training institutions, vehicles and wireless equipment [Third Report (1980) of NPC].

In July 1978, the National Police Commission constituted a nine-member committee of experts headed by Prof. S. Sampath of the Union Public Service Commission (and earlier of the Indian Institute of Technology, Madras) to assess the progress of modernization of law enforcement and to determine requirements for future development and improvement. In its report of November 1979, the committee gave several recommendations pertaining to the areas of communication, forensic science and medicine, computers and transport. In specific terms, it urged that the police should be allowed to build up its own multi-channel microwave trunk-routes to provide linkage down to the police station level. It suggested the creation of a Directorate of Coordination at the apex level to ensure a greater use of computers in police investigations. The committee desired that the police should take full advantage of all the techniques of electronic-data-processing and recommended the provision of key-to-tape data input devices and optical readers and the expansion of on-line disk storage capacities of computer centres. It envisaged six high capability regional computer centres which could be connected to the national grid.

While endorsing the Sampath Committee's views, the NPC recommended the following in its Third Report (1980):

(i) Acquisition of scientific equipment should receive priority over construction of buildings in the matter of grants to states by the central government.
(ii) All districts should have teleprinter links with the State Police Headquarters.
(iii) Portable pocket-sets should be given to police officers on patrol duty.
(iv) Control Rooms, with attendant patrol vans, should be made available to all cities with a population of 100,000.
(v) Central government assistance for installing computers in the states should continue till all states are covered, and the requirements of the State Crime Records Bureaux and the National Crime Records Bureau are met.

Most of the NPC recommendations have been implemented over the years.

Scientific Aid to Police Investigation

The forensic science laboratory in each state is a major centre for the scientific analysis of material picked up at a scene of crime. It is headed by a Director who invariably works under the administative control of the Director-General of Police. However, in some states, the laboratory functions independently of the police and directly under the Home Secretary. A few have decentralized forensic science work by setting up regional laboratories at select district headquarters towns. In Tamil Nadu, for instance, there is a Scientific Assistant in most of the districts. He handles the less complicated cases by visiting the scene of crime and gathering material clues available there.

Except for a few of the smaller states, the rest have each a Finger Print Bureau (FPB). There is also a Central FPB at Calcutta for storing finger prints of inter-state criminals. A relatively recent development is the computerization of fingerprint records. The National Crime Records Bureau (NCRB) is coordinating a project that attempts a national storehouse of fingerprints available for comparison by a crime investigator in any part of the country through the national police computer network.

DNA fingerprinting assistance is available to the Indian Police for the past few years. A slightly modified version of the technique used in the Western world has been devised by Lalji Singh, a scientist at the Centre for Cellular and Molecular Biology (CCMB), Hyderabad. The CCMB is not merely the focal point for research in the area. It also helps investigative agencies to solve many problems of identity. One sensational case in which DNA fingerprinting was used most effectively was the assassination (21 May 1991) of former Prime Minister Rajiv Gandhi. It helped to fix the identity of two key accused, Dhanu, the human bomb who carried out the assassination and whose mutilated body was recovered at the scene, and Sivarasan who masterminded the plot and committed suicide a few weeks after the assassination. The Delhi Police also sought the assistance of the CCMB in the recent Naina Sahni case (popularly known as the 'Tandoor murder') in which a woman's body was found in the cooking oven of a hotel.

Although the Indian Evidence Act has not yet been amended to give legal validity to the findings of DNA fingerprinting, courts have started accepting these as relevant and admissible.[1] Another striking feature of the Indian scene is that no single institution has been accredited for the purpose of undertaking examination of the DNA samples. As a result, the CCMB, because of the reputation it has acquired during the past few years, has been burdened with far too many samples for tendering opinion.

The US Scene

Police departments in the country acquired a formal shape only around the middle of the nineteenth century. It was a nearly primitive beginning in terms of equipment to support the field operative who discharged his duty without the minute-to-minute contact with his headquarters that we are now so much accustomed to. Naturally, supervision of his professional conduct was almost non-existent. A slight change in the situation was brought about sometime in the 1850s, following the establishment of a telegraph network.

Initially, there was only a call box which, comprised a signalling lever that confirmed the presence of the officer at his prescribed post. There was an improvement in 1880, when call boxes were expanded to include telephones, thus providing a two-way communication between the patrolman and his police station. There was a further milestone in the early 1900s with the arrival of the automobile and the radio. These two new facilities did not merely enable the street-level officer to cover a large area with minimum physical strain. They also helped to provide a closer network of supervision (Alpert and Dunham 1988).

The early part of the twentieth century marked the arrival of a new class of police leaders. Appalled by the growing police corruption, these highly motivated chiefs wanted to impart a sense of professionalism to police work. Acting in pursuance of the goal, 'Get politics out of the police', and 'Get the police out of politics', they initiated several measures, which, apart from hiring a better quality of personnel, improving training methods, and giving them security of tenure, envisaged the creation of specialized units to tackle the emerging complexities of police tasks (Walker 1983:11).

Between 1920 and 1960, when professionalism was the key-word, public expectations were slowly rising. The rapid technological developments of this period naturally figured in the minds of police chiefs who were exercised over the question of how to improve the quality of police performance. It was in this process that the introduction of the patrol car, the two-way radio and the telephone revolutionized police routine (Walker 1983).

It was just a few years before World War I that the concept of motor patrol to supplement foot patrol gained cognizance. In course of time, police departments became convinced of the efficacy of the patrol car in facilitating control over the unlawful conduct of individuals. By the 1920s, the patrol car became a familiar sight in the urban setting. A change-over, almost totally to motor patrolling, came about in the 1950s (Walker 1983).

The 'two-way radio' was the second novelty that transformed police routine. This was in the late 1930s and it soon became a favourite with police supervisors who were struggling to establish a secure and reliable mode of control over the beat staff. Apart from ensuring that police officers were physically present in the area allotted, the radio quickened the despatch of police assistance to citizens in distress.

The telephone received its patent as early as 1877 and quickly became a popular means of communication among citizens. Naturally, the police also began to use it, but with little effect, in the absence of a portable radio. The telephone's utility was, therefore, extremely limited in day-to-day police routine, till two-way radios and patrol cars made their appearance. The three together set up a self-contained circuit whereby a citizen could call the police station by telephone and his request for assistance transmitted by the two-way radio to the patrolman driving around in a motor vehicle (Walker 1983). 'Over the space of a single generation . . . citizens became socialized into the habit of "calling the cops" ' (ibid.:14).

The American police departments have come a long way since the 1950s. A major part of their work is presently performed with the aid of automobiles. Motor cycles, aeroplanes and helicopters beef up the transport system. Sophisticated car-radios and hand-held walkie-talkies provide a trustworthy and swift means of communication between locations. They provide freedom of movement and also lend a feeling of security to the patrolmen, who can now venture into any location with the knowledge that, in a distress situation, help from headquarters would be only a minute or two away. A large number of police headquarters boast of a computer-assisted-dispatch (CAD), which enables dispatchers located at the control room to keep track of mobile patrolmen and respond to urgent calls from them or from the public with amazing speed and accuracy. Very often, patrol cars have also mobile digital terminals linked to databases at the headquarters, whereby, retrieval of vital information by a patrolman is possible within seconds of a query (Echelberry 1989).

Communication

A typical city police department in the US has five basic sub-systems in its communication network.

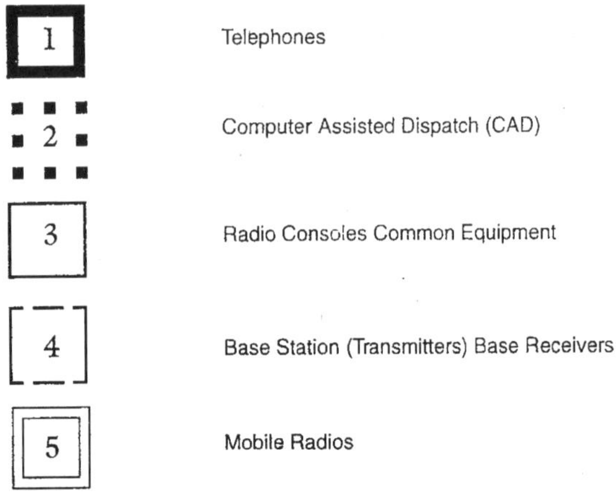

The flow chart depicting the communication system in a typical city police department follows:

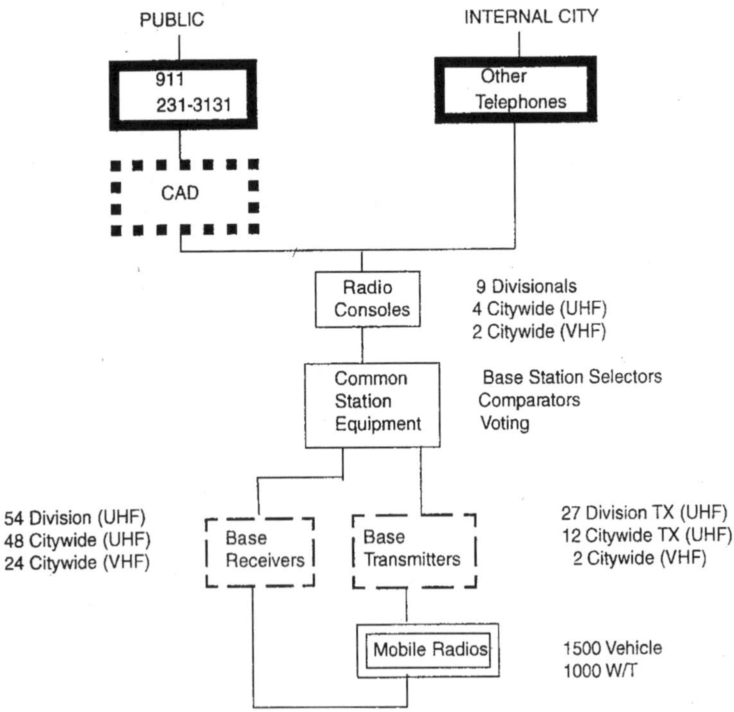

An emergency number 911 is available to the public to ask for various services. In a big city department, there are about 20 operators on round-the-clock duty in the radio room at the police headquarters who take the calls. These are then routed by the CAD to various police units for immediate attention. A few major cities have an 'enhanced' 911 capability that provides the operator with a read-out of the caller's number and address and the facility to hold on to the line till the operator himself releases it. This system reduces the possibility of incomplete calls and discourages prank calls (Task Force Report on Philadelphia Police 1987).

A Computer-Assisted-Dispatch (CAD) has five primary functions. They are: to verify whether the address given by the caller actually exists; assign priority to the most urgent of the several calls received; route the call to the correct dispatcher having the appropriate patrol sector; monitor availability of the various patrol cars so that the nearest vehicle is directed by the dispatcher; and, once the dispatch is over, monitor the progress of the call till it is attended to.

The radio communication comprises high power transmitters and receivers used by headquarters to send and receive messages, and the equipment (mobile vehicle radios and hand-held radios) with the field staff. To overcome environmental obstructions, such as tall buildings and hills and atmospheric conditions, most forces use repeaters located at various points. It is not uncommon to hear complaints of 'dead spots'—shadow regions where there is a total breakdown of communication—and 'bleed over'—interference of external signals caused by the overcrowding of a particular frequency. The accent now, therefore, is one of acquiring state-of-the-art equipment which filters external noise. There is also an effort to provide portable radios to more field officers (Philadelphia Task Force Report 1987).

Crime Laboratories

Almost all major police departments—city or state—have each a crime laboratory. The first of these was set up in 1923 in Los Angeles with just one employee. There has been substantial progress from this modest beginning. Apart from a significant rise in manpower, these laboratories have a battery of experts and consultants in a wide variety of disciplines.

For instance, the Scientific Investigation Division (SID) of the Los Angeles Police Department (LAPD) has more than 20 sworn personnel and 110 civilian specialists. The division has 7 sections and 6 units to assemble all possible scientific evidence.

The New York State Police (NYSP) is another department to make rapid strides in this area. Its laboratory system is headquartered in Albany and there are three regional laboratories. More than a hundred professionals work for the system, and nearly 20,000 cases, such as vandalism, criminal tampering and drug trade or consumption, are handled every year. Experts attached to the laboratories include toxicologists, criminalists (who examine arsons and explosives residues, and analyse paint, glass and tool marks), firearms examiners, serologists, drug analysts and document examiners.

DNA Testing

The FBI has become the nodal point for an exchange of information between law enforcement agencies in the country. Its DNA programme covers four basic areas: case work, technical assistance, the National DNA Index and Research. The FBI laboratory receives DNA samples from agencies all over the country. Of the nearly 2000 cases handled till 1991, two-thirds related to investigation of rape and the remaining to murder and other violent crime. The FBI claims that, in about 75 per cent of the cases, 'sufficient interpretable information' is available to help determine whether the individual in question could be linked or not to further investigation (FBI 1991). Noteworthy here is that, in about one-third of the examinations during 1988–July 1991, the FBI was able to delink the suspect from the source of the biological evidence collected at the crime scene.

About 20 state and local crime laboratories are reported to undertake forensic DNA analysis. An FBI survey (1990) revealed substantial support for its pioneering and coordinating role in DNA testing. The proposal to develop DNA-related software and automation tools to make state and local crime laboratories self-reliant has been particularly commended. Most promising is the project to establish a National DNA Index, which will permit an exchange of DNA profiles relating to unknown subjects and convicted sex offenders.

The impressive progress in the field of DNA testing will have to be viewed against the growing judicial acceptance of DNA evidence. According to one study, courts in almost all states have admitted DNA evidence at more than 400 hearings/trials so far. Of these, the

FBI laboratory alone accounted for admissions in over 120 trials and 85 separate admissibility hearings in 40 states (Sylvester and Stafford 1991).

What is of major concern to crime investigators is the enormous delay in obtaining laboratory findings. An *USA Today* report quotes the FBI as saying that, of the 298,000 DNA samples collected all over the country since 1990, only about 62,000 have been disposed of. A laboratory in Virginia alone has a backlog of 115,000 samples and 500 cases referred to it. Several reasons are cited for this enormous backlog. One is that many of the laboratories have not been able to buy the equipment needed because of lack of funds. Secondly, they accord a higher priority to work assigned to them by courts. One factor mentioned most is the lack of compatibility between the two different computer systems employed by the FBI and the Bureau of Alcohol, Tobacco and Firearms (BATF). It is said that, of the laboratories which can afford the requisite equipment, 21 use the ATF system and 91 that of the FBI. Since the two systems cannot communicate with each other, the databank of neither is complete. Efforts are now in progress to establish a network (*Times of India*, 30 August 1996).

Police Computerization

Information technology is a source of enormous power, and such power enables control over institutions (Archambeaults 1990). Overcoming their earlier apathy, criminal justice agencies now display a welcome sensitivity to keeping pace with this revolution so as to sharpen performance and live up to client expectations. Their current responsiveness is dictated by a growing complexity of police operations and the magnitude of the data generated in the bargain. A sequel is the need to process the large volume of available information without any loss of time or accuracy. This accounts for the crucial role played by computer technology in day-to-day criminal justice operations. Although some problems have arisen from this, such technology 'has become . . . a management survival tool' (ibid.: 4). Archambeaults (1990) believe that knowledge of computers will soon become a basic requirement for employment in criminal justice agencies, particularly the police. This observation is meaningful in the context of the recent expansion of the role of computers in the US and Indian police departments.

POLICE COMPUTERIZATION IN INDIA

The Annual Conference of Deputy Inspectors-General, CID, held in New Delhi in 1970 set up a sub-committee to explore the feasibility of computerization of crime records against the background of the data becoming too large to be handled manually. The sub-committee reported back to say that this was possible. It went on to lay down a standardized input format for the entire country. In 1972, a sub-committee of the same conference went into the question of computerizing fingerprint records and suggested a new system of classifying fingerprints for this purpose. These formulations for computerizing crime and fingerprint records were largely influenced by the pioneering work already done in these fields in the Tamil Nadu Police under the personal leadership of N. Krishnaswamy, a senior IPS officer of that state.

During 1975-6, modernization of crime records through computerization was included in the programmes to be funded by the Government of India under the modernization scheme, which had come into effect in 1970. A landmark was the creation (1976) of a Directorate of Coordination of Police Computers (DCPC) with a view to introducing computer-based crime-criminal information systems in the states and to assist them in procuring and installing computers. In the same year, a study group examined the appropriate strategies and modalities of crime record-keeping in the context of the latest developments in EDP and telecommunications. This was followed by a Committee on Crime Records of 1978 which reviewed existing crime records and associated procedures and recommended a few changes. Finally, flowing from an NPC recommendation, and on the basis of modalities suggested by a Task Force (1985) constituted by the Ministry of Home Affairs, a National Crime Records Bureau (NCRB) was established in 1986 under the Ministry of Home Affairs (MHA) of Government of India to serve as a 'national repository of crime and criminal information'.

The NCRB has played an active role in guiding computerization programmes in the state police forces, especially in the area of maintenance of crime records, so that they effectively feed the channels of information to the NCRB. For this purpose, it had first suggested, and later succeeded in creating state and district CRBx. A major task undertaken was to devise a set of new Integrated Police Forms for common use by all the state police forces in the country. This was to ensure recording of all relevant information in police stations on a uniform basis and in a manner suited to computerization. Adoption of these forms by the state police forces has been slow but steady. The pace is likely to pick up when computers are supplied to police stations, an area where a beginning has already been made. Concurrently, the NCRB has also taken up the major task of supplying related computer hardware and software to all state and district CRBx in the country and to integrate all these into a national network called POLNET based upon state-of-the-art satellite-based communication equipment.[2]

The NCRB has made its presence felt also in the area of software development. The more than ten applications software packages till now to its credit include the Fingerprint Name-Indexing, Portrait Building, Terrorist Information and Detention Information Systems. These have been shared with the State Crime Records Bureaux. The NCRB also operates as a premier computer training establishment for the country and runs about 21 programmes every year. Its annual compilation, 'Crime in India' has been placed on a firm footing.

Computerization of the US Police

Police departments in the US did not initially show any great enthusiasm. A modest beginning was made only in the early 1960s with the opening of traffic accident files. A few departments also used computers for compiling crime statistics and to assist housekeeping activities.

St. Louis was about the first department that took advantage of computers (Colton 1978). The apparent indifference of the rest of the US Police invited harsh comments from the 1967 President's Commission which was critical of the fact that, unlike the military, which employed a large number of scientists and engineers, agencies responsible for crime prevention and detection chose to hire just a handful of them to fight crime. The Commission's observations perhaps gave the much-needed thrust required by police agencies to move forward in a big way to exploit the advances in science and technology.

The late 1960s witnessed intense activity by several police departments anxious to introduce computers. This gradually pushed up the number of departments that had computerized at least a part of their records. Apart from the President's Commission Report, a few other factors helped in the process (Colton 1978). Chief of these was the availability of federal funds through the newly-created Law Enforcement Assistance Administration (LEEA). The police emphasis on professionalism and modernization, coupled with the pressure from marketing personnel of computer manufacturers, also provided a congenial setting.

An International City Management Association (ICMA) survey of 1971 revealed that 44 per cent of the responding police departments used a computer. This went up to 56 per cent by 1974 (Colton 1978). The survey, however, found that computer application was rudimentary because information-processing still related only to routine efforts.

Computerization has been accelerated substantially since 1974. Except for the very small departments, the others have either their own computers or share time with neighbouring computers. According to one survey, in 1990, over 90 per cent of state and local law enforcement agencies reported using PCs. Further, more than a half of such agencies had access to an Automated Fingerprint Identification System (AFIS). Also, 25 per cent of local and 14 per cent of state agencies had car-mounted digital terminal computers (International Fact Book of Criminal Justice, 1993). However, during a survey conducted a few years ago in the US, only 16 per cent of the responding departments indicated that police agencies were using computers to their best advantage (Sharp 1996).

The Position in Some Police Departments

The Miami Police Department

The Miami Police has been using computers for more than a decade. The 1100 sworn officers in the department now handle about 400 incident reports everyday. The information thereby generated is processed with the help of 250 terminals, 55 desk printers and 33 micro-computers. In addition, there are 137 mobile digital terminals (MDT) available in patrol cars (*Police Chief*, January 1989).

Principal applications by Miami Police take the form of Computer-Assisted Dispatch (CAD) and Computer-Assisted Report Entry (CARE). An off-shoot of CAD is the Hazardous Location File. This is a programme which alerts a despatcher that a potentially dangerous situation exists at a specific location. It helps in prompting the nearest officer to send extra manpower. Yet another unique innovation in Miami is the One-hour Call-up, a programme that assists in monitoring officers who would normally check in regularly (*Police Chief*, January 1989).

The New York State Police

The New York Statewide Police Information Network (NYSPIN), a computer-oriented communications and data base system, came into being in 1966 (Law Enforcement Technology, April 1989). This facilitates information-sharing by about 185 police offices in the state in more than 700 terminal locations, with more than 64000 criminal justice agencies in the country. This has been made possible through links with other computer systems, such as the National Crime Information Center (NCIC), the National Law Enforcement Telecommunication System (NLETS) and the New York City Police Department. On an average, NYSPIN records annually about 190 million messages.

New York City Police Department (NYPD)

The NYPD information systems are made up of several computer platforms. They are a combination of mainframe, LAN-based and stand alone computers. The platforms support approximately 40 NYPD applications, from personnel management to arrest processing systems. There are approximately 70 software support products.

The Special Police Radio Inquiry Network (SPRINT) is core to NYPD's operations. This links the public with the most sensitive and high-pressure 911 system that renders emergency services to citizens in distress. The system is required to process more than 18,000 calls received each day by 64 operators working round-the-clock. This gigantic task is fulfilled with the help of an IBM 370/148 computer and associated telecommunications hardware.

The system's efficiency may be gauged from the fact that the response time is usually 30 seconds. SPRINT enables the centralized control of street-level police work through the prompt dispatch of patrol officers. The latter receive assistance from the system through access to information required to fulfil an assigned task. SPRINT comprises essentially an Automatic Call Distributor (ACD), which identifies the borough from which a call has emanated and diverts it to the operator assigned to that particular borough. The operator then determines particulars such as the caller's location and the nature of service required. The information thus obtained is fed into the SPRINT terminal, and, immediately thereafter, a 'total incident display' appears on the monitor screen. When the emergency operator keys the SPRINT terminal, the information is processed and flashed to the dispatcher's monitor. Such display carries information on the location of the incident-precinct, appropriate patrol car and alternative units available. Helpful to the dispatcher is also the computer's ability to assign a priority level to each complaint based on its critical nature.

The Los Angeles Police Department (LAPD)

The LAPD computerization programme is in a transitional state.The traditional mainframe and coaxially attached non-intelligent terminal mode form the bulwark of the system. The mainframe applications run on dual IBM 3090 computers. The department is, however, moving towards the present paradigm of distributed/shared databases and PC-based LANs and WANs. The PC networks are based on Pentium desktop computers and the Operating System is Novell Netware 4.1.

The Emergency Command Control Communications System (ECCCS), which aims at reducing the response time for dispatch of police assistance over an area of 465 square miles, represents the most sophisticated computerized activity of the LAPD. Analogous to New York City's SPRINT, ECCCS comprises the Central Dispatch Center (CDC), Area Command Centers (ACCs), field units, ECCCS computers, CDC consoles and voice and digital radio equipment.

The ECCCS computers carry both a main and a communications processor. Verifying incident addresses, recommending field units for dispatch and identifying special or hazardous locations are the chief functions of the computers. They are used also for storing information pertaining to incidents and the status of field units. The Central Dispatch Operators act on the basis of a computer-displayed recommendation for field unit assignment. Each of the 55 operators has two display screens, a key-board and a radio control panel. The screens are used for data input and output and for digital communication with field units equipped with Mobile Data Terminals (MDTs) and the 18 Area Command Centres all over Los Angeles. Each field unit has an MDT, which gives officers of the unit access to external data bases, besides permitting them digital communication on the unit and incident status to Central Dispatch Operators.

The Houston Police Department (HPD)

The HPD has four key systems: Amdahl, UNISYS, DEC VAX and PC-based. These take care of a wide range of activities: personnel management, service of warrants, identification, etc. Databases built up include firearms records, performance evaluation, overtime tracking and subpoena tracking.

The Santa Ana Police Department (SAPD)

The SAPD's computer system consists of five minicomputers, 16 GB of on-line storage, associated equipment and software. Three VAX 8250 minicomputers currently supply word processing and database management. Installed in 1988, these are extremely reliable. The busiest SAPD computer system is CAD that is linked to 132 Mobile Data Terminals (MDTs). Field personnel use MDTs to receive calls from the CAD and communicate with other officers. Finally, SAPD can boast of a photo imaging computer that stores photographs of arrestees on magnetic medium from which an officer can quickly retrieve digital photographs of all persons in the system that match the description of wanted persons.[3]

The National Institute of Justice (NIJ)

The NIJ is the research arm of the Department of Justice. In 1972, it created an 'international clearing house to share its latest findings with officers who can put the information to use' (Law Enforcement Technology, April 1989:22). Called the National Criminal Justice Reference Service (NCJRS), the NIJ information is derived from an enormous computerized data base. According to one estimate, the data base now includes more than 100,000 documents (ibid.). The disciplines covered include criminology, crime prevention, drugs and crime, law enforcement and statistics. Behind the service are a number of specialists, each of whom has access to the database. Search for information is in three formats: topical searches (summaries of documents and full bibliographic information), topical bibliographies (summaries of materials complete with subject and title indexes), and custom searches (a list of about 400 titles with bibliographic citations which include summaries of contents).

The Federal Bureau of Investigation (FBI)

The FBI's Uniform Crime Report (UCR) is produced annually by a manual process of combining returns from thousands of agencies. This cumbersome process is being progressively replaced by an automated system based on a newly-introduced National Incident-based

Reporting System (NIBRS). Under this innovation, each agency reporting crime figures to the FBI on a voluntary basis, instead of tallying offence, arrest and other crime-related data on a monthly basis, will hereafter report information for each individual crime on the prescribed NIBRS format through automated data processing means (*FBI Law Enforcement Bulletin,* November 1992).

Specialized Services available in the US Police

Growth of Mobile Data Terminals

The swiftness with which manpower is despatched to incident-spots determines the reputation of any police agency. We have come a long way from the earliest method of using light or audio signals to alert patrol officers. The computer is now a valuable tool that takes care of this task with remarkable efficiency. It has vastly improved upon mobile radio equipment which held sway in the area till a decade ago.

Radio dispatch was no doubt effective for quite sometime. Once the volume of traffic increased enormously, the human component (the operator) came under too much of a stress, leading to delay and errors. It was this situation that prompted police agencies to look around for help, and this was available in the form of 'mobile data terminals' (MDTs). The ability of computers to convert radio frequency signals to digital signals is exploited here. It has been found that the response time under a MDT system is 10-20 seconds, as compared to the usual three to four minutes in voice enquiry (Kolpack 1989).

The switch-over to MDTs began around the mid-1970s, when successful experiments were conducted to link elementary communication equipment with computer systems. This brought about marked changes in the mode of transmission of information from the headquarters to field units and *vice versa*. Access to other vast databases has been one of the major advantages of the switch-over.

The declining cost of computers is another significant gain. Basically, in the area of MDTs, the following types of equipment are available:

- (i) a mobile printer unit which prints data on to a paper, utilizing standard radio frequencies;
- (ii) status boards which provide display of unit status on pressing a button; and
- (iii) a screen with key-board which presents an alphanumeric display of requested or dispatched information (Kolpack 1989).

The system has many capabilities. These include protection of information, display of dispatch information and access to local, regional, state and national data bases. Perhaps more important is the 'Automatic Vehicle Locator' (AVL), which functions with the help of a Loran receiver mounted on a vehicle. Position information is transmitted to the control computer through a dedicated radio channel and gets displayed in a graphic form. The AVL comes in handy during radio problems and helps to track down an officer. This has also been found useful during vehicle pursuits, when the officer will have to concentrate on driving safely and is unable to operate his hand-mike. The AVL helps the dispatcher to monitor trends of the pursuit and intervene with additional manpower when he feels it warranted (Kolpack 1989).

Autmoated Fingerprint Identification System (AFIS)

Research into automating a system of comparing fingerprints goes back to more than twenty years (Doherty 1986). This is vital to investigators who are overwhelmed by the task of rummaging an ever-growing pile of records of individuals who had come to adverse notice. Automation greatly reduces search time by narrowing down the area of enquiry. The equipment now available is so sophisticated that the benefit of automation has become more obvious than before. As a result, more than 30 states are now served by an AFIS (Marx 1990). An expansion of this net, which would encourage the sharing of data, depends not on technology, but on the willingness of the users to enter into a contract on the basis of one of several standard formats available (ibid.). SEARCH—a non-profit consortium of states—has already initiated efforts in this direction.

The City of Miami Police Department has a system called PRINTRAK 250S. It holds 1.3 million fingerprint files and can scrutinize 200 prints per second. At the end of search, it produces a print-out that contains a list of suspects in a descending order of probability (Doherty 1986). In view of its enormous cost, several agencies in a region are found to share a single system.

Another sophisticated system is the one used by the San Francisco Police Department. This is an NEC equipment which employs custom processing chips.

Facial Identification System

Very often, a witness or a victim is able to describe the offender in some detail. This does not, however, help the investigating officer to form a clear mental picture of the offender. In such cases, it had been the past practice to manually draw a picture (IDENTIKIT) taking into account the available description. This has been of limited utility because of its approximation. The computer has opened up the possibility of arriving at a more accurate picture.

The computer photograph system contains a data base of facial features culled out from photographs of real individuals. Each photograph is analysed, and facial features are broken down through a digitizing process and stored under categories such as eyes, noses, mouths, chins and foreheads. The equipment comprises a console unit containing a computer, a drive unit, two monitors, a key board and a video copy processor that reproduces the image on monitor. It is possible to customize the arrangement for representing sexes and racial/ethnic groups (Sewell 1988). The dual screens of the computer permit display of all selected facial images on one side, while the operator juggles with additional options and images on the other. A pioneer in the use of the system is the Chesterfield County (Virginia) Police Department.

Police Patrol Scheduling System (PPSS)

Police administrators are often baffled by the problem of determining the exact number of personnel to be deployed in the field in a particular situation. Rotation *v.* fixed days-off, and one *v.* two officers per patrol car, are allied issues on which they find decision-making a difficult exercise. This is a grave shortcoming because human resources are scarce and will have to be utilized judiciously so that every area of police charter gets adequate manpower. A breakthrough is the evolution of a Police Patrol Scheduling System (PPSS), which uses micro-computers to evaluate various deployment issues (Huxley and Taylor 1989). The objective of the system is the drafting of an optimal schedule on the basis of 'right starting times and days for the right number of officers so that, on an hour-by-hour basis, the number on duty matches needs as closely as possible' (ibid.:59).

Pioneering work in the area was done by the San Francisco Police Department. PPSS helped it to arrive at shortages arising from limited deployment. This computation of shortages per hour, as against per shift, was a major advance, because optimal use of resources resulted from plotting hourly requirements against rotation *v.* fixed-scheduling. PPSS was also useful to identify the 'worst case', the 'one requiring the greatest number of officers to achieve total coverage' (Huxley and Taylor 1989: 59).

Current Problems

Computer technology has undoubtedly brought in appreciable benefits to the delivery of police services. A 53 per cent reduction in investigation time spent on writing and typing reports is claimed by St. Louis Department officers. The latter also report a $50,000 drop in administrative expenses. Computerized criminal investigative information systems, introduced by the San Diego Police Department, are known to have led to more than 3000 arrests and case cancellations (Archambeaults 1990). Several other departments have also been using computers effectively.

While results achieved have thus been impressive, the exercise has not been totally free from problems (Archambeaults 1990, Pearson and Bradley 1989 and Patterson 1989). For instance, one department could not utilize its newly-bought equipment for nearly two years, because it had not provided adequate funds for its installation and for training personnel. There was also the case of a department finding itself totally at a loss, when the hardware manufacturer from whom it had bought equipment stopped its production and the accompanying support service. A third agency discovered that a programme bought by it could handle only one-half of the records produced by the department every year (Pearson and Bradley 1989). These are only some broad examples of how computerization, unless backed by advance planning and imagination, could land a department in easily avoidable problems.

The most important area in which some police departments have committed fundamental mistakes is with regard to the selection of appropriate hardware. This has become a difficult decision in the context of the enormous number of computers now available and the sophistry employed by salesmen anxious to sell their wares. A common error is one of buying a computer that is incompatible with the software proposed to be used. It is known that some departments had bought computers for which there were no law enforcement programmes. The accent on economizing costs and opting for bargain sales have also landed a few departments in trouble. Frequently, they get stuck with machines that have no future support in terms of software or spares. In a few instances of lack of appreciation of requirements, some agencies are known to have gone in for a mainframe, when what they needed was just a personal computer (Pearson and Bradley 1989).

The choice of right software also presents problems. Departments need to be clear in their minds as to what their objectives are, while going in for computerization. Only such clarity will help them in arriving at the right selection.

Two important criteria for selection are availability of support service and scope for flexibility. Some departments have found that the software bought by them is not backed by service personnel who are ready at hand to answer questions or to correct errors. Another shortcoming occasionally noticed is that the software bought is rigid and is not adaptable to local requirements, contrary to tall claims made at the time of sale (Pearson and Bradley 1989).

Comparative Analysis and Prospects for the Future[4]

The foregoing review of how police forces in India and the US have adapted themselves to the advances of science and technology shows considerable similarities in approach behind seeming differences, which are essentially one of degree, attributable to the disparity in the availability of resources. In basic terms, the problems that police forces are called on to handle in the two countries, as indeed in most countries, are marked by the same increases in volume and complexity of crime. Again, the solutions that they seek inevitably address the same objectives of not only coping with these increases, but also enhancing the speed of responses and the quality of information on which such responses rest.

In seeking the aid of science and technology in the pursuit of these objectives, transport, communications and computerization have come to occupy, what may be considered a basic infrastructural role in both the countries, while a wide range of forensic services have assumed an important superstructural role. The progressive adoption of these facilities has corresponded to the sequence of development of the related technologies.

Motor transport was the very first facility which police forces readily took to, because it fulfilled the very first need of police operations, namely, speedy physical intervention over dispersed areas. The telephone and the two-way mobile radio brought swift, orally-transmitted information and instruction into active play in field operations, enhancing the value of mere physical intervention to the level of informed intervention. But, whatever information and instruction could be communicated, remained restricted to that which the interacting officers could immediately draw from their personal knowledge and experience.

Computerization has added a new dimension of field operations, the ability to draw, as quickly and readily, from data bases representing the accumulated knowledge and experience of a whole police force and indeed of other police forces as well. At the same time, computerization has been a far more complex solution to implement, than the transport and communication solutions. A small group of technical people can quickly establish and maintain a transport fleet or a communication network, however large these may be. From the point of the end-user, the police officer in the field, operating a vehicle or a telephone or a radio set involves no special knowledge or skill, and hence police forces have been able to adapt very fast to transport and communication facilities.

Implementation of computerization, however, poses a technical dimension that demands much more effort, involvement, knowledge and skills from all levels of a police force. At the end-user level of a police force, using a terminal for the constant feeding of data to build and update data bases and for retrieving background information relevant to particular situations calls for a higher level of understanding and skill, than in driving a vehicle or using a telephone. At the administrative and supervisory levels of the police force, there has to be a considerable degree of involvement in the process of defining objectives, determining specifications of hardware and software and designing, maintaining and operating the hardware and software. Though these processes, at the higher levels, are highly technical, needing to be handled by qualified technical personnel, they cannot be successfully established without the sustained interaction and informed support of police officers at all levels, because it is the latter who have to very clearly determine the operational requirements that have to be supported by computerization. Clear definition and prioritisation of objectives to enable effective computerization, surprisingly, does not come easily, especially in an organizational culture that is conditioned to 'first act and then think' or, perhaps, not think at all !

Experience in both India and the US shows that police forces in general have been slow to measure up to the exacting levels of knowledge, skill and attitude required for the effective implementation and utilization of computerization programmes. Absence of adequate involvement of all levels of a police force at every stage of the implementation process has resulted in the all-too-frequent mistakes in the choice of hardware, design of software, poor utilization of the new facilities, often limited to simpler applications not relevant to the sophisticated demands of support to critical field operations, etc. All this adds up to wasteful expenditure and reinforces the observation of Archambeaults cited earlier that computers have become a management survival tool and a knowledge of computers will become a basic requirement for employment in criminal justice agencies, specially the police.

In the area of operation of the forensic services, science and technology continue to make significant contributions in both the countries by way of new equipment, with tremendous capabilities, most of which relate to processes of observation, record and analysis in respect of physical or circumstantial evidence that has a bearing on criminal activity or culpability. Personal observation has been greatly extended by methods that involve the use of X-rays, infra-red and ultraviolet light, lasers and radars, microscopes and spectroscopes. Monitoring systems are able to scan the entire electromagnetic spectrum for both use and misuse of radio communication. The capabilities of conventional photography and tape-recording have been extended by new generations of digital audio and video recording. And new methods of analysis are being added to the old, derived from not only the old disciplines of physics and chemistry, but from the newer ones of electronics, atomic physics, bio-chemistry and genetics.

The capability of digitization of audio, video or virtually every form of recordable evidence, makes it possible to accumulate, process, and retrieve these with the aid of computers. Data, related not only to physical and genetic fingerprints, but also every digital record for every other form of evidence retrieved from scenes of crime, or from suspects, or offenders, will find a place in comprehensive computerized data bases of the future. The data bases will also get integrated into expanding networks, providing instantaneous access to new 'World Wide Web' of crime and criminal information. This is the vista that science and technology will open up to police forces across the world in the twenty-first century. It will be up to the police forces then to provide themselves, not merely the physical equipment, but far more importantly, the knowledge, skills and attitudes to exploit this vista effectively in the fight against crime.

NOTES

1. The Tamil Nadu Police recently successfuly cited DNA evidence in the sensational 'Swami Premanand Case' to prove that the accused had raped a 19-year girl who became pregnant as a result of the assault. The CCMB conclusion that the DNA of the foetus matched the blood sample of the Swami was upheld in the case (*Indian Express,* 25 August 1997).
2. Tamil Nadu was the first police department in the country to experiment with computerization of crime records. Taking advantage of a move (1970) of the State Finance Department to computerize its budget operations, a decision was taken by the police to put data on about 50000 crimes and fingerprints of 300,000 criminals on computer tapes and disks. Initially, they were processed on an IBM-1440 system. Subsequently, the data bank was moved into a larger IBM-370 system. Thanks to the 1975 scheme of the Ministry of Home Affairs for supply of TDC 316 computers built by the Electronic Corporation of India Ltd. (ECIL) to all state police forces, the first such system was supplied to the Tamil Nadu Police in 1976. The crime-criminal-fingerprint record system, which had become operational on the IBM-370 system, was then moved to the TDC-316 system, making it the first such system to become operational under the National Police Computerization Programme.
3. Information on computer systems functioning in the various US police departments was collected partly when I was at Temple University in 1989-90 and partly through recent correspondence with some departments, such as Houston, Santa Ana, NYPD and LAPD.
4. This section was mostly written by N. Krishnaswamy who is an authority on police modernization. Realizing my limitations in the area, I approached him, and he readily agreed to help with a draft, which I expanded wherever I could.

7

Problems of Personnel Management

> The Constabulary . . . form the foundation and base for the entire police structure. Any attempt at a meaningful police reform has necessarily to start at their level only.
>
> *First Report of the National Police Commisssion* (India), 1979

A CHARACTERISTIC of many modern police agencies is their rapidly growing size. An expanded role in society and the constantly enlarging population that it has to serve have brought in periodic manpower accretions. As a result, many police forces have become Leviathans. What is unfortunately overlooked here is that this phenomenon, in conjunction with the dynamics of the modern environment, demands a continuous upgradation of personnel quality and practices, in tune with the modern principles of human resource management. It is debatable whether many police leaders are alive to this requirement. A cold fact is that apathy in this area has often diluted police morale and discipline. It is from this perspective that issues of personnel management in the American and Indian police forces are examined in this chapter. The canvas being vast, focus here will be only on a few major areas, such as recruitment and selection, discipline, and collective bargaining.

THE INDIAN SCENE

Historical Background

A re-drawing of the subcontinent's political map in 1947 into India and Pakistan, and the several subsequent phases of reorganization of the states constituting the Indian Union, ushered in many administrative changes. A corollary was the creation of many state and central police forces. The trend is one of a ceaseless expansion of manpower and equipment, throwing up the distinct prospect of many new problems of personnel management. An appreciation of the current issues is best facilitated by a brief historical review of how personnel management was handled during the formative years of the Indian Police.

One of the earliest documents is the report of the Torture Commission (1854) (already referred to in Chapter 2) appointed by the then Madras (now Tamil Nadu) Government in 1854. While concluding that torture was widely practised, it said: 'the whole Police is underpaid, notoriously corrupt, and without any of the moral restraint and self-respect which education ordinarily engenders' (Griffiths 1971:80).

An overview of the other literature of the times makes clear one dominant attitude of the government. Right from the beginning, it was averse to spending more than what was absolutely essential to raising and maintaining a force, with a total disregard for quality or morale. For instance, one of the two terms of reference of the first Police Commission (1860) was 'to suggest to Government any measure whereby expenditure may be economized or efficiency increased' (Griffiths 1971:88). Consequently, this commission concentrated on the police organization as a whole, and did not choose to prescribe standards of recruitment or a salary structure (Raghavan 1985).

The second Police Commission (1902)—otherwise known as the Fraser Commission—pointed out several deficiencies in personnel management. Apart from the understaffing at the field level, it also referred to the 'inadequate pay, poor methods of selection and the lack of any proper training'. It added:

> The police force is far from efficient; it is defective in training and organisation; it is inadequately supervised; it is generally regarded as corrupt and oppressive; and it has utterly failed to secure the confidence and cordial cooperation of the people. (p. 150)

This gives a fair idea of the dimensions of personnel problems which the police leadership had to tackle during the early years of the twentieth century.

Surprisingly, after the 1902 Fraser Commission, no Police

Commission was appointed at the national level until 1977 to go into the whole gamut of police reforms. The Gore Committee—known otherwise as the Committee on Police Training (CPT)—appointed earlier in 1971, had been asked to look into the narrow area of training alone. It laid down (1973) for the first time a clear philosophy for police training and highlighted the all-round neglect of training. It urged re-orientation of training perspectives in the light of the need to transform the police, from a mere crime prevention and order-oriented force to a service agency sensitive to the feelings of the weaker sections of society. The committee's accent on efforts to upgrade the quality of trainers and to provide strong incentives to attract the right talent for faculty positions in training institutions was a refreshing departure from the beaten track. The National Police Commission (NPC) (1977) wholeheartedly endorsed the CPT's views on how to upgrade police training in the country.

The NPC contributed a lot to the thinking on police personnel management. In its first report (1979), the commission pinpointed the Constable as the functionary who needed most attention. Referring to him as the 'cutting edge of police administration' and the level at which 'any attempt at a meaningful police reform has necessarily to start', it declared (p. 18) that the 'crux of efficient policing . . . is the effective and amiable street presence of a well-qualified, trained and motivated constable'. Stating that he should be prepared for performing not merely mechanical duties as in the past, but also those involving discretion and judgement, the commission went on to prescribe a higher educational qualification at the point of entry. While commending the CPT's report, the NPC emphasized the importance of on-the-job training, and laid great stress on instilling in the constabulary and higher levels, the need for proper conduct towards the citizen.

In respect of Sub-Inspectors, the NPC agreed (Fifth Report, 1980) with the CPT's standards, namely, a college degree, entry age group of 20-3 and the same physical requirements as applicable to the constabulary. In its Sixth Report (1981), the NPC also paid fair attention to the higher echelons, particularly the IPS which formed the leadership corps. It was concerned over the fact that the quality of recruits to this elitist service was declining and that IPS officers developed 'acute frustration . . . within a few years of being in service'. To make the IPS more attractive, the commission believed that there was 'a strong case for rationalizing and improving the internal structure of the IPS and bringing it on par with the IAS (Indian Administrative Service) in pay structure and promotion prospects' (ibid.: 9).

Significant was the NPC's suggestion that IPS officers should be considered for filling certain jobs outside the police force so that their outlook was broadened. This was in response to a long-standing demand from IPS officers themselves who believed that their advancement prospects within the department were poor, and that these could improve only if non-police jobs were thrown open to them.[1]

The NPC was emphatic that unless the calibre of leadership was upgraded, no perceptible improvement in the quality of policing could be brought about. It, therefore, outlined in its Second Report (1979) an elaborate new procedure for the appointment of the Chief of Police of a state, namely, the DGP. This contemplated selection from a panel of three names picked by a committee headed by the Chairman of the Union Public Service Commission and comprising, among others, the central government's Home Secretary, the seniormost among the heads of Central Police Organizations, the State Chief Secretary and the serving Police Chief. More important was the recommendation that the DGP should enjoy a statutorily-fixed tenure 'without the Damocles' sword of transfer hanging over his head all the time, subject to political whim'. For this purpose, the NPC proposed a specific provision to be incorporated in the Police Act itself.[2]

Possibly the NPC's most significant contribution was in the area of grievance redressal. There was evidence of efforts to form associations of policemen at the lower levels from the early part of this century. The NPC's review (First Report 1979) revealed no uniformity in practice. It therefore outlined a machinery of Police Associations (which were to be democratically elected bodies) and Staff Councils (with nominated representatives of different ranks) at the district and state levels. There was to be arbitration in matters concerning pay and allowances, leave and any other matter agreed to between the State Police Staff Council and state government.

While most NPC recommendations have been implemented, some far-reaching and revolutionary suggestions, such as the new procedure to choose the Police Chief and a fixed statutory tenure for him, the abolition of recruitment to the level of DSP by state governments and the creation of a State Security Commission which would oversee the police, have not yet found favour.

The Current Scene in India

Recruitment and Selection of Police Personnel

Open market selection in the state and central police organizations is presently at three levels: Constable, Sub-Inspector (SI) and Deputy/ Assistant Superintendent (DSP/ASP). In a few, there is the additional level of Assistant Sub-Inspector (ASI), although this rank is fast disappearing.

In most states, Constables and SIs are recruited by the DGP, who also issues formal orders of appointment. (The state government lays down, in consultation with the DGP, the basic standards and the testing procedure.) Constables are normally selected at the district level, but the process is centralized at the state level whenever there is massive recruitment of the kind Tamil Nadu and a few other states have been undertaking in the past few years.

A minimum height of 162.5 cm and a pass in the XII grade at school are generally insisted upon for the constable-aspirant who will also have to successfully complete a few physical efficiency tests (such as the 100 m sprint, 1500 m run, long and broad jumps and rope climbing) before being allowed to take the written and oral tests. Broadly speaking, the same process applies for the selection of SIs, except that they are chosen at the state level and the educational qualification prescribed is normally a college degree. A significant feature of the selection scheme is the absence of a psychology test.

A DSP, who is appointed by the state government, takes a competitive examination which is common to the State Civil Service (a generalist corps like the IAS) and is held by the State Public Service Commission. Candidates short-listed on the basis of this written examination have to face an oral test.

As described in Chapter 1, IPS officers are picked up from successful candidates at the Civil Services Examination held each year by the Union Public Service Commission. After selection and appointment, they are allotted to the various states, the number for each state depending upon the vacancies existing in that State.[3] Appendix VII gives the IPS strength in each state.

There is however an additional avenue of induction into the IPS at the level of Superintendent of Police (SP) from the pool of state government-recruited DSPs belonging to the State Police Service (SPS) who have a reasonably good track record of about 8 to 10 years. According to IPS Cadre Rules, 33 per cent of senior posts (of and above the rank of SP) in each State Cadre are earmarked for this class of 'promotees'.

General Observations

The post-Independence experience of Indian Police throws up a few generalizations. The most undisputed of these is that, except in the case of some central forces which involve hardship locations in inhospitable terrain, the high rate of unemployment in the country ensures a large pool of candidates for selection. About 15 to 20 offer themselves for every available slot, especially at the Constable level. The ratio is only slightly smaller in the case of the other ranks.

A certain amount of political pressure is brought to bear on selection staff by the competing candidates. More blatant is the attempt by serving personnel to influence decisions in favour of their wards. An informal employee quota does exist, and those in charge of selection, being themselves police officers, look upon this as a means to promote the morale of serving personnel. A few forms of corruption are known to prevail, and these tend somewhat to affect the quality of selection. Relevant here is a recent episode in Haryana where a DIG of Police came out in the open to level certain allegations with regard to recruitment of Constables in the state.[4]

Here and there, in some states, occasional efforts are made to professionalize the selection process. An instance in point is the formation of a Uniformed Services Recruitment Board (USRB) in the southern state of Tamil Nadu which takes care of recruitment for the Police, Fire Service and Prisons. Headed by an officer of the rank of DGP/Addl DGP, this board was asked in 1992-3 to select nearly 10,000 constables. For the first time, a major part of this gigantic exercise was streamlined with the help of computers. More than 70,000 responded to the advertisement calling for applications. Of these, nearly 5 per cent were turned down because they did not fulfil the basic age and educational requirements. After the screening for physical efficiency standards, 17000 candidates qualified for the written test. For the oral examination, 12000 were short-listed and 10,264 (14.6 per cent of all applicants) were ultimately selected for appointment. The whole process was so structured—by prescribing the exact marks to be awarded for each selection criterion—that subjectivity was greatly eliminated. The only subjective test—oral interview—had a weightage of only 10 per cent. Experiments such as the USRB should serve to enhance candidate faith in the fairness of the selection system.

Another generalization that may be made without fear of contradiction is that police forces at all levels are getting more and more of the educated segments of the youth. For instance, in the Tamil Nadu Police, according to figures correct up to 1 January 1993, 5.8 per cent of the nearly 60,000 strong constabulary were college degree holders. Compared to this, of the more than 10,000 candidates selected by the USRB in 1992-3, that is, after the above statistics were compiled, about 8 per cent held a college degree. Some even had a Master's Degree. As for the IPS, of the 84 under training at the National Police Academy, Hyderabad during 1996, 32 held a Master's Degree in various arts and science subjects. In addition, 7 were MBAs, and 26 engineers. Appendix VIII gives a profile of IPS probationers who were trained at the National Police Academy, Hyderabad during 1991-7.

Minorities in Indian Police

As in the case of other government departments, recruitment to the police is governed by the rule of reservation already mentioned in Chapter 1. In view of their large presence in the population, filling all available positions from among the SC/ST or BCs/MBCs poses no problem. Actually, some of them find a place even among the non-reserved vacancies ('Open Competition') on the basis of their good performance in entrance tests. While it has been found difficult to procure All India figures, statistics of the position that obtains in Tamil Nadu Police are illustrative. Of the nearly 67,000 Constables in position on 31 March 1997 in all wings of the State Police, about 10 per cent were Christians and 5.5 were Muslims.[5] Also, about 18 per cent of the constabulary belonged to the Scheduled Castes (SC) and less than 2 per cent to Scheduled Tribes (ST). (During the massive 1992-3 recruitment in Tamil Nadu, 50.95 per cent of those selected were from Backward Classes, 26.42 from the Most Backward Classes, and 16.35 from SC and ST.)

Women Police in India

The creation of a women's wing in the Indian Police in a formal manner was essentially a post-Independence decision. Prior to this, there was sporadic recruitment of small numbers of women in just a few centres like Kanpur (1938), Bombay (1939), Lahore and in the southern Province of Travancore-Cochin (now Kerala). Elsewhere, women were no doubt being employed on a casual basis to fulfil certain legal requirements, as in the case of search of women prisoners in custody. But they were never a part of the force.

The enormous violence that accompanied the partition of the country in 1947 resulted in a spurt of offences against women, such as rape and kidnapping. Simultaneously, the need for an arrangement to protect abandoned women and children was also felt (NPC Fifth Report 1980). For instance, the Delhi Police recruited a few women Constables and a Sub-Inspector in 1948 to handle women refugees from across the border. Progress of the movement towards creating full-fledged women police wings in different parts of the country was considerably slow. It was only in the 1960s that one saw substantial accretions to the forces (Aleem 1991 and Ghosh 1981).

There are nearly 15,300 policewomen in position nationally against 18,400 authorized positions (*Crime in India,* 1995). These include women officers belonging to the elitist Indian Police Service (IPS). Many of them have handled tough assignments with extraordinary competence. Incidentally, the first woman IPS officer, Kiran Bedi of the 1972 batch, is a recipient of the prestigious Ramon Magsaysay award and the Jawharlal Nehru Fellowship.

The services of women police are utilized in a variety of chores, especially for interacting with women complainants/victims. Apart from escorting women prisoners, they are found useful for tackling women participating in public demonstrations which disrupt vehicular traffic and threaten public peace.

To encourage women shed their inhibition in going to police stations, because of the latter's essentially male composition, a few states have established all-women police stations. Tamil Nadu has been particularly active on this front. There are 57 all-women police stations in the state with a total strength of 4712 personnel. Chennai City alone has three. It may be useful to recall what the NPC said on this in its Fifth Report:

> the entire philosophy, culture and attitude of police should be such as to make a police station appear and function as a ready source of relief for persons in distress. In our view, the presence of policewomen in police stations would help to a great extent in achieving this object. (1980:58)

Several studies have been conducted or are in progress on the efficacy of all-women police stations. These point to the belief that they have started playing a positive role in tackling various forms of spouse abuse, especially the harassment of wives by their husbands/in-laws related to the demand for dowry. Other kinds of sexual harassment—popularly called eve-teasing—have also received some attention. The fact that, sometimes, a few women counsellors attached to these police stations complement the work of women police officers enhances the utility of the experiment. Interestingly, Mangai Natarajan (1996) of the John Jay College, New York, found that few policewomen were employed in core police duties, such as patrolling and traffic duties. Actually, many of these officers interviewed by her in Tamil Nadu revealed a desire for being 'fully integrated into the range of police duties'.

Police Training in India

The apex body for training is the National Police Academy (NPA), located outside Hyderabad, capital of the southern state of Andhra Pradesh. Apart from providing comprehensive initial training to IPS recruits, it runs several other programmes for middle and senior levels. Perhaps the most significant activity is the NPA's module for trainers working in state and central forces. The NPA also functions as an excellent research centre for several police scholars from all over the country. The Academy's faculty, besides police officers, comprises academicians from various disciplines such as law, management and sociology, either on a wholetime or part-time basis.

A two-tier training outfit operates in a majority of the states. There is a training college meant for Sub-Inspectors and DSPs selected from the open market by the state government. This college also provides orientation to IPS probationers as soon as they finish their spell at the NPA and are ready for being inducted into the field as ASPs in a state police force. There are also a few recruit schools in each state meant mainly to train Constables. The emphasis here is on strengthening physical fitness, although basic knowledge in law and community relations is also imparted. Both the training college and recruit schools run a few refresher courses as a mid-career requirement.

A very recent positive move is the creation of Police Academies to enhance the quality of training. The Andhra Pradesh Police Academy, set up in May 1986, is a model institution with impressive infrastructural facilities. A similar academy is coming up in Tamil Nadu. This enlightenment among police policy-makers in different parts of the country that favours strengthening of training arrangements augurs well for the future.

POLICE DISCIPLINE IN INDIA

Being a quasi-military organization, the management of a police force throws up many issues of discipline—individual and collective. We know that, right from its inception, the Indian Police has had its quota of internal management problems. Chief of these is the need to make the lower levels of the force conform to accepted standards of conduct. A principal constraint in the initial days was the low literacy of an overwhelming majority of the force and their consequent lack of professional interest and a knowledge of the minimum requirements of public service.

An indication of the problem that faced the police leadership during the 1860s is available from the figures of desertion and resignation reported around that time.[6]

Apart from individual aberrations, police leaders have had to contend with collective misconduct also. The history of Indian Police is replete with accounts of several agitations by discontented policemen, challenging political and internal supervisory authority.[7]

Since the major countrywide police agitation of 1979, the Indian Police has generally enjoyed internal peace. There have, however, been a few instances of intransigence on the part of lower rungs of the forces. During 1981-7, there were 307 organized protest actions by policemen all over the country. Bihar (55) and West Bengal (53) topped the list. During 1988-93, there were 122 such collective agitations. Bihar (32) was again the most affected. These were in pursuance of demands such as action against supervisory officers for maltreatment of the constabulary, withdrawal of disciplinary proceedings against individual lower level policemen, grant of ration allowance, etc.

ENFORCEMENT OF INTERNAL DISCIPLINE IN THE INDIAN POLICE

Matters of discipline confined to internal management are handled by supervisory officers themselves. Commonly known delinquencies falling in this category are desertion, unauthorized temporary absence from duty, negligence, such as allowing prisoners to escape or sleeping while on guard duty, failure to visit scenes of crime or respond to calls for assistance and insubordination towards supervisors. The lowest level to which such inquiries are entrusted is the Inspector. Penalties awarded at the end of inquiry are classified as minor (black mark, reprimand or censure) and major (reduction in pay or rank, removal, compulsory retirement or dismissal). Where the delinquency is grave and it merits a major penalty, the inquiry is elaborate, involving examination and cross-examination of witnesses. The inquiry officer sends up his findings to a higher authority for their acceptance and infliction of penalty or the dropping of further action.

The Constitution of India [Article 311(1)] protects a civil servant against capricious and arbitrary disciplinary action. It stipulates that no civil servant may be dismissed or removed by an authority subordinate to that by which he had been appointed. Another safeguard [Article 311(2)] is that, any dismissal, removal or reduction in rank of a civil servant could be only after 'an inquiry in which he had been informed of the charges against him and given a reasonable opportunity of being heard in respect of the charges'.

Corruption and Brutality

Maintaining discipline within police forces is a formidable task. Two specific problems which confront civilized democratic governments are police brutality and corruption, both of which greatly affect police image. The citizen expects the executive to constantly engage itself in devising measures to combat the twin evils so that the police are made effectively accountable to the rule of law. Where the leadership is lax, police forces invite disrepute, not only on themselves but on elected governments as well. This section explores the dimensions of the situation in India and sets out how the administration attempts to fuse police conduct with the requirements of a Constitutional rule.

Police Corruption in India

Corruption is a definite matter for concern for the leadership. A 12 December 1901 letter from the Government of Bengal to the Central Government could not have described the scene better:

> In no branch . . . is improvement so imperatively required as in the police. . . . There is no part of our system of government of which such universal and bitter complaint is made. . . . The evil is essentially in the investigaing staff. It is dishonest and it is tyrannical. (Police Commission Report 1902)

The 1902 Police Commission heard the same complaint wherever it went. It came down heavily on the practice of entrusting crime investigation to Constables, which considerably widened the scope for corruption by a class, which it regarded, as undereducated, ill-trained and poorly paid. It was exercised more about the lack of integrity among Station-House Officers who were known to hush up cases for a consideration, receive presents from parties concerned in a case, and 'levy illicit fees from from shopkeepers and others for services rendered'.

The NPC (1977) did not come to any different conclusions. It observed: 'What the Police Commission said in 1903 would more or less fully apply even to the present situation. If any thing, the position has worsened' (Third Report 1980:25).

The commission identified several areas and stages of investigation, such as registration of a complaint, arrest/non-arrest and release/non-release of accused on bail, recording of statements of witnesses, as vitiated by corruption. It recommended 'a system of surprise checks and inspections and effective supervision by honest and well motivated officers at the different levels of command within the hierarchy itself' (p. 26).

Complaints voiced through the media, court pronouncements at all levels and periodic reviews of vigilance agencies in the states and in the central government reinforce the impression that there has been no perceptible improvement in integrity levels since the NPC's report.

Corruption in the police takes two forms. One is the misuse of official facilities such as manpower, vehicles and telephone. Over the years, such misuse has become so widespread and insidious in the entire bureaucracy that no serious note is taken of it any longer, although there are elaborate departmental rules which prohibit such deviant practices.

What still invites major attention of senior functionaries and the public is the gross abuse of police authority to collect money and other favours to benefit an individual policeman or groups of policemen. The most well known means of doing this is non-enforcement of drug, liquor and prostitution laws which benefits those who have a stranglehold over the underworld. Monthly payoffs to all the staff of a police station by bootleggers and those who run vice dens prevail, especially in the larger towns and cities all over the country. Unauthorized detention of suspects and their release for a consideration is also known. Arbitrary arrest and bail decisions are a further means of making money. Perhaps most obnoxious is the practice of detectives misappropriating the whole or part of stolen property recovered from an offender during investigation.

The machinery that exists for combating corruption in the police is fragile and inadequate. The regular hierarchy does not normally have the time, inclination or the expertise called for here. In the states, the burden is cast on the Anti-Corruption Bureaux (ACBx) which look after the whole civil service (usually of a strength of the order of 100,000 to 150,000) and can therefore give only part attention to police corruption. As a result, these bureaux touch only a fringe of the problem. The CBI has jurisdiction over central police forces and suffers from the same resource constraint as the State ACBx.

The NPC made several suggestions to tackle police corruption. One radical proposal was to amend Article 311(2)(c) of the Constitution of India, whereby, apart from protection of the security of the State, the need to maintain integrity in public services could also be a ground on which a public servant could be dismissed without holding a formal departmental inquiry. This was, however, not agreed to.

Induced by the belief that reducing the enormous discretionary powers to effect arrests that even grassroots level policemen enjoy, could greatly bring down corruption, the NPC recommended that broad guidelines should be laid down for the exercise of such powers. These would require that an arrest should be made only in grave cases such as murder, dacoity, robbery or rape, or when the accused is likely to abscond, or where, being given to violent behaviour, if not arrested, he may be expected to commit a further crime. These guidelines are no doubt reiterated from time to time by senior officers. The impact is just marginal.

Police Brutality in India

Perhaps the most serious charge against investigating officers is that they are readily inclined to use force (popularly referred to as 'third degree') in dealing with crime suspects. The charge gains some credence from the number of deaths in police custody reported each year. Enquiries initiated by governments have proved that many had indeed been the result of police violence.

In its Fourth Report (1980), the NPC called for frequent surprise visits to police stations by senior officers with a view to checking unauthorized custody of suspects. It also pleaded for a clear departure from the current evaluation of work in police stations solely on the basis of statistics. This was with a view to weaning away field officers from an informal quota system that led to foisting of cases and use of third degree to extract false confessions. The history of police in post-Independence India is replete with unsavoury incidents of police misbehaviour with individual citizens in custody which have attracted extensive media attention. The Rajan episode in Kerala and the Bhagalpur blindings of Bihar are a few that will continue to be talked about for many decades to come.

Investigation of Public Complaints against the Indian Police

Both central and state governments are highly sensitive to the matter and have issued several instructions to curb police misconduct. In almost every case of custodial death, an administrative or judicial inquiry is held, and when charges of torture or illegal custody are proved, the erring police personnel are arraigned before a regular court of law or a departmental inquiry that may lead to dismissal or reduction in rank. Government awareness of the dimensions of the problem is reflected in its decision (1993) to constitute a Human Rights Commission. The Commission, headed by a former Chief Justice of the Supreme Court, has proved to be extremely proactive. There is public cynicism however about the long-term efficacy of such measures in the context of the absence of any signs of attitutidinal change on the part of the police.

Conscious of the public distrust of the impartiality of police supervisors, the government invariably directs an Executive Magistrate (Revenue Divisional Officer or Deputy Collector) to probe into complaints of brutality. Since this magistrate also forms part of the administration, very often, there is a public demand for an inquiry by a High Court Judge. Whenever this is conceded, such a judicial enquiry is held in public, whereat, evidence of witnesses in possession of information pertaining to the alleged incident is recorded, and the judge submits a factual report to the government which initiates appropriate action, that may include prosecution in a court of law.

Aggrieved parties, fearing physical harm to one of their kith or kin in police custody, do sometimes approach the High Court directly on a writ of *habeas corpus.* The court demands a factual report from the government and, if this reveals police highhandedness, it directs stern action, including a full-fledged investigation by the CID and subsequent prosecution of police personnel concerned under the IPC. There have been some instances of the CBI being requested by state governments to investigate sensational cases. One recent example is the investigation of the complaint (1995) of excessive force by the Uttar Pradesh Police against agitators demanding the creation of a Uttarakand State. In April 1996, finding the allegation to be true, the CBI filed a chargesheet against the District Magistrate and the Superintendent of Police.

Finding the existing arrangements unsatisfactory, the NPC, in its first report (February 1979), suggested the creation of a District Inquiry Authority (DIA) in every district to probe grave misconduct by the police. This has, however, not been implemented.

Grievance Machinery for the Police in India

Following the unprecedented nationwide police strike of 1979, the central government convened a conference (6 June 1979) of chief ministers of states to discuss the issues relating to police morale. While emphasizing the need for various welfare measures through a 7-point programme adopted by the conference, it was decided to commend the NPC's proposal of a grievance machinery. Following this, the central and state governments announced a series of welfare measures. Swift action was also taken to form police associations and staff councils.

Feverish activity was seen in some states, including Tamil Nadu where, in October 1979, three associations were accorded recognition by the IGP. A fourth one, the Police Subordinates Association, owing allegiance to Sub-Inspector Nainardass and his associates, who were behind the police strike earlier in the year, was denied recognition. In the initial period, the associations were active mainly in urban centres, particularly Madras City. The issues taken up by them at their periodic meetings included the demands for more staff, end to 'arbitrary' transfers of personnel and for more amenities at places of work and living quarters (Raghavan 1985). An opinion survey by me revealed that policemen were sharply divided over whether the new grievance machinery was of any utility. Lack of authority was regarded as one major reason why the new arrangement had little impact on improving the policeman's lot (ibid.). Nevertheless, there was no great intensity of feelings on the subject.

Since my survey cited, there has been no momentous development. Police associations are either non-existent or exist only on paper in many states. They are, however, not discussed, and there is no evidence of either policemen or governments taking serious notice of them. This indifference is difficult to explain. A plausible interpretation is that there is a high state of contentment among policemen in the field. However, what contributes to this apparent feeling of satisfaction in these days of high costs of living and expectations of an equally high standard of living and the enhanced risk to policemen from terrorist violence, is entirely a matter for conjecture. There is here a fertile area for research.

Machinery for Police Personnel Management

Perhaps the most glaring lacuna in the organization of the police in India is the absence of a specialized agency for carrying out personnel tasks. This major shortcoming accounts for the ad hocism that one sees in police man management.

In a typical district police force, personnel functions are solely the SP's responsibility. The latter is assisted by a Personal Assistant or Manager who has a few Office Superintendents in charge of several branches. Assistants functioning under a Superintendent are each assigned a subject such as recruitment, appointment, processing of salary/travelling expense claims, transfers, departmental enquiries, etc. There is hardly any distinction between personnel functions and housekeeping activities. The staff involved in the process, generally known as the ministerial staff, as distinct from executive police officers who don uniform (analogous to the civilians and sworn personnel in US police departments) are raw recruits from the field. They have a modest educational background—some have a college degree in science or humanities—but no knowledge or training in personnel management whatsoever. They pick up the required expertise on the job and receive no exposure to modern concepts of management.

A similar situation exists at the State Police Headquarters. The DGP is assisted by an ADGP/IGP Personnel and an ADGP/IGP Headquarters who are IPS officers with about 20-5 years of work experience. They look after personnel and housekeeping functions respectively with a large complement of ministerial staff.[8]

The absence of a specialized and trained machinery of personnel managers has a definite impact on the quality of internal management. A favourite subject for seminars of police officers is the case for a modern personnel cell in each force. Unfortunately, however, this has not been pursued with vigour. As a result, police personnel management, especially at the field level, remains in the hands of untrained non-professionals with only a modest exposure to modern HRD concepts.

THE US SCENE

The History

The nineteenth-century American Police was a body dominated by the small-time local politician. The latter decided who should be appointed and who removed (Staufenberger 1980 and Walker 1983). The 'spoils system', which had become entrenched in the federal government by 1830, slowly found its way into the state and local administration. Police management could not remain insular, and monetary considerations dictated selection. Also, there was hardly any training worth its name. Salaries were reasonably good, somewhat higher than blue collar jobs. There was, however, no security of tenure.

The reformist movement that one saw toward the close of the nineteenth century did not concern itself with personnel practices. The endeavour was aimed mainly at pulling the police out of the quagmire of petty politics. Since the hold of the latter was quite strong, reformers achieved only limited success (Walker 1983).

One development in the 1880s brought about a semblance of merit and fairness in the system of police selection. This was the decision of some state and local governments to adopt the Pendleton Act (1883), which had introduced civil service regulations for employment with the Federal Government (vide Chapter 1). The NYPD was the first to take advantage of this (Walker 1983, and Thibault 1985). Here, as well as in a few other police departments, the written test came to be a major criterion for selection. This test took the form of multiple-choice questions (Thibault 1985). The measure of success of the new testing procedure was modest because of the resistance put up by the political elements who did not want to lose the patronage they had enjoyed for decades (ibid.). However, by the end of World War I, civil service standards for recruitment had gained ground in a number of departments, particularly the larger ones (Johnson 1981).

As already seen in Chapter 2, a welcome development of the early twentieth century was a second attempt at reform. The initiative came from a few enthusiastic chiefs, such as Richard Sylvester of the District of Columbia and August Vollmer of Berkeley, who saw to the introduction of a civil service system covering the wide gamut of personnel matters.

As President of the International Association of Chiefs of Police (IACP), Sylvester was instrumental in converting the IACP into 'the leading voice of police professionalism and the vehicle for disseminating new ideas in policing' (Walker 1983:10). Vollmer's emphasis was on raising a more educated police force. With this end in view, he sought the recruitment of college-educated youth. He went as far as introducing a police science course in the curriculum of the University of California. Thanks to these pioneering efforts of Sylvester and Vollmer, professionalism became a subject for discussion and consideration. Nevertheless, progress was slow and uneven, with a majority of departments still hesitant to fall in line with the reformers.

The 1931 report of the Wickersham Commission was significant from the point of view of personnel management in two respects. First, it highlighted the wide prevalence of 'third degree' in police dealings with the public, thus bringing out the importance of inducting personnel with a balanced mind and a set of values. The second was its plea for professionalization of the force with its attendant requirement of setting high personnel standards (Walker 1983). The report, therefore, gave an impetus to the reform movement and strengthened the hands of a set of enlightened officers who had attained positions of leadership (ibid.).

A direct consequence of the emphasis on professionalism was the crystallization of opinion among policemen that they needed a forum to look after their workplace interests. The appearance of police unions and other fraternal associations was traceable to this belief.

Although fraternal groups had appeared even in the nineteenth century, police unions came to notice only during World War I. One factor that contributed to this was the demand for higher wages following an abnormal increase in the cost of living. The American Federation of Labour (AFL) received applications from nearly 65 local unions. One of these was from the Boston policemen who had been annoyed at the rejection of their demand for a steep rise in wages. Reacting to the policemen's move to unionize themselves, the authorities suspended their leaders. This led to the well-known Boston Police strike of 1919 which was accompanied by vandalism and other forms of indiscipline. Firm handling with the help of the militia brought about its quick collapse (Burpo 1971 and 1973, Walker 1983, and Langworthy and Travis 1994).

The Boston events produced extremely hostile public reactions to police unions, and the whole movement therefore suffered a major reverse (Bouza 1985). For the next twenty years, there was a fragmented organization that took the shape of the Fraternal Order of Police (FOP) and similar bodies. There was a brief phase of unionism during World War II. This was a short-lived success which ended with a series of adverse judicial pronouncements (Walker 1983).

A third attempt (1960s) at unionism was in reaction to several trends which cumulatively undermined police morale. These included a comparatively low wage level, the increasingly authoritarian style of police supervisors and a heightened judicial suspicion of police mechanics evident from a series of Supreme Court decisions which greatly cut into police discretion. The many riots of the time in which the police became a target for black wrath and public criticism sharpened police determination to organize themselves under the umbrella of a full-fledged union. By 1970s, unions came to be a force to reckon with, and all major personnel decisions could be reached only with their consent. As we would see later in the chapter, this situation remains unchanged amidst widespread misgivings over their impact on police management and performance (Walker 1983 and Bouza 1985).

The recommendations of two National Commissions—the President's Commission on Law Enforcement and the Administration of Justice (1967) and the National Advisory Commission on Civil Disorders (1967-8)—deserve a mention in any historical account of personnel management in the American Police.

The 1967 commission clearly called for an upgradation of personnel standards. It pleaded for the recruitment of college graduates and laid down that the ultimate aim should be to insist on a college degree for entrants (Walker 1983). The second commission concentrated on improving police-community relations. Towards this end, it suggested the enhanced hiring of minorities.

In 1968, the Omnibus Crime Control and Safe Streets Act gave birth to the Law Enforcement Assistance Administration (LEAA) which greatly boosted the movement for improving the quality of police personnel. To be specific, it was instrumental in the creation of criminal justice programmes in college campuses through its Law Enforcement Educational Programme (LEEP) (Trojanowicz and Bucqueroux 1990). The National Advisory Commission on Criminal Justice Standards and Goals (1973) also declared that, by 1982, every police agency should insist on a four-year college education for its recruits (Swanson *et al.*, 1993). As a sequel, one could find a perceptible increase in the educational attainment of entry-level officers (Walker 1983 and Thibault 1985).

In a country known for an uneasy race relationship and for the widely prevalent belief that, disproportionate to their share of the population, blacks get arrested by a white-dominated police, the issue of black representation in the police assumes great significance. This is particularly because, as we have already seen in Chapter 3, the many racial riots in the US reported during the twentieth century had alienated the police from the black community and led to a demand for measures to build a bridge between the two. A positive development in this direction was the stand of the President's Commission (1967) that entrance examinations for police selections should be so designed as to remove any unintended racist bias in them.

No historical account of human resource management in the US Police will be complete without a reference to the Equal Employment Opportunity Act of 1972. One immediate consequence was that police departments pursuing a blatantly discriminatory personnel policy against minorities and women had to bring about a change in their stance (Swanson *et al.*,1993).

The case for extra sensitivity to black feelings had already been dictated by the uneasy relationship with the police since the early 1900s. The strains had became pronounced in the 1950s which marked the beginning of a phase of black protest and violence. Since then, considerable scholarly attention has been given to identifying factors which continue to adversely affect police-black interactions.

Following the Equal Employment Opportunity Act 1972, there was a spate of litigation challenging many selection criteria as biased against the minorities. Significantly, in 1979, a Federal District Judge ruled that the Dallas Police Department's entrance requirement of 45 semester hours with a C average or better, discriminated on the basis of race. However, in 1981, on a plea for a reconsideration of the ruling by the department, Justice Porter of the US District Court for the Northern District of Texas upheld the requirement of college education stating that 'such education fills the gap of inexperience in the handling of a crisis', and added that 'quality does not have to be sacrificed for quantity'. The Supreme Court endorsed this stand in 1986 (*Law Enforcement News,* 7 July 1986).

A final development in the long history of police personnel management was the special requirement of community policing which had gained ground in a majority of cities. According to Trojanowicz and Bucqueroux (1990), a new breed of police officers was called for to take the police into the twenty-first century, particularly in the context of community policing. They however believe that these 'are already on board', thanks to the recruitment of educated men and women of diverse ethnic and racial backgrounds. A rising crime graph and the wide acceptance of community policing as one sure way of enhancing police resources to combat crime do point to the belief that police recruitment policies, for quite sometime, will be oriented to this new style of policing.

The Current Situation in the US Police

Selection Methods

The responsibility for selection in major city police departments rests with the city administration's personnel department, although, in a few cities, there is a special team in the police department itself, exclusively to take care of minority entry. In some cases, where the central personnel department is either on a low-key or has virtually disappeared, the authority to select vests in the Civil Service Commission (Philadelphia Police Task Force Report 1987 and Swanson *et al.*,1993). In smaller departments, it is the Police Chief who performs this task.

Several methods are employed to reach potential applicants. The first of these is the use of continuous examination announcements. Advertisements in local newspapers, posters in public places, spot announcements over television and radio and asking for referrals from public employment services are the other methods (Pate and Hamilton 1991).

The prospective applicant should first demonstrate that he satisfies certain basic criteria. For instance, for the Los Angeles Police Department, requirements relate to age (21-35), education (High School Diploma or California GED equivalent) and height (60-80 inches). The Chicago PD prescribes a minimum age of 20 years as on 31 December and an educational attainment of at least two years in college. The minimum age for most of the big city departments varies between 18 and 21. Many do not prescribe any weight requirement, but stipulate that weight must be in proportion to height (Pate and Hamilton 1991). Some departments need the applicant to possess a valid driving licence, at least at the time of appointment.

A minimum requirement prescribed—educational attainment—is

perhaps the one that has traditionally been the subject of acute controversy. Notwithstanding the unequivocal recommendations of three Commissions—the Wickersham Commission (1931), the President's Commission (1967) and the National Advisory Commission on CJ Standards and Goals (1973)—favouring a stronger educational background for the average police recruit, opinion among police chiefs is divided.

The NYPD's 1985 experiment is relevant here. At the initiative of Mayor Edward J. Koch and Police Commissioner Ward, a novel recruitment programme targeted at college graduates was floated. Called the Police Cadet Corps, this scheme had five major objectives: to raise the NYPD's educational level; to test a more rigorous selection process for recruits; to widen the representativeness of the uniformed force; to increase the orientation toward community policing; and to improve the leadership skills of new officers. It envisaged scholarships ($3,000 toward the cadets' last two years in college) and practical training in police work to college sophomores who gave an undertaking to join the police after graduation. Two years' service in the police after graduation results in the loan being treated as paid in full. Failure to work for the police will entail repayment with interest (Lynch 1987, Police Foundation 1992 and Ralph S. Osborn 1992).

The first group of 133 cadets was selected from 1500 applicants, after a screening process similar to other police candidates, including a psychology test.[9] The cadets joined the NYPD in the summer of 1986 and started working inside the community under the supervision of precincts' community service officers (Lynch 1987).

A Police Foundation study (1991), funded by the National Institute of Justice (NIJ), examined the background of this cohort and three succeeding ones, viz., the 1987 A (140), 1987 B (101) and 1988 (131) cohorts. Taking all the four together, it was found that 51.1 per cent of the recruits were white, 24.8 Hispanic and 24.0 black. While the racial break-up of the first cohort was disproportionately in favour of the white male, when fresh batches came in, the cohorts became more and more representative of the city population (Pate and Hamilton 1991).

The Police Foundation study revealed that, by 1991, the scheme had brought in 217 college graduates into the NYPD, much less than the average of 200 expected per year. Nevertheless, the fact that 16.1 per cent of these were black and 21.7 were Hispanic disproved the popular belief that departments could recruit either graduates or minorities only, but not both (Police Foundation 1992).[10] This way, the objective of making the department more representative was fulfilled. Interviews of the cadets also highlighted the fact that they were positive toward community orientation, although it was difficult to predict whether such an attitude could be sustained after becoming police officers and getting exposed to the prevailing police culture. As regards the final objective—enhancing leadership skills—the Police Foundation study opined that it was premature to come to any conclusion (ibid.).

Another significant governmental action took the form of a Crime Bill passed by the US Senate in 1990. This contemplated a scheme of Police Corps by which the Federal Government would provide an annual scholarship up to $10,000 for college students who agreed to serve on a State or city police force after graduation (*New York Times*, 12 October 1990). During 1991, a House-Senate Conference Committee proposed an Omnibus Crime Bill which, apart from several other measures, suggested creation of the Police Corps. Although the House endorsed this bill, Republicans in the Senate blocked it with a filibuster. Presumably distressed by a worsening crime situation, the Senate introduced a fresh bill in 1992 which, among other features, incorporated the Police Corps scheme. This scheme evoked a generally favourable response in the press.[11]

In some form or the other, the Police Corps scheme operates in many cities. For instance, the Houston PD Community Services Division has a programme called the 'Explorer' affiliated to the Boy Scouts of America, which is open to youth in the age group of 14-20 or those in the ninth grade. Explorers direct traffic, ride with police officers, attend classes at the Police Academy, and take part in community service projects. This programme offers scholarship opportunities to those who contemplate a law enforcement career. The LAPD has also an Explorer Scouts scheme affiliated to the Boy Scouts of America. Entry requirements include age (14), education (ninth grade), no record or serious arrest convictions and a written recommendation from a responsible adult who is not a relation of the applicant.

The police selection process in many departments usually comprises a combination of the written examination (normally multiple-choice questions), background investigation and oral interview. Some agencies also use a physical agility test and a psychology test.

For instance, in Chicago, the written examination and the Biographical Data Form constitute the first step in the hiring process. Once a candidate passes this, he will be recruited, provided he successfully completes a psychological evaluation, background investigation, medical examination and a physical fitness test.

The Houston PD's selection process has six phases, beginning with a preliminary interview and ending with a medical examination, drug testing and psychological testing and evaluation. Between these stages, there are a reading comprehension test, a polygraph examination and a final interview.

A psychological stress evaluator (PSE) is being increasingly used now. Developed by two Army intelligence officers, it displays 'graphically certain stress-related components of the human voice's two modulations—the audible and the inaudible' (Swanson *et al.*, 1993). Supporters of the polygraph test claim that their instrument is superior to the PSE.

Perhaps the most acute controversy is over the psychology test. Employed since 1917 with varying degrees of success and viewed as 'an objective and standardized measure of a sample of behavior', psychology tests include intelligence tests, interest and preference tests, personality tests and situational tests (Swanson *et al.*, 1993). Personnel managers who employ them 'are looking for a stable personality that is flexible enough to adjust to the stress situations in police work along with the complex peer relations' (Thibault 1985). There is fair agreement that this type of tests could be used mainly to eliminate the 'psychotic and potentially dangerous human beings' (ibid.), and to detect instances of ' extreme pathology' (Swanson *et al.*,1993). Beyond this, its utility is highly speculative (Thibault 1985).

Selection of Police Chief

Where the City Manager system operates, the latter being a professional chosen for his managerial ability, the selection is less political. In cities governed by a Mayor, apart from professional considerations, political expediency also plays a role. In this environment, the twin issues of political neutrality and security of tenure become strident. As Geller would say:

> police administration is an inherently political (although, hopefully, nonpartisan) activity and that the Chief's municipal superior needs to play a significant role in assuring quality policing. Neither the Mayor nor the Chief can afford to remain aloof from the other's concerns, for, a serious mistake by either one, could cost both their jobs, to the public's detriment. (1985:4)

Andrews, Jr. believes that most Mayors 'prefer a dutiful minion to having an independent community leader in their administration' (1985:13). He also refers to the premature termination of police chiefs in several big city forces. Chicago had more than ten regular or acting chiefs in about 25 years, thus veering around the national average of 2.8 years. This situation arises from a lack of appreciation of policing complexities and the vital need for a Chief to be assured of a long-term so as to first build a team, and thereafter implement innovative programmes. An IACP study for the National Advisory Commission (NAC) on CJ Standards and Goals revealed a preponderance of opinion among political chief executives against a fixed tenure and due process protection for police chiefs against arbitrary removal (ibid.).

Andrews, Jr. recommends 'a multiyear contract with early severance indemnity' (1985:14) that would act as a deterrence against capricious action. Some state laws afford a degree of protection. For instance, in Illinois, no fireman or policeman can be removed or discharged without cause or without being served a chargesheet and heard in person. In Minnesota, civil service protection is available to the Chief. In New Hampshire, before being dismissed, a Chief will have to be given a written notice detailing the material available to back such a course of action, followed by a hearing. Finally, the findings arising from the process will have to be communicated to him before his services can be terminated. In general, wherever the Chief had risen from the ranks of the department which he heads, he has enjoyed greater protection than an outsider brought in as a Chief (Swanson *et al.*, 1993).

Minorities in the US Police

Hiring of minorities has become highly controversial because of the several court decisions and litigation alleging reverse discrimination. Nevertheless, a majority of departments, state as well as local, have made significant progress toward strengthening their ethnic composition through various mechanics. These include special recruitment teams which regularly visit schools, colleges and community centres. Advertisements in the minority news media and pre-examination counselling to minorities are the other means employed (Pate and Hamilton 1991).

There are, however, instances of some departments overreaching themselves with indiscriminate recruitment of minorities leading to grave personnel problems. For example, in the early 1980s, the City of Miami decided to hire 80 per cent minorities. While this was welcomed by the latter, police administrators were opposed to such a sweeping change in recruitment policy. Apart from hiring as per this quota, promotions of minority officers were also stepped up. Thereafter one saw, in the mid-1980s, more than twenty Miami police officers getting arrested for various crimes, including murder and burglary. This rash of misconduct is generally attributed to the recruitment spree of the earlier years (Alpert and Dunham 1988).

Pate and Hamilton (1991) studied policing in six major cities, New York, Los Angeles, Philadelphia, Chicago, Detroit and Houston. The figures collected by them in 1986 confirmed the popular belief that policing remained white male-dominated. The white segment ranged anywhere between 78.7 per cent (New York) and 52.6 per cent (Detroit). Black officers were between 10.7 per cent and 46 per cent in the two cities. Hispanics were also similarly underrepresented, except that in Houston and Los Angeles, they fared somewhat better possibly because of their substantial numbers in the local population.[12]

The BJS-sponsored Law Enforcement Management and Administrative Statistics (LEMAS) programme (July 1990) surveyed a nationally representative sample of law enforcement agencies. It revealed that, in the case of local police departments, 83 per cent personnel were white, 10.5 black, 5.2 Hispanic and 1.3 other minorities. These were an improvement over 1987 in the case of black (1.2) and Hispanic (0.7). In the case of Sheriff's departments, the overall distribution (84.5, 9.8, 4 and 1) was not very different. State police departments portrayed the disadvantageous position of the minorities more blatantly. Only 7.5 per cent of their personnel were black and 4.4 Hispanic (Alpert and Dunham 1993). In the big six cities studied by Pate and Hamilton (1991), according to statistics compiled in 1986, Detroit had the largest component (46 per cent) of black officers and Los Angeles the highest (16.5 per cent) representation for Hispanics. All these figures will have to be reckoned against the 1990 Census figures of a national black population of 11.1 per cent and an Hispanic population of 8.3.

Women in the US Police

The past two decades have brought about a substantial change in the concept of women police. Not only has there been a considerable accretion to their ranks, their role has further expanded. In 1968, for the first time in the country, Indianapolis put women on patrol duty (followed by Washington in 1972).

A woman patrol officer is no longer a novelty. While an International City Management Association (ICMA) survey of 1973 revealed that women constituted 2 per cent of the sworn law enforcement personnel in cities with a population of 250,000, a 1986 study found that this had gone up to 9.5 (Martin 1990).

One interesting phenomenon is that minority women constitute 40 per cent of women police officers, as against just 21 per cent accounted for by minority men. One plausible interpretation of this is that, among the limited opportunities available to minorities, policing is perhaps the most attractive and prestigious option (Martin 1990).

Several factors are cited to explain the momentum gained by women policing. The first of these is the pressure generally on the police to change in favour of a closer interaction with the community, a trend that was ushered in the late 1960s, following heightened tensions between the two. Another is the strength of the feminist movement which has greatly altered the economic and legal status of women in society. Legal recognition of the right of women to seek a career in law enforcement through statutes such as the 1972 Amendments to Title VII of the Civil Rights Act of 1964 and the Crime Control Act of 1973 and the guidelines of the Equal Employment Opportunity Commission has also contributed not a little to this development. A final but the most significant factor is the finding of several studies to the effect that policewomen perform as well as, if not better than, their male colleagues in many complicated situations (Homant and Kennedy 1985, Grennan 1987, and Martin 1990).

The LEMAS survey cited under the previous section indicated that women accounted for 8.1 per cent of the sworn personnel in the country. In the six biggest cities, according to 1986 figures, Detroit had the highest percentage (17.5) of female officers. Los Angeles and Houston had the lowest (9.2) (Pate and Hamilton 1991).[13]

The steady enlargement of female representation has been made possible by a few changes in personnel standards. Initially, the insistence on minimum physical standards greatly restricted the applicant pool. During the past two decades, these have been given up. Less than 5 per cent of the departments now impose minimum height and weight requirements. A majority now only require that a candidate's weight should be in proportion to her height. The selection process includes written, oral and medical examinations, a screening psychology test, combined with a pre-training physical agility test. Some departments hold an oral interview as well. But this is of no great consequence, as, unlike in the past, the interview has become routine and objective (Martin 1990).

The Police Foundation study conducted by Susan Martin no doubt finds a steady increase in the dimensions of policing by women. At the same time, it is not optimistic about the numbers going up without an aggressive and focussed personnel policy. It is also distressed to find that, notwithstanding a quick promotion rate, female representation in the supervisory ranks is not substantial. The study therefore believes that, while there have been a few gains at the middle management level, entry into leadership and decision-making positions will be greatly delayed (Martin 1990).

Police Training in the US

Although the Progressive Era at the beginning of the twentieth century made some contribution toward upgrading police personnel, and August Vollmer made a plea for exposing police officers to higher education as early as 1920, it was only in the 1960s that there was a semblance of an effort to improve standards of education of policemen and their training.

There are a large number of formal and informal programmes of cooperation and training available to law enforcement agencies (Sweatman and Cross 1989). These are run by both federal and state authorities. The special task forces, such as the ones for Organized Crime and Drug Enforcement, provide an expertise that is shared by many departments. The Federal Law Enforcement Training Centre (FLETC) at Glyco (Georgia) is available to a large number of agencies. Apart from holding its own basic courses to sharpen skills in law enforcement, it extends its facilities to other agencies for conducting their programmes. The FBI National Academy at Quantico (Virginia) offers several courses covering a wide spectrum of subjects, including forensic science, crisis management and applied criminal psychology. The academy's affiliation with the University of Virginia enables it to offer college credits to trainee officers. The US Secret Service also conducts programmes which cover examination of questioned documents, dignitary protective techniques and training of firearm instructors (ibid.).

A majority of states have local police training boards charged with the task of ensuring minimum training standards. They approve the curricula before being administered to trainees. Generally speaking, these include criminal law, humanities, first aid, weapon handling, self-defence and investigation procedure. Training programmes extend anywhere between 10 and 18 weeks (Sweatman and Cross 1989).

Some states have a special legislation prescribing standards of police training (Langworthy and Travis 1994). For instance, in June 1974, the Pennsylvania legislature adopted a Municipal Police Education and Training Law that imposed mandatory training and also created a Municipal Police Officers' Education and Training (MPOET) Commission.

Generally speaking, the style and emphasis of police training have changed since the 1980s. The shift from its original quasi-military and stress character has been marked. Training is now less traditional, and focusses attention on issues such as use of discretion, police ethics, community relations and crisis management in live situations.

One NYPD innovation deserves a mention. The department recently addressed itself to the growing problem of dismissal of its summonses. The Patrol Services Bureau started disseminating the essentials of training manuals to patrol officers, 'demonstrating how to prepare more effective summonses and to eliminate processing problems'. The NYPD claims that, as a sequel to this, dismissal rate for parking summonses came down from 30 per cent in 1994 to 2 during the first four months of 1996 (City of New York 1996).

There has also been a qualitative change in the mode of administering on-the-job training programmes. While the assigning of a trainee to a veteran patrol officer continues, field training officers now are 'specialists who are selected and trained for the job of acclimatizing rookie officers to the new world of policing' (Langworthy and Travis 1994:219).

Again, a February 1995 NYPD experiment is relevant. Called TOPCOPS (Tactical Operational Policing Causes Optimal Personal Safety), this programme covered simulated real life situations. Administered by expert instructors, including veteran officers, it placed emphasis on teaching how to react to armed confrontations, commercial robberies, persons with guns and mentally disturbed individuals. The programme also covered verbal judo which 'teaches the officers to choose language and gestures that defuse rather than escalate hostile confrontations' (City of New York 1996:10).

Santa Ana is another department that believes in orienting its training as much as possible to genuine field problems. One of its vital training inputs is the department's Tactical Alert Plan which involves familiarization with the use of a Tactical Alert Trailer, a vehicle equipped with supplies for use in the event of a disaster or other unusual occurrence (SAPD 1994).

Enforcement of Internal Discipline in the US Police

Some of the widely known acts of misbehaviour in a typical US police department include:

(i) disobedience of lawful orders of supervisors;
(ii) unjustified sick leave;
(iii) reporting late for duty or leaving early;
(iv) sleeping on the job;
(v) drinking on the job or reporting to work while under the influence of liquor; and
(vi) improper attire and neglect of personal equipment.

These acts amount to shirking and negligence arising from general laziness and are not always directed at particular citizens. They are tackled through the available internal disciplinary mechanism (Guyot 1991). The procedure adopted here is adversarial. Although several layers are involved in the process, only the more serious transgressions go to the higher echelons.

A 1976 IACP recommendation, which prescribed a nine-step system of handling indisciplinary conduct, is followed by a majority of departments. This contemplates an investigation by the immediate supervisor and a review at command level. When warranted, the delinquent officer is suspended from service. If investigation establishes misconduct, the delinquent's unit officer files formal charges and recommends sanctions (Guyot 1991).

Police Brutality in the US

Public criticism of illegal force on innocent citizens had been strident even towards the end of nineteenth century. A formal probe was however undertaken for the first time only in 1929 by the Wickersham Commission which was positive that third degree was 'extensively practised' (Walker 1983). In deference to renewed community pressure following this report, the police leadership mounted a major campaign against brutality. The concerted move by a few eminent police chiefs to introduce greater professionalism in police operations was a sequel. This yielded fair results, though one could not claim that the evil had been totally eliminated (ibid.).

In the 1950s, allegations of harassment and brutality, particularly from the minorities, were not uncommon (Trojanowicz and Buqueroux 1990). The late 1950s and early 1960s saw the NAACP, ACLU and a host of other liberal groups mounting a campaign against the police, alleging that the latter systematically deprived the minorities of their civil rights. Although there were many scandals involving police integrity around this time—including the 1960 Chicago Police indictment of 8 officers for burglary and loot—the focus during the rest of the 1960s was on police brutality (*Congressional Quarterly Researcher*, 6 September 1991).

The violent riots in the urban ghettos all over the country during the mid-1960s called for some firm police handling. This again gave rise to a sharp criticism of the police inclination to use excessive force. The civil rights demonstrations and the anti-Vietnam protests which followed, only exacerbated the situation against the police (Fogelson 1977, and *Congressional Quarterly Researcher*, 6 September 1991). Several Supreme Court decisions between 1961 and 1966 (including the famous *Mapp* v. *Ohio* and *Mirando* v. *Arizona*) also highlighted the police highhandedness in dealing with crime suspects. According to Fogelson (1997), the situation was not as bad as it was in the 1920s and early 1930s when the police in big cities were more repressive.

The early 1970s were distinct for the public disenchantment with the reformist movement that had been set in motion during the post-World War II period. The specific charge was that 'the reformers had not put an end to the corruption, incompetence, and lawlessness of the big-city police' (Fogelson 1977:274).

A little later, Kohler's study of 1975 which addressed itself to the police use of deadly force against a civilian—not necessarily under custody for interrogation—found that, in a majority of 1500 cases analysed, the evidence collected did not justify the use of force (Lee and Visano 1981). Later, in August 1985, the Philadelphia Police was rocked by the death of one David Perkins following his arrest for violating a traffic signal. Medical evidence concluded that the death was not accidental, but was probably caused by police brutality (Philadelphia Police Task Force 1987).

Recent reports also point to the belief that excessive use of force by the police continues to worry civic officials keen on cordial police-community relations. Two incidents of 1989 drew national attention.

In one, a black Police Sergeant on leave was detained by the Long Beach Police without any apparent justification and badly hit on the head. In the other, a black motorist who refused to heed a police request to stop, after he had committed a traffic violation, was shot along with a friend riding on the pillion. Both succumbed to their injuries (Trojanowicz and Bucqueroux 1990).

The March 1991 incident of Los Angeles in which an amateur videographer vividly captured the merciless beating of a black motorist, Rodney King, by a group of policemen, caused a national uproar. As Lance Morrow of *Time* would say, 'the police, not acting on some lashing impulse of the moment, but seeming desultory and methodical at the same time. Cops stroll around. It looks like an impromptu social occasion' (April 1991).

In August 1997, the NYPD came to adverse notice for the torture of an Haitian immigrant, Abner Louima, at Brooklyn's 70th Precinct. Strong public protest against the incident compelled the City administration to effect the arrest of four police officers. This once again brought to fore the debate on police brutality. (For a detailed account, see *Time*, 1 September 1997.)

The Christopher Commission (1991) appointed by Mayor Tom Bradley to conduct 'a full and fair examination' of the LAPD concluded that the King beating was 'a landmark in the recent history of law enforcement' and added that officers of the department observed a 'code of silence' which rendered detection of misconduct extremely difficult. The commission found that there were a number of LAPD officers who were known for their proclivity to violence in total disregard of instructions against it (Worsnop 1991 and Peak 1993). Equally significant was the fact that, between 1986 and 1990, there were more than 2500 citizen claims on LAPD arising from citizen complaints of injury to person or property caused by the police use of excessive force. The commission's final report expressed concern over the LAPD's inability to discipline officers who had come to repeated notice for excess force and to keep out applicants who revealed a predilection for employing violence in dealing with citizens. Further, the training received at the LAPD Academy did not seem to moderate conduct in the field (Peak 1993).

According to Bayley (1994b), perspectives and focus on police brutality keep shifting. In the case of the US, brutality described by the Wickersham Commission related to the use of third-degree. The brutality of the 1960s was the alleged excessive force against political demonstrations. Unjustified shootings constituted the core of complaints in the 1970s. In the current 1990s, as a sequel to the Rodney King incident, police brutality in the US is reckoned as 'synonymous with unjustified force in the making of an arrest' (ibid.). The Louima incident of August 1997 makes one wonder whether the NYPD, if not the rest of the American Police, has gone back to the Wickersham days.

While different countries report various forms of brutality, of the greatest relevance to the US are police shootings. Against a backdrop of frequent resort to firearms came the Supreme Court ruling of 1985 in *Tennessee* v. *Garner* which struck down a Tennessee statute that authorized the use of force even against a non-dangerous fleeing suspect. According to Professor Fyfe, a former NYPD officer now teaching at Temple University, Philadelphia, this ruling (that deadly force was to be used only against violent suspects) should be welcome to the police, because it made the process of deciding whether or not to shoot, much simpler than before (Worsnop 1991).

Bayley (1994b) believes that, unlike in many other countries, police brutality in the US is 'adventitious, rather than systematic. . . . Although some individuals may excuse it, government and dominant political opinion generally does not.' Nevertheless, Bayley is unhappy at the country's 'inability to monitor the occurrence of brutality or even complaints about it, on a national basis'. As in other democracies, in the US, there is pressure for reform. These have however focussed on 'changing police management, rather than creating new mechanisms of civilian oversight' (ibid.).

Corruption in the US Police

Police corruption in the US has been studied by many writers in conjunction with political corruption. Accounts of police deviance in the nineteenth century (and a substantial part of the twentieth too) establish a kind of symbiotic relationship. 'The police in many communities functioned as the military arm of incumbent political parties and actively supported corrupt activities' (Moore, Jr. 1980).

The reform efforts that one saw in the first two or three decades of the twentieth century did not greatly alter the situation. The 1911 Curran Committee detected monthly extortion by the NYPD from gambling and brothel operators. The introduction of prohibition opened up a fresh avenue of corruption. On the whole, the scene was far from edifying in the 1930s when the Wickersham Commission observed that the 'well-known and oft-proven alliance between criminals and corrupt politicians, which controls, in part at least, where it does not wholly do so, the police forces of our large cities'. This could be looked upon 'as a primary cause of police inefficiency'(Peak 1993).

The 1973 report of the Knapp Commission (1972) which probed into the alleged widespread corruption in the NYPD is a classic document. (The commission was a sequel to the sensational disclosures made by a former NYPD Police Officer Frank Serpico.) While confirming the allegation, the commission said that 'the climate of the Department is inhospitable to attempts to uncover acts of corruption, and protective of those who are corrupt. The consequence is that the rookie who comes into the Department is faced with the situation where it is easier for him to become corrupt than to remain honest.' The commission classified bribe-takers into 'meat-eaters' (those who aggressively sought situations which they could exploit for making financial gain) and 'grass-eaters' (those who were not aggressive, but were not averse to accepting gratuities from contractors, truck operators, gamblers and others). The commission believed that grass-eaters constituted the overwhelming majority, and recommended a tightening of internal administrative controls as one way of fighting corruption.

Another significant study of police corruption in the US was that of the Pennsylvania Crime Commission in 1974. Referring to the three Grand Jury investigations into corruption in the PPD that had already taken place during the twentieth century, it bemoaned that 'systematic corruption' continued. It identified liquor, gambling and narcotics as three areas in which policemen received pay-offs for laxity in enforcing current regulations. The commission opined that the Department's perception of corruption as one that affected only a few odd spots contributed to a certain permissiveness.[14] A Task Force which went into the organization of the PPD in 1987 echoed the sentiment expressed by the Crime Commission.

It is widely believed that the situation which the Knapp Commission found in New York prevails almost in every other department. The difference is only one of degrees (Pursley 1991).

The most extensive form of police corruption remains one of receiving small gratuities or tips. Others include the failure to arrest and prosecute offenders, dropping investigation prematurely and not pursuing leads, altering testimony in court, and influencing departmental recommendations on granting of licences, etc. (Peak 1993).

The year 1992 witnessed a major scandal in the NYPD when a group of six police officers of the 94th Precinct in Green Point, Brooklyn were arrested for dealing in drugs. The arrests were compounded by the belief that the Internal Affairs Division (IAD) was aware of the misconduct for several years but had chosen to ignore it (Martin Gottlieb 1992). This led to the establishment of the Mollen Commission for investigating police corruption. In its interim report of December 1993, the commission observed that there was a pattern of 'police officers assisting and profiting from drug traffickers, committing larceny, burglary and robbery, conducting warrantless searches and seizures, committing perjury and falsifying statements'. According to the commission's investigators, about 10 of the city's 75 precincts were involved in these practices (*New York Times,* 16 April 1994).

In three separate incidents of March 1994, seven NYPD officers were arrested on similar charges. One of these was the sequel to a sting operation that videotaped officers breaking into an apartment, beating up an occupant, searching for drugs and stealing cash (*New York Times,* 16 April 1994). Further, on 15 April 1994, 12 police officers of the 30th Precinct in north-west Harlem were arrested for forcible collection of protection money from drug dealers. The Precinct Captain was transferred to a desk job (ibid.).

According to John Guido, who headed the IAD during 1972-86, corruption was 'a way of life' in the NYPD. He added: 'When cops come in, 20 per cent are potential criminals, 20 are totally honest and 60 will stay honest, if there are controls in place . . .' (*New York Times*, 21 June 1992). This perhaps sums up the current position in many major police departments in the US. A special TV feature *CNN Presents* of October 1995 which carried interviews with several researchers and police officers (including those arraigned for corruption) strengthened this assessment.

Investigation of Public Complaints against the US Police

The 1967 Task Force Report on Police to the President's Commission highlighted the controversial nature of the debate on who should look into complaints against the police. The fact that, as recently as 1991, the brother of a major victim of police misconduct—Rodney King—was frustrated in his attempt to lodge a complaint is indicative of the dilemma that confronts chiefs, who are jealous of their autonomy, and human rights activists, who are insistent that police misbehaviour ought to be brought to light and punished (Pate and Fridell 1993). At the same time, it possibly touches on the relative lack of success of decades of efforts of public-minded individuals to make the police more accountable to the community.

Complaints of excessive use of force by policemen remain the focus of attention of police chiefs and mayors in the US. Basically, every police department is responsible for probing personnel misconduct and imposing a penalty when a complaint is established. Generally speaking, public opinion favours the police themselves taking the lead in monitoring and punishing misconduct. The Rodney King episode that provoked a public clamour for action against delinquent policemen however reflected how public opinion could be mercurial (Bayley 1994b).

A specialized internal investigation team (usually the Internal Affairs Division—the IAD) exists in a majority of departments for responding to citizen complaints. This arrangement has been the subject of eternal controversy because of known domestic pressure for protecting an erring officer (Kerstetter 1985). Instances of police departments successfully resisting attempts to impose an external review of personnel conduct are legion. A 1988 review by West revealed that over 80 per cent of departments in the country had an exclusively internal arrangement. However, a 1992 study by Walker and Bumphus pointed to 68 per cent of the 50 largest cities having some arrangement or the other for civilian review (Pate and Fridell 1993). Over the years, a variety of experiments to introduce an external element in the overseeing mechanism have been attempted. There are three known models: civilian input, civilian monitor and civilian review.

In the 'civilian input model', receipt of complaints and the follow-up investigation are with a civilian agency which provides an independent source of information to the Police Chief. This agency may sometimes, as in Chicago, work within the department itself.

Where the 'civilian monitor model' operates, although functions of investigation, adjudication and discipline remain within the police, there is a provision for external civilian review. Such review does not focus on the delinquent officer's conduct. It rather seeks to satisfy itself that the department has discharged its responsibility to launch an objective investigation, taking into account the complainant's views and to bring to book a delinquent officer. This mechanism is analogous to the Ombudsman that one is familiar with in Sweden (Kerstetter 1985).

The 'civilian review model' is the one that is bitterly fought by the police as an unwarranted intrusion. Basically, the police stand is that investigation by inexperienced private individuals would lead to morale problems (Kerstetter 1985). One of the first to try this model was Washington, D.C. in 1948. A decade later, several departments—Philadelphia, Minneapolis Rochester and NYPD—followed suit.

Grievance Machinery in the US Police

American police literature is not very explicit on the availability of grievance redressal channels to individual police officers. The focus is almost exclusively on collective articulation of grievances through a union which, at periodic intervals, enters into contracts on a wide variety of issues with the departments. When the two parties cannot come to terms on contract provisions, an arbitrator steps in. This provision for arbitration is bartered by unions for giving up the right to strike (Coulson 1993).

A major characteristic of the police labour scene is the extremely fragmented nature of unionism, a phenomenon attributed to the essentially local origins of police unions (Guyot 1991). A second established fact is that a majority of sworn officers are aligned to one or the other of the several police unions.

After two brief spells in the 1910s and 1940s, police unionism staged a come-back in the 1960s. This resurgence was traceable to a combination of economic, social and political factors (Walker 1983). The most important of these was the growing disparity between police wages and those of other professional and semi-professional occupations. Next came a certain disgruntlement over management practices, which, in the opinion of many policemen, were either arbitrary and authoritarian or too unprofessional, bordering on patronage and favouritism. Discernible around this time was a feeling of social and political alienation. This arose from widely-circulated and generally believed accounts of brutality, a general lack of popular support to the police and a series of Supreme Court decisions which favoured suspects *vis-a-vis* the police. These circumstances convinced the ranks of the need to organize themselves. In the final analysis, what contributed substantially to the strengthening of unionism was the growing legal support to public employees coming together for articulating their grievances (ibid.).

Unlike in many private industries, there is no single national police union. The picture is one of a large number of local organizations standing by themselves or nominally affiliated to one or the other national federation with little or no control. There are at least seven national federations with varying degrees of influence.

The Fraternal Order of Police (FOP), founded in Pittsburgh in 1915, is the oldest. All sworn officers are eligible for membership. Groups admitted to the FOP are called Lodges. Although, when founded, the FOP was opposed to unionism and collective bargaining, the pressures of 1960s brought about a change of stance. As a result, a sizeable number of lodges are unions with collective bargaining contracts (Walker 1983). A 1990 estimate puts FOP membership at 170,000.

Next comes the National Association of Police Organizations (105,000), which serves independent local associations without trying to amalgamate them (Guyot 1991).

According to a 1985 survey of the nation's 100 largest cities, 98 had unions. Of them, 77 had concluded collective bargaining agreements with their departments. Interestingly, 45 of the 98 unions were affiliated only up to the state level and 36 were local lodges of the FOP. Consequently, there is no single, identifiable police spokesman or police policy document (Walker 1983).

Police unions are not credited with bringing about changes in policing. According to Guyot and K. Martensen (1991), they frequently exploit government institutions to scuttle or delay police management decisions. Unions have made their presence felt mainly in three areas: finances, management and law enforcement policy (Walker 1983). Higher starting and end salaries are reported by departments with unions, as compared to those without them (Guyot 1991).

Machinery for Personnel Management in the US Police

In many of the large departments, there is a distinct personnel bureau or division that takes care of all personnel matters, including training. Invariably, this works under a Deputy Chief or Deputy Commissioner.

The NYPD has a comprehensive Personnel Bureau whose tasks include recruitment, selection and training—both entry and in-service. The bureau has eight sub-units. The largest of these is the Applicant Processing Division (consisting of 230 uniformed and 119 civilian staff). Others include the Employee Management Division (performance evaluation, maintaining personnel records of all NYPD staff and the data bank relating to disciplinary matters, processing of terminations and dismissals of problematic employees), Employee

Relations Section (assisting personnel with serious medical/alcoholic problems, suicide awareness training), and the Occupational Safety and Health Unit.

The LAPD has a Human Resources Bureau which administers the department's personnel services, develops, implements and conducts recruiting and training programmes and investigates the background of candidates. The Bureau has four components: the Personnel Group, the Reserve Coordination Section, the Training Group and the Police Training Administrator.

In Philadelphia, there is a Deputy Commissioner Administration who has three bureaux under his control: training, administrative and staff service. Both civilians and sworn officers (a few of whom are management specialists) fill in the positions in these bureaux and they deal with personnel, fiscal management, data processing and safety functions. The Washington, D.C. Metropolitan Police has an Administrative Services Bureau, headed by an Assistant Chief, that looks after community relations, planning and development, training, labour relations and disciplinary review.

The Chicago Police Department's Employee Development Section of the Personnel Division (Bureau of Administrative Services) is involved in maintaining performance evaluations, administering procedures for promotional examinations, writing and updating job specifications and the orientation of police recruits. This unit is manned essentially by civilians. Many of them have college degrees in human resources or related fields.

COMPARATIVE ANALYSIS

The endeavour here—comparing the problems thrown up by two large groups of public service personnel, born, educated and trained among markedly different cultural milieu—is ambitious. It is nevertheless being attempted because, wherever they may operate and whatever be their ethnic and cultural backgrounds, policemen are linked by a unique bond, the 'police sub-culture'. The belief here is that they react identically to the various pressures which impinge on them while out on beat. This explains the universal complaint against police brutality and corruption. The impact of this sub-culture is so strong that the usually minor, and sometimes major, variance in recruitment, training and compensation practices does not seem to matter very much in shaping the police image.

Force Size

The size of an organization makes for a lot of difference to the quality of personnel management. A small organization is normally informal and therefore less bureaucratic, although this ambience does sometimes promote arbitrariness arising from personal prejudices. These observations are meaningful to the US Police, a collection of more than 17,000 police and sheriff departments which together employ about 600,000 full-time sworn officers and 237,000 non-sworn civilian personnel.[15] The non-federal police strength in India is nearly twice as large. This is distributed over 25 state police forces.

More than 10,000 (59 per cent) US police agencies have fewer than ten full-time sworn officers. Further, there are about 1600 which employ only one full-time officer (BJS 1993). I have found it difficult to locate studies which provide an insight into personnel practices prevailing in these small agencies. Although the sharing of resources by two or three neighbouring agencies, especially for recruitment and training, is not uncommon, the presumption is that the smaller departments do not set much score by modern management concepts and they would rather sort out their problems applying the general rules of prudence and common sense.

US police departments with a strength of about 15 to 20 full-time sworn personnel are no doubt analogous to the police stations in India, which constitute the lowest unit of policing in the country. There is, however, this difference, that the latter are not autonomous stand-alone forces, but are part of a highly hierarchical district police machinery. The picture becomes clearer from the fact that personnel management up to the level of Inspectors is extremely centralized at the District Police Office (DPO), which has to take care of the needs of about 750-1000 personnel, the average size of a force that works under the District SP in India. A comparative study will, therefore, be meaningful only by focussing attention on the less than one hundred police and sheriff's departments in the US, which have about 1000 or more personnel, and the district police forces in India. There is, however, one qualification to this statement.

Two major areas of personnel management—recruitment and training—which had traditionally been decentralized activities in India, insofar as the constabulary were concerned, are becoming highly centralized, with the State Police Headquarters directly getting involved in both the processes. This is a trend seen in a majority of states, and its impact on the quality of men and women coming into the forces will have to be studied in course of time.

Recruitment

One most obvious difference that strikes even a casual student is that, in the Indian Police, entry is at three levels: Constable, Sub-Inspector and Assistant/Deputy Superintendent. This includes a nationwide recruitment by a single agency—the Union Public Service Commission (UPSC)—to the IPS, whose officers are assigned to the 25 state police forces for beginning their career with the District Police. This middle-level entry is something unique to India and a few erstwhile colonies under some Western powers. I am told that only a handful of police departments in the rest of the world have a similar arrangement. In any case, this is unknown to the US Police. Almost in every one of the larger departments—those with 1000 or more manpower—entry is at the lowest level, namely Police Officer.[16]

A number of US departments resort to 'continuous examination announcements', whereby, whenever an eligible candidate turns up, he is tested and, if found fit, he or she is kept in a waiting list. This practice ensures a steady flow of talent and its acceptance. This was the case in India till recently. Once every year, the District SP used to conduct a test and keep an approved list of candidates from which appointments were made, depending on authorized vacancies. This is slowly giving way to a massive recruitment at the state level at erratic intervals. There is an unevenness in the numbers selected, which accounts for the bulges seen in certain years.

We see only minor differences in the minimum standards prescribed for applicants to police jobs. While 18 is the earliest age at which one could enter the constabulary in India, the applicant to the IPS cannot be younger than 21 at the time of taking the Preliminary Examination conducted by the UPSC. The normal maximum age, unlike in the US, for most of the Indian forces is 26. This limit is relaxable up to 35 only in the case of certain groups such as Scheduled Castes/Scheduled Tribes and those with work experience in the Defence forces (otherwise known as 'ex-servicemen').

There are some differences in the testing procedure. In a majority of forces in India, applicants for the constabulary are not allowed to sit for the written examination unless they attain minimum standards in the physical efficiency test (running, jumping and rope climbing). In the US, the written test is only one of a battery of tests, and its weightage varies with department. Also, in some, a candidate can skip the written test by obtaining a waiver after proving a high educational qualification, such as a college degree or past work experience in any law enforcement agency. This is not possible in the Indian Police. One significant US requirement—a valid driving licence—is unknown to India, unless the position specifically sought to be filled is that of a driver.[17]

Perhaps the most significant component of Police Officer selection in the US is the 'psychology test', which sometimes forms part of the medical examination of the candidate. Although its reliability has been severely questioned, departments are reluctant to jettison it. Except for a few central police forces, the psychology test is unknown to the Indian Police. It is heartening, however, that the concept is fast catching the attention of policy-makers.

Police Chief Tenure

This is a subject of animated discussion in both countries. A major difference is that state police chiefs in India, called the Directors-General of Police (DGP), enjoy civil service protection. This is because all of them belong to the Indian Police Service (IPS) which is an All India Service recognized by the country's constitution itself. They cannot be dismissed, removed or reduced in rank except under procedure prescribed by law. What is, however, debated in India is the action of some governments to shift an incumbent-DGP to an inconsequential assignment outside the police department for reasons which are not always explicit or professional. Such an action has however been upheld by courts and administrative tribunals since the Chief displaced suffers no loss in rank or salary. He merely moves on to another assignment, very often of a non-police character.[18]

The debate in the US is slightly different. What is at issue is the capricious action in some cities to terminate the contract of appointment of a Chief without assigning reasons. This situation arises because many chiefs are outsiders to the departments they may be heading. They serve on a contract basis, without the benefit of civil service protection enjoyed by those who had risen from the ranks in one department.

This leads us on to an area which is the most controversial in Indian Police, namely, the nature and quantum of external pressure that operates on a DGP with regard to personnel matters. Patronage does play a role in the choice of personnel for the so-called sensitive and prestigious appointments. It is the experience however that, where there is a healthy rapport between the DGP and the state government, the evil is somewhat kept under check. Also, where the DGP is transparent, consistent and objective and has the ability to explain lucidly the rationale for the position that he has taken in a particular matter, problems of man management are not acute. Nevertheless, a placement policy that is clinically free from non-professional considerations is a distant dream. (Interestingly, there are regional differences. For instance, the southern states, except for a few short phases of aberration, display a certain stability that accounts for the relatively long tenures for DGPs.)

Literature available in the US suggests that the issue is no doubt live, but is not one that now causes as much concern as it did a few decades ago when James F. Ahern, a former chief of the New Haven (Connecticut) Police Department wrote:

> Five years ago, anyone with the most superficial knowledge of the workings of the New Haven Police Department could point to the political power behind every Captain on the force. Every cop who wanted to get ahead had his 'hook'—or, as they say in New York, his 'rabbi'. Everyone owed his success to a politician . . . or to an underworld figure. (1972: 96-8)

A year thereafter, James Q. Wilson (1973) pointed out how differing political cultures of communities accounted for three distinct styles of policing; the 'watchman', 'legalistic' and 'service' styles. In his view, apart from causing qualitative and quantitative differences in law enforcement, this phenomenon had a perceptible impact on personnel standards, especially with regard to entry, promotion, specialization and the level of managerial skills.

A decade later, Patrick V. Murphy (1985) spoke of 'negotiable' and 'non-negotiable' issues for a Chief. In his view, except for giving a few inputs, the Mayor had no decision-making role in matters of appointments, transfers or assignments. He was equally emphatic that in the area of discipline, the Chief had unbridled authority.

Swanson *et al.* (1993) believe that American forces have come a long way from the New Haven experience of the 1970s. Nevertheless, they refer to the unique position of the Chief which does not afford him the desirable political insularity.[19] Two factors—the city council's control over the police budget and its enormous lawmaking powers—do weigh heavily in the Chief's mind while handling political matters. As a result, many chiefs would rather maintain good relations with the council members rather than risk even an occasional confrontation that could undermine the department's efforts to get authorization for proposals involving staff and equipment augmentation.

I see here a parallel with India. It is not uncommon for some DGPs to accommodate requests—not always out of the way—from political quarters, not for their self-aggrandizement, but for ensuring the smooth passage through government of proposals to expand departmental resources. This is a style of leadership that does not always go well with some junior officers who look upon their DGP as a 'political' person, even if the latter happens to be an outstanding professional.

CORRUPTION

Any exercise to estimate the dimensions of corruption in a public agency, such as the police, could be looked upon as preposterous. This is because police corruption is invariably the insidious activity of a group that is knit together by a code of silence. Hence I shall desist from making any generalization that seeks to establish one force as more corrupt than the other. It will be somewhat correct to say that the evil is present pronouncedly in the police departments of both countries.

There are, however, two striking differences. In the US, during the present century, there have been at least two public investigations—the Knapp Commission and the Pennsylvania Crime Commission—devoted solely to analysing the issue of police corruption. Distressingly, after the Torture Commission Report of 1855, in India, there has been no specific probe into corruption, as distinct from brutality. We have to be content with merely the reports of the central government's 1902 and 1977 Police Commissions and of a few State Police Commissions addressing the larger issue of police reform, and incidentally referring to the widespread prevalence of corruption. As a result, there is no credible in-depth analysis of the problem in the Indian context.

Secondly, there is a greater transparency in public discussion of police corruption in the US. This cannot be said of India where there is a general inhibition and a fear complex characterizing the debate, although, an allied area—police brutality—receives abundant attention. There is naturally a drought of literature on the subject. One does not also come across a bold and dispassionate media evaluation of lack of integrity in the police. Further, whenever the issue is debated in public forums, the tendency is toward vague generalizations. (In private discussions, one no doubt very often hears specific complaints of demand of bribe by traffic police personnel and crime investigators.) There are signs, however, of the picture undergoing a slight change in the past few years, thanks to the induction of younger and dynamic journalists into daily newspapers and the arrival of private television channels which believe in relatively fearless and investigative reporting.

Theft, robbery and drug payoffs are forms of police corruption known to both countries. A survey of US literature, however, suggests that the demand for money for not proceeding further in an investigation that had gone into police records is not a major concern. This is not so in the case of India. Corruption of the greatest magnitude, in terms of money demanded, is in relation to a promise to drop action or dilute the charge against an offender in a registered crime, such as murder or rioting, by suitably tampering with witnesses or by citing material that will cast a doubt on the prosecution story in the mind of the judge.

It is widely known in India that many personnel at police stations demand money from crime victims, especially those who have been the subject of theft, robbery or burglary, for registering their complaints and proceeding further with the investigation. This form of corruption becomes difficult in the US, because a majority of city departments have a 911 service which automatically assigns a number to each complaint that becomes difficult to suppress.

One other major point of contrast is with regard to the agency responsible for investigating police corruption. In the US, almost every large department has an Internal Affairs Division or Bureau that monitors police conduct and also probes charges of corruption. The position in India is somewhat different. Almost every State Government has a Directorate of Vigilance and Anti-Corruption (DVAC) or an Anti-Corruption Bureau (ACB), that is located outside the police but is manned by police officers, which enquires into corruption charges against all state civil servants, including policemen. There is no analogous agency exclusively for and within the police, although the CID in the police is occasionally asked to make a preliminary enquiry. Wherever there is material pointing *prima facie* to guilt, the CID report is passed on to the DVAC/ACB for a further enquiry and action, if necessary, by registering a regular case under the Prevention of Corruption Act 1988. Although any police agency can invoke this Act, it is invariably the DVAC/ACB which is entrusted with this responsibility by state governments.[20]

Brutality

This is a problem common to both countries. It was brought on official record in India as early as the 1850s in the form of the Torture Commission report. In the US, such formal admission came only in the 1930s when the Wickersham Commission referred to the widespread prevalence of 'third degree' in police mechanics. Taking into account the fact that Indian authorities had come down on this kind of police deviance very much before their American counterparts, one would expect a greater restraint on the part of the Indian Police. Unfortunately, this is not the case. One does see, even today, unprovoked and uninhibited violence on individual citizens by misguided policemen which brings discredit to the entire Indian Police.

One striking difference is with regard to the setting against which police brutality takes place. In India, the greatest uproar is over what is known as 'custodial deaths', resulting from the torture of a prisoner while in police custody. (Such custody itself is more often than not downright illegal, one that is not usually brought on police record.) This was the problem of the American Police as well in the early part of the twentieth century. There has however been a change in the past few decades. The current concern there, more than custodial violence, is over force employed while effecting arrests. The Rodney King incident is illustrative of this. It is significant that such force on an hapless individual is invariably in public, whereas, in India this occurs within the confines of a police station and away from public gaze. (The recent Louima incident in the NYPD changes this perception to an extent.)

Politically oriented agitations in public are an everyday affair in major parts of India. Since these are usually against the government, the confrontation becomes one between the political party that rules the government and those in opposition to it. The use of excessive force sometimes on a crowd of demonstrators, therefore, takes on a political hue and the police are accused of partisanship. The situation is exacerbated when an unruly and violent crowd is dispersed by the police through the use of firearms. Such a situation is infrequent in the US. Except for the civil rights demonstration and the anti-Vietnam protests of the 1960s when the police had to use force on huge crowds, one does not often see a major police-public battle in the streets. The political partisanship for which the Indian Police is blamed is also, therefore, not evident in the US environment.

Yet another feature of India's law and order situation—terrorism—accounts for major charges of police brutality. The police, in terrorist-affected states, especially in Punjab and Jammu & Kashmir, have opened themselves to complaints of excesses. This is because conventional methods of policing to blunt terrorist violence have proved ineffective here. Controversy surrounds the many 'encounters' between the police and extremists in which there is a large number of casualties. Except for the Waco incident of 1993, where federal forces were accused of unprovoked violence, the US situation does not pose a problem as intense as that arising from the terrorist menace in India.

Unionism

The first chronicled effort to form a police union in the US was during the second decade of the twentieth century. As against this, a semblance of unionism was seen in India for the first time—in the shape of a Revolutionary Policeman's Association formed in Bihar—only in July 1942. This headstart of nearly 30 years which unionism gained in the US possibly explains the solid base that it has acquired in that country. This is notwithstanding the fact that it was only in the 1960s that police unions were officially allowed to gain roots. The growth since that time has been substantial, compared to the still incipient stage of the movement in India.

While unionism is an officially accepted reality in the US, the expression 'union' is still an anathema to India's police leadership. What is permitted in India are 'associations', as outlined by the National Police Commission (1977), which do not have the connotations of a labour union. It is equally true that even such a diluted body as associations have not taken off the ground. Also, they do not have a recognized and strong national affiliate that can send a message down to the rank and file with regard to any matter of relevance, especially their service conditions. The police labour scene in India is thus heavily weighted against the average policeman at the grassroots level. This is in sharp contrast to the US situation wherein a majority of policemen are members of one union or the other. Also, these unions have a choice of at least seven major national federations to which they could affiliate themselves.

While strikes by policemen are prohibited in both countries, the US policeman enjoys two advantages over his Indian counterpart. The first is the right to collective bargaining which results in a specific contract entered into by the union representing him and the department concerned. This contract enables periodic negotiation of wages and day-to-day service matters.

The second advantage is a somewhat recent development. This is the acceptance of the need to incorporate in every contract, a Police Officer's Bill of Rights. This has become so widely recognized that, in some states, the Bill has been codified. (An example is the California Public Safety Officers' Procedural Bill of Rights Act.) This bill usually covers a wide spectrum of subjects such as political activity, investigations and interrogations, insubordination, administrative appeal, polygraph examination, financial disclosure, mutual aid agreements, etc. (Peak 1993).

NOTES

1. The practice of assigning IPS officers to non-police jobs varies from state to state. In some states, the post of Home Secretary, which is normally the preserve of the IAS, is held by an IPS officer. Sometimes, IPS officers are also considered for heading public transport corporations, sports directorates and tourism agencies.
2. Between 1968 and 1977, the northern state of Uttar Pradesh had 8 Police Chiefs. The record of the southern states is somewhat better. For instance, Tamil Nadu had only three in the same period. It is customary for every new government to appoint a new DGP. Ironically, the debate on the subject was revived in the southern state of Karnataka in March 1997 when its DGP who had been in office only for five months was suddenly shifted to head the central government's Railway Protection Force in the country's capital New Dehi. An editorial on the subject (Appendix V) by the *Hindu* presents a balanced view.
3. The total IPS strength for each state is determined by the central government in consultation with the states and this is subject to revision once in three years.
4. I do not have any information whether the DIG's charges are true. Nevertheless, I thought I should refer to this in order to make the reader, especially the one outside the country, understand the nature of controversies that large-scale recruitment to the police generates sometimes.
5. Although special efforts are made in the states, such as Uttar Pradesh and Bihar, which have seen bloody riots between Hindus and Muslims and where there have been complaints of bias on the part of the Hindu Constabulary, the number of Muslims in the force has gone up only slightly. This is why there is a persistent demand from the Muslims that the entire group, not merely sections of it, as at present, should be brought under the definition of 'backward classes'.
6. During 1863-4, as many as 17.5 per cent of the Madras Police resigned or deserted. Also, 16.4 per cent were dismissed for inefficiency or involvement in crime. During the same year, 428 policemen were convicted for various

offences, including murder and rape. In 1920, resignation/desertion stood at 31.4 per cent. Dismissals were 279. Also 179 officers were convicted in court. (Reports of the Administration of Madras Presidency, 1863-4 and 1921).

7. For a detailed account of police strikes/agitations in India, see Chapter 4 pp. 59-71 of my *Indian Police: Problems, Planning and Perspectives* (1985). New Delhi: Manohar.

8. Till about the late 1970s, a sole IPS official called Assistant Inspector General—AIG—of the rank of Superintendent of Police performed this dual role. I myself handled this assignment briefly and found it to be interesting and challenging.

9. The psychology test may consist one or more of the following: the Minnesota Multiphasic Personality Inventory (MMPI), a test for neuroses; the California Personality Inventory, a general set of measures of personality characteristics; the Detroit test, a group test of general intelligence, the Cornell test of motor skills; the House-Tree Person test, a projective test of self-concept and a general personality inventory.

10. According to information received by me directly from the NYPD, during the ten years of its existence, the scheme has absorbed 68 per cent (723) of all cadets as Police Officers in the department. I have been further told that the cadets are working with some of the best police officers in the department solving community problems, assisting senior citizens, and organizing youth-related activities.

11. Writing in the context of the Rodney King incident of Los Angeles, the *New York Times* (11 May 1992) expressed the belief that the corps 'would constitute a national investment in more enlightened police work and against racial hostility and grievous excess'.

12. The latest information received by me directly from some large police departments indicates the following position with regard to minority employment:

	White	Black	Hispanic	Others
New York City	24800	4950	6050	845
Chicago	8515	3323	1239	141
Los Angeles	4462	1232	2359	456
Houston	3375	938	943	107

13. The latest figures received by me directly from some major departments indicates the following position with regard to female sworn personnel:

NYPD	22%
LAPD	17%
Houston	13%
Chicago	18%

14. Interestingly, again in 1974, Lawrence Sherman identified three types of police corruption, one of which was confined to individuals ('rotten apples') and this squared with the complacence of some chiefs that corruption was only in a few 'rotten pockets' and was no cause for undue alarm. Pervasive unorganized

corruption and pervasive organized corruption were the other two types identified by Sherman.

15. These statistics do not cover those agencies under the Federal Government such as the FBI, Secret Service, etc. I have not been able to get any source from which the strength of the federal law enforcement agencies can be assessed.

16. There is, however, the practice of a number of departments directly bringing in a rank outsider to the job of Police Chief. A few also provide for lateral entry to middle levels. But these are all for experienced personnel with policing experience. Lateral entry is almost unknown to Indian police departments, because civil service regulations are rigid. A few such inductions are confined to technical personnel, purely on a short-term contract basis.

17. Police automobiles in India are driven by authorized drivers belonging to the constabulary. Seldom does an officer above the constabulary level drive a departmental vehicle. Also, vehicles are more often than not assigned to a unit, such as police station or circle, and not to individual officers. (Only officers of the rank of ASP/DSP and above enjoy the privilege of having a vehicle allotted to them for their exclusive use.) The existing position may require a review because of the continuously expanding fleet of police automobiles all over the country.

18. Under the central government's directive, every state can have at least two positions of Director-General, one, the regular chief (designated as 'cadre post'), and the other, an equivalent position (designated as 'ex-cadre post') which could be inside or outside the police department. The central government's directive is that, each state can have the same number of ex-cadre posts as cadre posts of DGP. This provision enables a state like my home-state of Tamil Nadu (which has two cadre posts of DGP) to have, at any point of time, four officers operating in the rank of DGP, one of whom, not necessarily the seniormost, heads the force. The other three are in positions like Chairman, Police Housing Corporation, Director, Vigilance and Anti-Corruption and Chairman, Madras City Transport Corporation.

19. A study (1992) by Tunnell and Gaines of the career graph of 115 police chiefs in Kentucky is relevant here. According to their conclusions, 'political pressures are exerted from a variety of directions, and as a result, over 50 per cent of the police chiefs in our study who had left their jobs were forced out by governmental politicians'.

20. One point of frequent criticism is that the DVAC, being almost wholly manned by police personnel deputed from the State Police, is not all that objective in handling complaints against the latter. This is only partly valid if one considers the number of cases processed against policemen.

8

Looking Ahead

> We cannot rely upon the police, even when they are dedicated to preventing crime, to save society from crime. No single institution can do that. At the same time, we must charge them with taking the lead in exploring what must be done. In institutional terms, they are best for the purpose.
>
> David Bayley, *Police for the Future,*
> New York: Oxford University Press, 1994

IT IS CUSTOMARY to end with a few broad generalizations. This convention commends itself for its many advantages. The most obvious is the facility that it affords the author to present his theme succinctly at one place and outline the material in support. While bowing to tradition, this final chapter goes a little beyond that, so as to record some stray thoughts on policing, not appearing strictly germane to the comparative study attempted here. I crave the indulgence of the reader if, in the process, I appear a little rambling. Also, if this chapter sounds a trifle casual and informal in its tone, this was meant to break the monotony of my recital till now. It is again because of this that I have chosen to put down a few impressions which may not exactly stand the rigours of current social science research, especially of the US variety.

In the early days of this study, I was frequently told by friends that what I was trying to do was one of comparing apples with oranges, and that I was not likely to come out with any revolutionary findings. I am afraid that my friends are not wholly correct.

I am convinced that, notwithstanding the marked cultural differences that characterize the milieu in which they operate, the American and Indian police forces face problems which are identical. Even at the risk of being somewhat repetitive, I would like to deal with them here briefly.

THE SIMILARITIES

Demands on the two police forces may be described as exacting. This is not unusual for two regions with high crime. Media scrutiny of the police response to events is one major factor that pushes up popular expectations. Unlike in the US where, for decades, newspaper and television coverage of crime had been extensive, in India, this was conservative and low-key till recently. Happenings of the past one year, have, however, transformed the scene. The reporting on white collar crime, especially graft in high places, is now intense and dramatic. Critical analyses of police investigations, often based on unfavourable court pronouncements, have served to enhance the average Indian citizen's interest in police mechanics. Pressures on the police in their daily routine are consequently mounting. The accountability of the US and Indian police forces to public opinion, attributable mainly to the extraordinary media interest, is, therefore, almost at the same high level.

One sociological reality weighs down the typical American and Indian policeman. The reference here is to the role and perceptions of the dominant minority in each country. The black in the US and the Muslim in India are equally distrustful of the police. Both feel under-represented in the police and therefore maltreated by them. There is a difference.

Several studies point to the interaction of blacks with the police to be intense, nearly on a day-to-day basis. This flows from their high participation in crime, both as victims and offenders. On the other hand, Muslim involvement in the system becomes a matter for debate mainly during physical exchanges—popularly referred to as communal riots—with Hindu groups. As a result, the Muslim perception of police conduct represents that of a collectivity, while black antagonism is reflective of the emotions of the individual, as well as the entire race. In either case, the police in both countries are inhibited by the need to be extremely circumspect in handling the dominant minority. Strangely, this produces in them two diverse reactions; extreme passivity, fearing punitive administrative action, or excessive violence.

This brings us to the universally familiar subject of the police use of 'third degree' methods. Employment of unlawful force on citizens, especially suspects, is a problem that bothers the higher echelons in both countries. There is, however, a distinction with regard to the context in which it occurs.

Police violence in the US is mostly in public places, against those fleeing from the scene of crime after committing an offence or those not heeding a police direction to stop for being questioned for a traffic violation. In slight contrast, what is of serious concern to human rights activists and police supervisors in India is the practice of some misguided and some unscrupulous policemen torturing hapless suspects within the confines of police stations to extract a confession or to extort sums of money. This evil accounts for the many deaths in police custody, reported nationally every year. Notwithstanding this difference, the focus of reformers in both countries is on tightening the procedure that governs crime investigation so as to reduce the scope for abuse of authority. A desire to impart greater transparency to police mechanics is also shared by them.

Corruption in the police is a nearly universal phenomenon. Supervisory ranks have to contend with this on a day-to-day basis. With a greater selectivity in the matter of selection and an entry-level wage that is not considered too low, one would expect a much higher measure of integrity in the US police. This does not seem to be the case, if one goes by the periodical reports of drug pay-offs to precinct-level staff and the number of policemen hauled up for receiving illegal gratification. Nevertheless, the impressions that I gained during my visits to the US would support the generalization that police corruption there, albeit present, is not as pervasive or visible as in India, although it receives considerable attention in the printed media.

Police leaders in both countries are fully conscious of the fact that there is a limit up to which they could demand more resources, especially manpower, from the administration. They are convinced that whole communities will have to be involved in the police routine in a big way so that a resources crunch does not affect police performance. Several structured projects, and a few unstructured—especially those in India—have been launched in the two countries, and these have started yielding results. There is a need, however, to highlight a difference, viz., one of mechanics.

In most of the big police departments in the US, there is invariably an action-oriented blueprint for community policing. In India, except in a few urban forces, such a document is a rarity, and programmes are loosely knit. Also conspicuous, in striking contrast to the US, is the disinclination of police chiefs in India to encourage academic research on projects such as community policing. These distinctions notwithstanding, a basic faith in the ability of the community to complement police initiatives is shared by the two countries.

An identical strand in the area of crime may be perceived in the two countries. While crime rates are no doubt high, fluctuations in the total volume of crime during the past two years are not too pronounced; a slight drop in the US and a slightly higher rise in India. This induces a certain complacence in those handling crime and a feeling that crime is under control. Public perceptions in the US and India are to the contrary, especially in the latter country where the popular impression is that a lot of crime is suppressed. As stated by me earlier in the book, the scope for such a dishonest practice is comparatively limited in the US.

The Differences

This is so much for what the two countries have in common. How far do they stand apart? A hard-boiled Indian policeman like me would necessarily start with a problem that bothers many of my colleagues in their daily routine, one that could be incomprehensible to many of my American counterparts. I have in mind the frequent complaint of external interference in police work, both in operations and day-to-day personnel management.

The grievance has substance nationwide. It is the direct off-shoot of the populist democracy that has emerged in the country. Its dynamics are too complex to understand and cope with, even for experienced officers. The younger ones are exposed to it very early in their career, and they receive little guidance from their superiors. Judicial activism of the kind now in display in the country, however, offers hope that the police will gradually carve out for themselves inviolable areas of professional autonomy that will be subject only to court scrutiny.

During my interaction with the Philadelphia Police, I had repeatedly quizzed my friends there on this subject. The responses confirmed my belief that the problem of external directions did not bother most of them. Nevertheless, I was told that the Mayor-Police Chief relationship did have certain political (not necessarily partisan) connotations, and that, a Chief, out of tune with the Mayor's political proclivities, seldom survived for long. I was further told that FBI investigations involving those in the highest layers of the political firmament were not all that clinical, and were occasionally susceptible to the prevalent undercurrents at the Capitol Hill. I cannot hazard a guess as to how far this impression corresponds with reality. I can speak with some measure of authority only on the India scene.

One feature of the American Police, its fragmented nature, is something that may not be intelligible to the average Indian policeman. He is so much conditioned by a massive bureaucracy, which is heavily centralized, that he will be hard put to understand how small forces of less than twenty policemen in the US can stand by themselves for operating effectively and for gathering the resources required for producing such effectiveness.

THE FUTURE OF POLICING IN INDIA AND THE US

INDIA

This is perhaps the easiest section of the book to write. I can indulge in some fantasy here, a luxury not available while working on the earlier parts.

As a member of the Indian Police Service for more than three decades, I have been in a vantageous position to closely observe the vicissitudes of the service during a crucial period. But this can, at the same time, detract from the need for objectivity, as, somewhere along the way, one acquires biases which are not easy to shed.

THE FUTURE CRIME SCENARIO

Crime is the most discussed subject in India. Thanks to the incredible expansion of the media, especially television, and the attention that crime receives from them, there is a widespread feeling that the situation is getting out of control and that the police are incapable of handling it. The latter are, therefore, likely to come under increasing pressure to solve, if not prevent, crime. The spread of literacy and improved communication facilities—there is a phenomenal increase in the number of telephones at public place—are two factors which could effectively dilute the opportunity for the police to disregard or suppress crime. The way public opinion asserted itself during the 1996 General Election to overturn non-performing governments indicated that citizens would not brook official apathy or negligence. The pushing up of the accountability of the political executive should have more than an echo on the administrative front.

Crime statistics for the past few years portray only minor fluctuations. For the country as a whole, I do not anticipate any violent swing, although individual cities or districts may, once in a while, reflect noticeable increases. This prognosis is based on the belief that more and more non-violent and petty crime, though cognizable under the IPC, may not get reported to the police, because of the growing cynicism about the latter's ability to solve crime and the costs involved in terms of time spent in lodging a complaint and following it up. The 3 per cent drop in the number of thefts in 1995 bears testimony to this.

I expect crime against women to be more in focus in the years to come. The 8 per cent rise in rapes during 1994 and the 4 per cent of 1995 possibly point to a greater willingness to go the police and expose the offender. Many women's organizations all over the country now display a certain aggression that was not evident till recently. They have been solidly supported by the media. There are now a number of young high-profile female journalists who do not miss an opportunity to pursue leads of atrocities against women. The setting up of exclusive all-women police stations in some states gives women the greater access to police service that was not there earlier. Sexual harassment of different kinds and more forms of domestic violence will be brought to police notice much more than before. Whether this will be reflected in the crime figures is a matter for conjecture, because considerable discretion is still available to the police, whether to register a formal case or not.

Economic crimes in 1995 no doubt showed a marginal drop. I expect this trend to be reversed very soon. The heightened economic activity, consequent to the freeing of government controls, has pushed up the opportunity for deviant behaviour. The Harshad Mehta episode of 1992 gave enough evidence of this. Frauds in banks and irregularities committed by non-banking financial institutions—in which a wide cross-section of the population invest their life-time savings because of a promise of attractive returns—are now a well-known feature of the urban scenario. The police are now sensitive to the problem and are slowly beginning to equip themselves to handle it. The creation of exclusive economic offences wings at police headquarters is indicative of this. I expect that such wings will be expanded and specially equipped, through training, to deal with larger volumes of economic crime.

Computerization of crime information has been placed on a firm footing. This is bound to gain further roots if the NCRB remains active, as it is now. This facility to exchange information with ease will push up inter-state cooperation and the neutralization of gangs who operate over a wide geographic area.

Impact of the Mandal Commission

The new scheme of quotas following the implementation of the Mandal Commission recommendations (see Chapter 1) should see the induction into the IPS of more of the rural youth from the relatively underprivileged sections of the society. While this is true of the IAS and other higher civil services as well, it has a particular significance for the police. It should, at least theoretically, ensure a greater police sensitivity to the problems of the lower strata. This is important in the context of the galling tales of police apathy to the poor *vis-a-vis* the privileged treatment of the moneyed class, who can often 'buy' police attention. I will not go the whole hog with many of my cynical colleagues who are positive that it is the better placed individual who will continue to be privileged in the police station context. I look upon this as a possible area for future research: Has the new class composition of the IPS altered police attitudes to the rural poor?

The Role of Central Police in States

Notwithstanding the strong sentiments heard frequently in favour of greater autonomy for the states *vis-a-vis* the central government, I strongly believe that collaboration between state and central forces will expand rather than diminish. Even states which are traditionally reluctant to be a part of the national mainstream acknowledge the indebtedness of their police to the Home Ministry of the central government in Delhi.

The Central Reserve Police Force will remain the mainstay for states to tackle major threats to peace. The continuous expansion of the CRPF is a direct recognition of the faith placed on it by the states. Recruitment to the CRPF may, therefore, have to be more broadbased, in concession to the various regional pulls, so as to ensure its greater acceptability. One issue that may be raised in the future is: How far is this dependence on a central force expedient for a state government, especially when the latter is controlled by a political party that is opposed to the one(s) running the central government? Another that will come for attention is the impact of an excessive reliance on the CRPF on the quality of State Armed Police battalions, especially their state of training and preparedness.

Two areas which will continue to cry for attention during the next few decades are terrorism and physical protection of dignitaries.

While these remain the state's responsibilities, the intelligence inputs given by the Home Ministry in New Delhi are enormous. No less significant is the valuable assistance by way of training programmes and supply of modern sophisticated equipment needed to blunt the terrorist might. In view of the global perception that has to be brought to bear on counter-terrorist strategy, no individual state will have the vision or the resources required for the purpose. Regardless of the political complexion of the central or a state government at any point of time, this collaboration will become an utter necessity.

One interesting speculation relates to the future role of the Central Bureau of Investigation (CBI). At present, it is under great pressure to take up investigations, many of which are purely within the competence of the State Police, but are transferred to it on the ground that they are enveloped in a controversy and the bona fides of a state investigating agency are liable to be doubted. As a result, the CBI is overworked, unable to focus on its more important tasks of tackling economic crime and detecting graft among central civil servants. Except on a few occasions—such as the assassination of former Prime Minister Rajiv Gandhi—states do not exactly need the investigating skills of the CBI. Hence, the decision to pass on a case to the CBI is sometimes not on strictly professional requirements. It is a matter for conjecture as to whether this unsatisfactory situation will remain so or whether concrete guidelines will be drawn to make the process less subjective. A lot will depend on the complexion of the central government at any point of time, whether it is run by a single party or a coalition of parties. Recent Supreme Court/High Court directions to the CBI in some important cases raise the hope that the Bureau will be relatively less subject to the directions of the executive. Against this development, there is reason to believe that state government decisions to entrust cases to the CBI will, in future, be on a more clinical examination of all facts.

Prospects for the US Police

The Violent Crime Problem

Law and order situations like the ones witnessed in India do not pose a major problem to the police forces in the US. In particular, religious and caste clashes, which are an almost daily occurrence in India, are of little relevance in the US context. The white-black relationship is no doubt uneasy and fragile and has the potential to suddenly erupt into major violence, but possibly only at infrequent intervals. As a result, the community's preoccupation is one with raw crime, such as homicide, rape and robbery.

The near obsession with crime is dictated by high crime rates. The fact that the volume of crime is actually decreasing, as per FBI statistics, does not tone down the paranoia. I, therefore, believe that the police will be evaluated solely on its ability to contain crime. Successes elsewhere will not matter in building the police image. Here I foresee one danger.

The excessive attention to crime could distort the police vision and make it minimally prepared for meeting contingencies arising from terrorism and social tensions caused by growing economic disparities. This does not mean for a minute that the US police chiefs do not have plans of action. What is hinted here is that such insidious problems require a long-term strategy, and it is not certain that one does exist.

What is the crime scenario likely to be in the decades to come? Gurr feels that everything will depend on the reactions of the community and governments in the country to the 'fundamental problems . . . social disarray, lack of economic opportunity and racial inequality. . . . In the long run, I place my bet not on the intractable nature of social reality, but on the ability of Americans, in times of crisis, to take control of their lives and change what they do not like about their society' (1989b:19).

Skogan (1989) was a little more specific when he drew attention to the census forecast that there was going to be a substantial reduction in the younger segment. While this high risk (crimewise) category peaked in 1977, it was likely to suffer a marked fall around 1995. Hence, prospects of a drop in crime from then onwards were quite bright, particularly because future fertility rates were not expected to reach the levels of the post-World War II Baby Boomers.

While this projection has proved reasonably correct, judging from recent UCR figures, two factors are relevant for the early part of the next century. First is the slower departure from crime of the present-day violent offenders. Second, by 2010, the black segment of the population in the 14-21 age group will have risen to 21 per cent as against the mere 12 per cent in 1963 when the rates of violent crime rose significantly (Skogan 1989).

Friedman (1993:454) is also not sanguine about the current situation changing very much for the better. In his view, 'modern violence is different from frontier violence or historic American violence'. Noting that many countries with a bloodier past than America are relatively crime-free, Friedman believes: 'Something has to be rotten in the modern state of affairs—some sickness that is peculiarly our own, the child of our period, our customs, our times' (1993: 454-5). These words acquire a new meaning in the context of the mindless Oklahoma City bombing (April 1995) by a white extremist organization and the Olympic Park explosion (July 1996) during the Atlanta Olympic Games.

The Future of Community Policing

Although it is a much-touted expression, used *ad nauseam*, any police department in the country, which does not profess community policing, is liable to be looked down upon as a laid back organization. As a result, there will be increasing pressure in the days to come on even the very small departments to proclaim their faith in the concept. Simultaneously, however, there will be intensified clamour from the cynics that its practitioners should convincingly prove the benefits from such a style of policing.

There is already a vocal school that does not set much score by community policing. This school should gain in strength from the fact that evaluations of projects in the area are few and far between, and the ones conducted till now do not exactly help the cause of community policing. I, therefore, visualize a period of confusion in the police ranks during a critical phase in the US police history. This could be a serious reverse, as community policing itself came into reckoning to fill a major inadequacy that became obvious when the system was under fire.

Federal-Municipal Police Ties

As in the case of India, the ties between the Federal Police and the rest of the police in various parts of the US are becoming increasingly significant. This is quite a reversal of what was contemplated for the whole administrative system by the Founding Fathers.

There appears less reluctance now on the part of many departments to indent on the resources of the FBI and other federal law enforcement agencies. This is an encouraging trend. I foresee a further expansion of such a relationship.

The tone set by President Clinton in financing the scheme of community police officers should become stronger in the days to come. The fact that terrorism has infiltrated into American soil and that it demands enormous resources and teamwork among several agencies, projects a closer bond between federal and other police agencies. The FBI will be increasingly under pressure to step up its coordinating role. It may have to enlarge its resources substantially to fulfil all round expectations.

Human Resource Management

A debate that will continue to dominate the area of police personnel management is how to push up the minority content of the departments. With the existing standards set for selection and the other restrictions imposed by civil service regulations, I do not see how this is going to be ensured. The absence of a popular movement that is politically and numerically very strong, like the one seen in India, makes the US scene qualitatively different. A quota system that permits relaxation of standards seems the major avenue by which more blacks, Hispanics and women will come into the police. How far will courts in the country uphold such a quota is a moot question.

Epilogue

At the end of it all it is possible that the most indulgent of my readers could ask me as to why I wrote this book. First and foremost, this exercise, with its heavy academic bias, has given me the utmost satisfaction which every scholar expects from his labours. This was one motivation.

More than this, during my exposure to the American Police, I genuinely felt that all my colleagues back home needed to be told how the system worked in a country that was not merely advanced in terms of science and technology and economic development, but was also a mosaic of varied cultures. There was thus here scope for learning and intelligent adaptation.

Next, I found in the US very little knowledge about the Indian Police. This was disappointing, although I did come across scholars not averse to being told about how we, in the Indian Police, operated, and what our problems were. The process is being facilitated to an extent by a few Indians who have joined universities that offer courses in criminal justice. Some have made a mark and have even found their way into teaching faculties. Dilip Das of State University of New York (SUNY) Plattsburgh and Mangai Natarajan of John Jay College, New York, are two worthy of mention. This is not enough.

There is actually a case for serious and credible literature on the Indian Police, that is not only intelligible to the American researchers, but which, at least partially, meets their exacting standards. This is one more objective of this book. I will leave it to my friends in the American campuses to come to their own conclusion on whether I have succeeded.

Finally, it was my desire that policy-makers in India should be exposed to the various cross-currents in the system and made to think on ideas of how to make the Indian Police more effective and acceptable to the community than they were now. The philosophy that is sought to be promoted here is that there should be a constant review of existing methods of policing. Without this introspection, I am afraid the Indian Police will remain static, if not regressive, rather than being dynamic and progressive.

APPENDIX I

Law and Order Incidents in India
1995-6

Date	Place	State	Details
1995			
7 Jan.	Imphal	Manipur	9 civilians killed in clash with CRPF.
10 Feb.	Faizganj	UP	Quarrel over construction of a wall around a Masjid. 6 Muslims injured. One dies in police firing.
27 Feb.	Vijaipur	J&K	Electric supply tower blasted.
10 March	Aligarh	UP	Teasing of Hindu girl by Muslim youth. 2 Hindus, 4 Muslims die. 22 injured. Curfew imposed.
20 March	Hubli	Karnataka	Hindu-Muslim clash. 2 Hindus and 3 Muslims killed. 50 injured in police firing. Curfew imposed.
14 Apr.	Madras	Tamil Nadu	Bomb blast at Hindu Munnani Office. 3 Hindus and 3 Muslims stabbed to death.
29 Apr.	Chiraduga	Karnataka	Hindus & Muslims indulge in arson following an altercation. 10 injured and 20 shops damaged.
2 May	Vandha	Gujarat	4 Muslims killed, 2 injured in a clash following suspected

Date	Place	State	Details
			chain snatching from a Hindu girl.
14 June	Aligarh	UP	Exchange of fire between Hindus & Muslims. 4 Muslims die.
20 July	Puwanimadi	J&K	Bomb explosion—17 dead.
31 Aug.	Chandigarh		Chief Minister Beant Singh assassinated.
1996			
13 Jan.	Narayanagiri	AP	PWG kill a Homeguard.
14 Jan.	Guwahati	Assam	ULFA Activists fired upon. Kill an ULFA surrenderee (SULFA) and one of his PSOs.
14 Jan.	West Tripura	Tripura	2 police personnel killed and 3 others injured in an ambush byNFLT activists.
20 Jan.	Gaya	Bihar	MDC Activists kill 5 police personnel (ASI-1, Havildar-1 and PCs-3) and injure 4 others.
20 Jan.	Hejamara	Tripura	ATTF Activists kill 6 CRPF personnel.
7 Feb.	Langting	Nagaland	Unidentified militants kill a DSP, his wife and 4 other CRPF personnel.
21 Feb.	Basugaon	Assam Road	Bodo militants kill 5 CRPF personnel.
4 Mar.	Pathakapally	AP	PWG attack police station. Kill a Constable and injure 3 others.
6 Mar. to 10 Mar.	Kamarajar & Madurai Dts.	Tamil Nadu	Caste clashes claim 10 lives.
3 Apr. to 9 Apr.	Kamarajar & TK Dts.	Tamil Nadu	Caste clashes between OBCs and Dalits cause 8 deaths.
9 Apr.	Tronglaubi	Manipur	Valley extremists ambush police party. 12 persons, including an SP and his 3 family members, killed.

Date	Place	State	Details
10 Apr.	Gattupally	AP	4 PWG extremists killed in an encounter with Police.
6 May	Singijan	Assam	Minister for Rura Development and 7 other members of his police escort killed by ULFA activists.
18-22 May	Kokrajhar	Assam	Ethnic violence between Bodos and Santhals cause 71 deaths.
7 Oct.	Jakaram Culvert	AP	In a landmine blast, 7 police personnel, including an Inspector, killed by PWG.
15 Nov.	Adilabad	AP	PWG activists kill 13 police personnel and a civilian.
12 Dec.	Kalyanpur	Tripura	24 Non-Tribal Bengalis killed by ATTF activists.

APPENDIX II

Vinayaka Procession turns Violent

(*Hindu*, Chennai, 4 September 1995)

Police used teargas and lathis to disperse participants in the tail end of the Vinayaka Chathurthi procession at Triplicane and the Marina here this evening. There was heavy stone throwing at some points on the procession route which led to lathicharge.

While scores of people were injured in the police action, about 20 police personnel, including a Joint Commissioner, a Deputy Commissioner and an Assistant Commissioner were hurt, and three police jeeps, and four buses were damaged in the violence which gripped Triplicane and adjoining area. Thirty persons were arrested in connection with the violent incidents. The wayside pulpit of the CSI Church at Gemini was damaged by some persons, who tore up a Bible displayed there.

Following the violence, the task of pulling a few Vinayaka idols at the end of the procession fell on the police personnel, though this provoked the volunteers further.

Lathicharge on the Marina started when the last two idols pulled by the police reached Seerani Arangam, as provocative slogans were raised against the police and stones thrown at them.

The Triplicane procession was among the three major ones in the city towards the Marina, the other two from near Nandanam Signal on Anna Salai and Muthuswamy Iyer Bridge. All was well with the procession when it started from Subadral Street in Triplicane at 1:31 p.m. Amid chants of 'Om Kali, Jai Kali' and 'Bharat Mata Ki Jai,' the procession was flagged off by the Hindu Munnani State President, Mr. Rama Gopalan.

The idols of different sizes from Central Madras and areas adjoining Triplicane and the 32 feet high 'Veera Vigneswara idol' of Thiruvateeswaranpet, were pulled along Quaid-e-Milleth Road (Triplicane High Road) for immersion in the sea by enthusiastic participants amidst blaring loudspeakers, beating of drums and sprinkling of colour powder.

Almost the entire procession had crossed the sensitive Ice House mosque junction when a few idols were left behind. Repeated announcements were made over loudspeakers appealing to the volunteers to move on quickly. The Police Commissioner, Mr. K.K. Rajasekharan Nair, urged the processionists at the Triplicane Post Office point to move faster. The volunteers protested and demanded that the police should not interfere. Slogans against Pakistan were raised leading to a tense situation.

As the entire procession had not crossed the Ice House mosque point by the scheduled time of 4:30 p.m., the police stopped the remaining few idols near the Ponnappa Chetty Lane. This was done to facilitate prayers at the mosque without risk of any untoward incidents. Even as the police exercised restraint, some processionists tried to press ahead, only to be pushed back by the police.

Chappals and stones were then thrown towards the police and as the brickbatting increased, the personnel resorted to lathicharge. The crowd ran helter-skelter into the lanes and by-lanes, but continued to throw stones.

Those who accompanied some idols which had been stopped at the junction. of B.V. Naicken Street grew restive and stones were thrown here also and an Assistant Commissioner of Police, Crime, Mr. Viswanathan, was injured in the chest. He was taken to a private nursing home at Ice House. Intensive lathicharge was made.

To bring the situation under control, the police fired teargas shells, though it did not stop the chappals and stones being lobbed from the by-lanes, especially Pallappan Street and Ellaiamman Koil Street. The volunteers insisted that Mr. Ramagopalan come to the spot and that police apologise. To relieve the Triplicane High Road of congestion, the police personnel themselves started pulling the two giant Vinayaka idols among the four left behind, around 5:45 p.m.

The trouble did not end there and when the idols reached Seerani Arangam, there was further stone-pelting and lathicharge. Mr.Rama Gopalan appealed to the police not to use force as he alleged that the violence had been triggered off by 'anti-Hindu forces'. But this had little impact and brickbatting continued.

Following intelligence reports, Police had an apprehension that there would be some disturbance in the procession. The DGP, Mr. V. Vaikunth, himself was present near the Ice House Mosque and he supervised the operations. His presence saved what would have otherwise turned into a nastier situation.

APPENDIX III

The Police Force is Communally Biased

(Julio Ribeiro in *Times of India*, 25.4.95)

A study of communal bias in the police by a senior police official from the UP cadre of the Indian Police Service, Mr. Vibhuti Rai, shows that there is enough evidence available to prove that such a bias exists. He has cited instances from UP and Bihar to make his point. In Bombay, the reluctance of the police to defer frenzied mobs killing Muslims in January 1993, and from looting and burning their property, led to the barbaric bomb blasts of March 1993. It was the response of a frustrated minority that took recourse to a terrorist act to wreak revenge.

Another Example

The killings of innocent Sikhs in Delhi after Mrs Gandhi's assassination was yet another example of police ineptitude, if not collusion, with the rioters. It is not correct to assert, as Mr Rai has done in his interview to *The Times of India,* that a communal riot can be suppressed in a day if the state government so desires. This is a rather tall statement which the officer will have to retrace if he is faced by situations like the ones in Delhi or Bombay.

Communal riots can be avoided if politicians do not misuse religion, and the religious sentiments of gullible people, to seek power; and if astute police leaders pre-empt them by timely warnings to the mischief-makers. But such preventive measures do not always succeed. Political compulsions are often so predominant, and the passions whipped up so strong, that no amount of sincere effort can avert the march of events.

The state and its law-enforcing arm is then left with no alternative but to use force to oppose the depredations of the riotous mobs. If it uses adequate force at the very inception and lets it be known that no quarter will be given, the message will go across. Unfortunately, the lumpen elements, who have a field day on such occasions, will not easily renounce a chance to loot. This alone ensures that the riots will take what seems an unduly long while to abate. And the longer it lasts the more the frustrations that build up among the population at large and the law-enforcers.

In the Watts riots in the USA, some two decades ago, the police took a conscious decision to allow the riots to abate without counterforce. The theory was that the riots, like the eye of a storm, would abate in any case. If the state used force it would be only of limited efficacy. The benefits of such action would be outweighed by its fall-out.

The conclusion arrived at by the Watts police is debatable. In India, police inaction would evoke severe condemnation and criticism. This has been the case in Delhi in 1984 and in Bombay in 1993. The police forces in our country will be well advised to act swiftly and firmly to curb the rioters. It may take many more days to restore normalcy than what Mr. Rai envisages, but if the intention is to be clear and unambiguous, half the criticism will be neutralized.

Mr Rai additionally suggests affirmative action to induct more Muslims and other minorities in the police forces. The recommendation is forceful though reservations, which he suggests, will be the wrong method to adopt. It will be unconstitutional, and may cause more problems than it seeks to solve.

The more sensible option for fair recruitment is to ensure that no impediments are placed in the way of minority registration at Employment Exchanges. Because of in-built prejudices, many young Muslim men and women are rejected even if they are otherwise fit. An in-house policy decision to recruit more Muslims will go a long way to correct imbalances.

Special Responsibility

Muslim community leaders have a special responsibility to encourage vernacular education. A reluctance to learn the local lingo comes in the way of employment in government departments for the simple reason that official work is conducted in that language.

Muslim representation in the uniformed forces, both the police and the army, must improve. It is the best way to encourage national integration and minimize religious, caste and regional differences. The uniform ensures camaraderie and esprit de corps between officers dependent on each other for their very survival. The British Government has attempted this in a big way in Northern Ireland. We can learn from its experience.

(The author is a former Police Commissioner of Bombay.)

APPENDIX IV

Excerpts from the Texas Code of Criminal Procedure

CCP ART. 38.22. WHEN STATEMENTS MAY BE USED

Sec. 1

In this article, a written statement of an accused means a statement signed by the accused or a statement made by the accused in his own handwriting or, if the accused is unable to write, a statement bearing his mark, when the mark has been witnessed by a person other than a peace officer.

Sec. 2

No written statement made by an accused as a result of custodial interrogation is admissible as evidence against him in any criminal proceeding unless it is shown on the face of the statement that:

(a) The accused, prior to making the statement, either received from a magistrate the warning provided in Article 15.17 of this code or received from the person to whom the statement is made a warning that:

(1) he has the right to remain silent and not make any statement at all and that any statement he makes may be used against him at his trial;

(2) any statement he makes may be used as evidence against him in court;

(3) he has the right to have a lawyer present to advise him prior to and during any questioning;

(4) if he is unable to employ a lawyer, he has the right to have a lawyer appointed to advise him to prior to and during any questioning; and

(5) the accused, prior to and during the making of the statement, knowingly, intelligently, and voluntarily waived the rights set out in the warning prescribed by Subsection (a) of this section.

Sec. 6

In all cases where a question is raised as to the voluntariness of a statement of an accused, the court must make an independent finding in the absence of the jury as to whether the statement was made under voluntary conditions. If the statement has been found to have been voluntarily made and held admissible as a matter of law and fact by the court in a hearing in the absence of the jury, the court must enter an order stating its conclusion as to whether or not the statement was voluntarily made, along with the specific finding of facts upon which the conclusion was based, which order shall be filed among the papers of the cause. Such order shall not be exhibited to the jury nor the finding thereof made known to the jury in any manner. Upon the finding by the judge as a matter of law and fact that the statement was voluntarily made, evidence pertaining to such matter may be submitted to the jury and it shall be instructed that unless the jury believes beyond a reasonable doubt that the statement was voluntarily made, the jury shall not consider such statement for any purpose nor any evidence obtained as a result thereof. In any case where a motion to suppress the statement has been filed and evidence has been submitted to the court on this issue, the court within its discretion, may reconsider such evidence in his finding that the statement was voluntarily made and the same evidence submitted to the court at the hearing on the motion to suppress shall be made a part of the record, the same as if it were being presented at the time of trial. However, the state or the defendant shall be entitled to present any new evidence on the issue of the voluntariness of the statement prior to the court's final ruling and order stating its findings.

APPENDIX V

An International Blueprint for Community Policing

(Prateep V. Philip, IPS, Superintendent of Police, Tamil Nadu)

Objectives of the Friends of Police (FOP) Movement

1. To separate the friends from the foes of the police, i.e. to separate the chaff from the grain.
2. To enable members of the public without regard to caste, creed or status, to establish rapport with the police force. It is a method of people empowerment.
3. To promote crime awareness within society and foster the prevention of crimes.
4. To promote a sense of civic responsibility and duty through education. To assist persons to learn as well as to teach human values.
5. To act as a force multiplier by involving FOP members in community policing, and increase the potential to deter and prevent crimes.

Qualifications to become a FOP

1. Every FOP candidate shall be a citizen and resident in the district in which a candidate applies for membership in the Friends of Police.
2. The FOP candidate shall not be involved in any civil or criminal case. This is to ensure that the prospective FOP has no axe to grind with the police.
3. No educational qualification or employment is prescribed, but the FOP candidate shall preferably be literate to enable written communications.
4. Age: minimum age of 18; maximum of 70.

In short, any member of the public who is not involved in any civil or criminal case can become a FOP. A person who aspires to be a FOP writes a letter to the Superintendent of Police that pledges his friendship to the FOP mission. The letter includes the name, age, address and occupation of the FOP candidate. Additionally, the aspirant states an area of interest: crime prevention, anti-vice campaign, victim assistance, patrol work, or traffic assistance. The appeal to the public to apply as a FOP is made through the local press and invariably hundreds of letters will be received. The chief of police approves FOP requests upon verification of application information.

APPENDIX VI

Wanted a New Police Culture
(*Hindu*, 8 March 1997)

The transfer of the Director General of Police in Karnataka within five months of his assuming this high post has come as a surprise. The incumbent, Mr A.P. Durai, has expressed the view that arbitrary transfers had the effect of demoralizing the police force and the stability in the force was also at stake. This is not the first time that such an abrupt transfer has taken place but it is time that the authorities stopped playing ducks and drakes with the security forces in the interests of society as a whole. Mr Durai has said that it is not possible to wish away external pressures but it was necessary to develop an inner mechanism to withstand these pressures. The National Police Commission did go into the problem in depth and made some concrete suggestions to ensure that the police force did not succumb to political pressures, especially. Pressure on the police takes a variety of forms, ranging from a promise of career advancement to preferential treatment in the matter of promotions. It is also true that if the official concerned fails to oblige, he will be penalised. Administrative action such as transfer to some innocuous place or even suspension could be taken and it is precisely for this reason most police officials are forced to fall in line with the dictates of the politician.

The consequent damage to discipline and morale of the chain of command within the police system can be imagined. The police functionaries at all levels perform a very important function in the maintenance of law and order even under the most trying circumstances and, therefore, any obstacles in the way of their free functioning should be carefully avoided. Linked with this is the question of accountability of the police. If it is expected that the police should not merely carry out the orders given to them but should really uphold the Constitution, then they obviously must be insulated from political leadership should rise to the challenge of the situation and initiate a process of reorientation and restructuring of the police system and its functioning instead of using it for its narrow partisan purposes as is happening on occasions now.

Of course, this is only one side of the coin and there is the other side which is equally disturbing. Policemen also indulge in doing things which they ought not to do or refrain from acting in a particular manner to favour politicians in power. They approach politicians to obtain choice postings and to avoid being transferred or to earn an advancement in rank. Thus a necessary basis is provided for a mutually advantageous barter. Even if such instances are rare, or at least not as common as instances of direct political interference, this tendency brings the police system into contempt. People's faith in the impartial and objective conduct of the police is eroded and they become extremely cynical when they find the party in power using the police to serve its ends. What is needed is a new police culture. A humane approach, public service orientation and citizens' police are the core areas of transformation of a new police culture with its own values of legality, integrity, responsibility and accountability. It is here that the suggestion made by the National Police Commission assumes special importance. It recommended the setting up of a statutory State Security Commission in each State composed of the Minister in charge of Police, two MLAs—one from the ruling party and the other from the Opposition parties—some retired High Court judges and men of public standing to monitor the performance of the police. This is bound to check the misuse of power by the police and also prevent the partisan use of the security apparatus. It is time that this proposal was implemented.

APPENDIX VII

Authorised Cadre Strength of the Indian Police Service (as on 01-1-97)

Name of State	Senior Posts							No. of Officers in position				
	Under the State Govt.	Under the Central Govt.	Total	Deputa-tion Reserve	Leave Reserve	Direct Recruit-ment Posts	Promo-tion Posts	Total Autho-rised strength	Direct Recruits No. in junior scale and above	Direct Recruits No. in senior scale	Promo-tees	Total
(1)	(2)	(3)	(4)	(5)	(6)	(7)	(8)	(9)	(10)	(11)	(12)	(13)
Andhra Pradesh	99	40	139	25	19	137	46	183	20	104	46	170
Arunachal Pradesh	88	35	123	22	17	121	41	162	8	89	40	137
Assam-Meghalaya	74	30	104	18	14	102	34	136	4	84	28	116
Bihar	135	54	189	34	27	187	63	250	23	137	63	223
Gujarat	72	29	101	18	14	100	33	133	3	90	33	126
Haryana	59	24	83	15	11	82	27	109	9	66	20	95

Himachal Pradesh	39	16	55	10	7	54	18	72	6	41	18	65
Jammu & Kashmir	51	20	71	13	10	59	35	94	9	35	33	77
Karnataka	79	32	111	20	16	110	37	147	10	80	37	127
Kerala	66	26	92	16	13	91	30	121	5	68	27	100
Madhya Pradesh	150	60	210	38	30	208	70	278	17	177	70	264
Maharashtra	111	44	155	28	22	154	51	205	16	120	50	186
Manipur-Tripura	57	23	80	14	11	79	26	105	8	60	25	93
Nagaland	27	11	38	6	5	37	12	49	1	20	12	33
Orissa	82	33	115	20	16	113	38	151	8	78	30	116
Punjab	79	31	110	19	15	108	36	144	20	74	35	129
Rajasthan	79	32	111	20	15	109	37	146	12	85	16	113
Sikkim	14	6	20	3	2	15	6	21	2	12	8	22
Tamil Nadu	102	41	143	26	20	142	47	189	17	104	44	165
Uttar Pradesh	214	86	300	53	42	295	100	395	27	239	97	363
West Bengal	138	55	193	34	27	190	64	254	15	147	64	226
Total	1815	728	2543	452	353	2493	851	3344	240	1910	796	2946

Source: ***Indian Police Service**, Civil List 1997*, Ministry of Home Affairs, Government of India, New Delhi.

APPENDIX VIII

Profile (1991-7) of IPS Probationers at the National Police Academy, Hyderabad

	1991	1992	1993	1994	1995	1996	1997
Sex							
Male	75	76	67	72	75	71	78
Female	08	06	04	06	09	13	13
Age							
Under 25	18	11	15	07	16	17	06
25-28	61	51	40	40	53	45	67
Over 28	04	20	16	31	15	22	18
Education							
Sciences	15	39	11	NA	NA	NA	14
Humanities	34	12	22	NA	NA	NA	33
Engineering	22	20	22	38	30	27	32
Medicine	03	04	03	07	03	05	03
Law	03	02	03	05	05	01	06
Management	03	03	07	03	03	07	03*

Note: No break-up under the heads 'sciences' and 'humanities' available for 1994-6.
*One of them was also an Engineering Graduate.

Source: Director, NPA, Hyderabad.

Bibliography

Adams, John (1996), 'Reforming India's Economy in an Era of Global Change', *Current History* (April).

Ahern, J.F. (1972), *Police in Trouble*, New York: Hawthorne Books.

Aleem, Shamim (1991), *Women in Indian Police,* New Delhi: Sterling.

Alpert, Geoffrey P. and Roger G. Dunham (1988 and 1992), *Policing Urban America,* Prospect Heights (NJ): Waveland Press.

Andrews (Jr.), Allen H. (1985), 'Structuring the Political Independence of the Police Chief', in William A. Geller (ed.), *Police Leadership in America,* New York: Praeger.

Archambeault, William G. and Betty J. Archambeault (1990), *Computers in Criminal Justice Administration and Management*, Cincinnati: Anderson Publishing Co.

Archer, D. and R. Gartner (1984), *Violence and Crime in Cross-national Perspective*, New Haven: Yale University Press.

Balasubramaniam, S.V. (1994), 'F.O.P.: Bridge between Police and Public', *Hindu* (4 November).

Bami, H.L. (1976), 'Development of Forensic Science Laboratories in India and Abroad', *Police Research and Development* (Oct.-Dec.).

Bayley, David H. (1969), *The Police and Political Development in India,* Princeton: Princeton University Press.

——— (1976), *Forces of Order*, Berkeley: University of California Press.

——— (1985), *Patterns of Policing*, New Brunswick: Rutgers University Press.

——— (1992), 'Comparative Organization of the Police in English-speaking Countries', in Michael Tonry and Norval Morris (eds.), *Modern Policing,* Chicago: University of Chicago Press.

——— (1994a), *Drugs, Crime and Law Enforcement in the United States,* Paper presented at the UNAFEI, Tokyo.

——— (1994b), *Police Brutality Abroad,* Paper presented to the National Institute of Justice, Washington, D.C.

——— (1994c), *Police for the Future,* New York: Oxford University Press.

Bayley, David H. and Jerome K. Skolnick (1988), *Community Policing: Issues and Practices around the World,* Washington, D.C.: National Institute of Justice.

Belenko, Steven (1990), 'The Impact of Drug Offenders on the CJ System', in Ralph Weishet (ed.), *Drugs, Crime and CJ System*, Cincinnati: Anderson Publishing Co.

Bennett, R. and J.P. Lynch (1990), 'Does a Difference Make a Difference? Comparing Cross-National Crime Indicators' (28) *Criminology*.

Berry, Mary Frances (1994), *Black Resistance, White Law*, New York: Penguin Press.

Beteille, Andre (1996),'Caste in Contemporary India', in C.J. Fuller (ed.), *Caste Today*, Oxford: Oxford University Press.

Birchler, Mark Robert (1988), 'The Future of Law Enforcement: Laptop Computers', *The Police Chief* (May).

Bizzack, John W. (ed.) (1991), *Issues in Policing: New Perspectives*, Lexington (KY): Autumn Hall.

——— (1991), *Criminal Investigations: Managing for Results*, Lexington: Autumn Hall.

Bouza, Anthony V. (1985), 'Police Unions', in Allan H. Geller (ed.), *Police Leadership in America*, New York: Praeger.

——— (1993), *How to stop Crime*, New York: Plenum Press.

Bradsher, Keith (1995), 'U.S. ranks first in Economic Inequality', *New York Times* (27 April).

Braiden, Chris (1990), 'Community Policing: Nothing New Under the Sun', *Problem-Solving Quarterly* (Summer).

Brown, Michael (1981), *Working the street*, New York: Russell Sage Foundation.

Brown, Richard Maxwell (1989a), 'Crime, Law and Society, From the Industrial to the Information Society', in Ted Robert Gurr (ed.), *Violence in America*, Newbury Park (California): Sage.

——— (1989b), 'Historical Patterns of Violence', in Ted Robert Gurr (ed.), *Violence in America*, Newbury Park (California): Sage.

Brownstein, Henry H. and Paul G. Goldstein (1990), 'A Typology of Drug-related Homicides', in Robert C.Trojanowicz and R. Bucqueroux (eds.), *Community Policing: A Contemporary Perspective*, Cincinnati: Anderson Publishing Co.

Bureau of Justice Statistics (1988), *Report to the Nation on Crime and Justice*, Washington, D.C.

——— (1990), *Special Report: Handgun Crime Victims.*

——— (1993a), *Jail Inmates 1992* (May).

——— (1993b), *Prisoners in 1992* (August).

Burpo, John (1971), *The Police Labour Movement, Problems and Perspectives*, Springfield (Ill.): Charles C. Thomas.

——— (1973), *Police Union in the Civil Service Setting*, Washington, D.C.: Department of Justice.

Button, James (1989), 'The Outcomes of Contemporary Black Protest and Violence', in Ted Robert Gurr (ed.), *Violence in America* (Vol. 2), Newbury Park (California): Sage.

City of New York (1997), *The Mayor's Management Report.*

Cole, George F. *et al.* (eds.) (1987), *Major Criminal Justice Systems*, Newbury Park: Sage.

Colton, Kent W. (ed.) (1978), *Police Computer Technology,* Lexington (Mass.): Lexington Publishing.

Congressional Quarterly Guide to the Presidency (1989), *The Civil Service System Today,* Washington, D.C.: Congressional Quarterly Inc.

Copper, Mary H. (1995), 'Combating Terrorism', in *Congressional Quarterly Researcher* (July).

Cressey, Donald (1969), *Theft of the Nation*, New York: Harper and Row.

Coulson, Robert (1993), *Police Under Pressure*, Westport (Conn): Greenwood Press.

Cronin, Thomas E. (1981), *U.S. v Crime in the Streets,* Bloomington: Indiana University Press.

Curry, J.C. (1932), *Indian Police,* London: Faber and Faber.

Doherty, Michael (1986), 'Applying Parallel Processing Techniques to Automated Fingerprint Identification', *The Police Chief* (May).

Dunham, Roger G. and Geoffery P. Albert (eds.) (1993), *Critical Issues in Policing*, Prospect Heights (Ill.): Waveland Press.

Echelberry, Norman (1989), 'Move Over, Crockett and Tubbs; Miami has a new Crime-fighting Weapon', *The Police Chief* (January).

Eck, J.E. and W. Spelman (1987), *Solving Problems: Problem-Oriented Policing in Newport News,* Washington, D.C.: Police Executive Research Forum.

Edwardes, S.M. (1983), *Crime in British India*, New Delhi: ABC Publishing House (rpt. of 1924).

Fairchild, Erika (1993), *Comparative Criminal Justice Systems*, Belmont (California): Wadsworth Publishing Co.

Federal Bureau of Investigation (1993), *Terrorism in the U.S.*

——— (1996), *Crime in the United States 1995, Uniform Crime Reports.*

Felson, Marcus (1994), *Crime and Everyday Life Insight and Implications for Society*, Thousand Oaks (CA): Pine Forge Press.

Fogelson, R.M. (1977), *Big-City Police*, Cambridge (MA): Harvard University Press.

Friedman, Lawrence (1993), *Crime and Punishment in American History,* New York: Basic Books.

Fuller, C.J. (1996), *Caste Today,* New Delhi: Oxford University Press.

Gainsburg, David (1994), 'Learning from the Kerner Commission', in *Civil Disorder, What do we know? How should we prepare?*, Washington, D.C.: Police Foundation.

Gates, Daryl and Robert Jackson (1989), 'The Street Gang Phenomenon', *League of California Cities* (April).

Geller, Allen H. (1985), *Police Leadership in America*, New York: Praeger.

George, B.J.(1990), 'Federal and State Legislation against Organized Crime in the United States', *Resource Material Series* (38) Tokyo: UNAFEI.

Ghosh, S.K. (1981), *Women in Policing*, New Delhi: Light and Life Publishers.

Ghosh, S.K. and K.F. Rustamji (1993), *Encyclopaedia of Police in India* (Vol. I), New Delhi: Ashish Publishing.

Gibbons, Sarah (1997), 'Zero Tolerance', *International Police Review* (May-June).

Glick, Nathan (1989), *An Outline of American Government,* Washington, D.C.: USIA.

Godson, Roy and William J. Olson (1993), *International Organized Crime: Emerging Threat to U.S. Security,* Washington, D.C.: National Strategy Information Centre.

Goldstein, Herman (1977), *Policing a Free Society*, Cambridge (MA): Ballinger.

——— (1979), 'Improving Policing: A Problem-Oriented Approach', *Crime and Delinquency* (April).

——— (1990), *Problem-Oriented Policing*, New York: McGraw Hill.

Gottlieb, Martin (1992), 'New York cycle of police scandal may be ready for a 20-year renewal', *New York Times* (21 June).

Government of India (1903), *Report of the Indian Police Commission, 1902*, New Delhi.

——— (1973), *Report of the Committee on Police Training*, New Delhi.

——— (1979-81), *Reports (Vol. I to VIII) of the National Police Commission,* Delhi: Controller of Publications.

——— (1997), *Indian Police Service: Civil List 1997,* New Delhi: Ministry of Home Affairs.

Greene, Jack R. (1981), 'Changes in the Conception of Police Work: Crime Control versus Collective Goods', in Kevin N. Wright (ed.), *Crime and Criminal Justice in a Declining Economy*, Cambridge (MA): Oelgeschlager.

——— (1988), 'Police and Community Relations: Where Have We Been and Where Are We Going?' in R. Dunham and J. Alpert (eds.), *Critical Issues in Law Enforcement*, Waveland Press.

——— (1989), 'Police Officer Job Satisfaction and Community Perceptions: Implications for Community Policing', *Journal of Research in Crime and Delinquency*, 26, 2 (May).

——— (1990), 'Community Policing and Cultural Change in Law Enforcement: Prospects and Challenges', *Paper for the Southwestern Legal Foundation,* Richardson (Texas).

Greene, Jack R. and Stephen Mastrofski (eds.) (1988), *Community Policing: Rhetoric or Reality,* New York: Praeger Press.

Greene, Jack R. and Scott H. Decker (1989), 'Police and Community Perceptions of the Community Role in Policing: The Philadelphia Experience', *Howard Journal of Criminal Justice,* 22, 2 (May).

Grennan, S. (1987), 'Findings on the role of officer gender in violent encounters with citizens', *Journal of Police Science and Administration*, 15 (1).

Griffiths, Sir Percival (1971), *To Guard My People, The History of the Indian Police,* London: Ernest Benn.

Gupta, Anandswarup (1974), *Crime and Police in India (Upto 1861)*, Agra: Sahitya Bhawan.

——— (1979), *The Police in British India, 1861-1947*, New Delhi: Concept Publishing.

Gurr, Ted Robert (1977), 'Crime Trends in Modern Democracies since 1945', *International Annals of Criminology 16.*

——— (1981), 'Historical Trends in Violent Crime', *Crime and Justice, An Annual Review of Research* (Vol. 3), Chicago: University of Chicago Press.

——— (1989(a), *Violence in America* (Vol. 1): *The History of Crime*, Newbury Park (California): Sage.

——— (1989(b), *Violence in America* (Vol. 2): *Protest, Rebellion and Reform*, Newbury Park (California): Sage.

Gurr, Ted Robert and Hugh Davis Graham (eds.) (1979), *Violence in America: Historical and Comparative Perspectives,* Beverly Hills: Sage.

Guyot, D. (1991), *Policing as though People Matter,* Philadelphia: Temple University Press.

Guyot, D. and K. Martensen (1991), 'The governmental setting', in William Geller (ed.), *Local Government and Police Management,* Washington, D.C.: International City Management Association.

Hacker, Andrew (1992), *Two Nations: Black and White, Separate, Hostile and Unequal,* New York: Macmillan.

Haller, Mark (1989), 'Bootlegging: The Business and Politics of Violence', in Ted Robert Gurr (ed.), *Violence in America* (Vol. 1), Newbury Park (California): Sage.

Hobbs, James (1992),'The Future of Crime Prevention and Problem Solving through Designing and Modifying the Environment', in *Source Book of Community-oriented Policing,* Washington, D.C.: ICMA.

Homant, R. and D. Kennedy (1985), 'Police perceptions of spouse abuse: A comparison of male and female officers', *Journal of Criminal Justice* 13 (1).

Human Rights Watch (1991), *Police Brutality in the U.S.: A Policy Statement on the Need for Federal Oversight* (July), New York: Human Rights Watch.

Huxley, Stephen J. and Philip E. Taylor (1989), 'Strategic Issues in Patrol Deployment: A Computer Analysis', *The Police Chief* (February).

Inciardi, James A. (1987), *Criminal Justice,* New York: Harcourt Brace Jovanovich.

Indian Institute of Public Opinion (1979), *Study on Police Image*, New Delhi: Ministry of Home Affairs.

Inspector General of Madras (1959), *The History of Madras Police*.

Johnson, D.R. (1981), *American Law Enforcement: A History*, St. Louis (MO): Forum Press.

Joshi, G.P. and J.C. Arora (1994), *Crime in India, A Trend Analysis (1951-91)*, New Delhi: Bureau of Police Research and Development.

Kanth, A.K. (1990), 'The Current Situation and Trends in Drug Offences', *Indian Police Journal* (January-December).

Kates, Don B. (1989), 'Firearms and Violence: Old Premises and Current Evidence', in Ted Robert Gurr (ed.), *Violence in America* (Vol. 1), Newbury Park (California): Sage.

Kaushal, Neeraj (1996), 'Women, the measure of progress', *Economic Times*, Chennai (29 October).

Kaushik, Surendra (1996), 'India's democratic economic transformation', *Challenge* (Sept.-Oct.).

Kelling, George, Tony Pate, Duane Dieckman and Charles E. Brown (1974), *The Kansas City Preventive Patrol Experiment: A Summary Report*, Washington, D.C.: The Police Foundation.

Kelling, George L. and Mark Moore (1985), *The Evolving Strategy of Policing*, Washington, D.C.: U.S. Dept. of Justice.

Kerstetter, Wayne A. (1985), 'Who disciplines the Police?', in William A. Geller (ed.), *Police Leadership in America*, New York: Praeger.

Kleck, Garry (1984), 'The Relationship between Gun Ownership Levels and Rates of Violence in the U.S.', in D. Gates (ed.), *Firearms and Violence: Issues of Public Policy*, Cambridge (MA): Ballinger.

Kolpack, Bryce (1989), 'MDTS: The Information Connection', *Law Enforcement Technology* (April).

Kosmin, Barry A. and Seymour P. Lachman (1993), *One Nation Under God: Religion in Contemporary American Society*, New York: Harmony Books.

Knapp Commission (1972), *The Knapp Commission Report*, New York: George Braziller.

Lane, Roger (1971), *Policing the City*, New York: Athenaeum.

Lane, Roger and John J. Turner (eds.) (1978), *Riot, Rout and Tumult*, Westport (CT): Greenwood.

Langworthy, Robert H. and Lawrence F. Travis III (1994), *Policing in America*, New York: Macmillan.

Lanier, Mark M. and David L. Carter (1994), 'Applying Computer Simulation to Forecast Homicide Rates', *Journal of Criminal Justice* 21 (5).

Law Enforcement Management Institute of Texas (1994), *Crime-specific Policing in Houston*.

Lee, John Allan and Livy Anthony Visano (1981), 'Official Deviance in the Legal System', in H.L. Ross (ed.), *Law and Deviance*.

Los Angeles Police Department (1992), *The City in Crisis: A Report by the Special Advisor to the Board of Police Commissioners on the Civil Disorder in Los Angeles.*

Lynch, Gerald W. (1987), 'Cops and College', *America* (4 April), Congressional Digest: Washington, D.C.

Madras Government (1865), *Madras Presidency Administration Report 1863-64.*

Manning, Peter K. (1992), 'Information Technologies and the Police', in Michael Tonry and Norval Morris (eds.), *Modern Policing,* Chicago: University of Chicago Press.

Martin, Susan E. (1990), *On the Move: The Status of Women Policing,* Washington, D.C.: Police Foundation.

Marx, Robert L. (1990), 'Principles and Predictions for Justice Information Management Systems', in *Criminal Justice in the 1990s,* Washington, D.C.: Bureau of Justice Statistics.

Mastrofski, Stephen D. (1993), 'Eying the doughnut: Community Policing and Progressive Reform', *American Journal of Police,* Vol. 12 (4).

Mastrofski, Stephen D. and Jack R. Greene (1993), 'Community Policing and the Rule of Law', in David Weisburd and Craig Uchida (eds.), *Police Innovation and Control of the Police*, New York: Springer-Verlog.

Mawby, R.I. (1990), *Comparative Policing Issues*, London: Unwin Hyman.

McBride, Duane C. and James A. Swartz (1990), 'Drugs and Violence in the Age of Crack Cocaine', in Ralph Weisheit (ed.), *Drugs, Crime and CJ System*, Cincinnati: Anderson Publishing.

McNamara, Joseph D. (1997), 'Too many Cops Think It's a War', *Time* (1 September).

Miller, Jay V. (1991), 'The FBI's Forensic DNA Analysis Program', *FBI Law Enforcement Bulletin* (July).

Misra, Shailendra (1986), *Police Brutality*, New Delhi: Vikas.

Monkonnen, E.H. (1981), *Police in Urban America, 1860-1920,* Cambridge (U.K.): Cambridge University Press.

Moore (Jr.), Harry W. (1980), 'The Delphic Analysis of Police Corruption', *Journal of Police Science and Administration,* Vol. 8, No. 1.

Moore, Mark Harrison and Robert C. Trojanowicz (1988a), 'Policing and the Fear of Crime', in *Perspectives on Policing*, Washington, D.C.: National Institute of Justice.

——— (1988b), *Corporate Strategies for Policing,* Washington, D.C.: National Institute of Justice.

Moore, Mark Harrison (1992), 'Community Policing', in Michael Tonry and Norval Morris (eds.), *Modern Policing,* Chicago: The University of Chicago Press.

Murphy, Patrick V. (1985), 'The Prospective Chief's Negotiation of Authority with the Mayor', in William A. Geller (ed.), *Police Leadership in America*, New York: Praeger.

Nag, N.K. (1983), 'A Study of the countrymade Guns of Seventies in West Bengal', *Indian Police Journal* (January-March).

Natarajan, Mangai (1996), 'Women police units in India: A new direction', *Police Studies* 19 (2).

National Crime Records Bureau (1997), *Crime in India (1995)*, New Delhi: Ministry of Home Affairs, Government of India.

National Institute of Justice (Sept. 1993), 'Toward the Paperless Police Department: The Use of Laptop Computers', *Research in Brief*, Washington, D.C.

——— (Dec. 1993), 'Street Gang Crime in Chicago', *Research in Brief*, Washington, D.C.

——— (Jan. 1994), *Violence Against Women: A National Crime Victimization Survey Report*, Washington, D.C.

New York City Police Department (1996), *Disorder Control Guidelines*.

Oliver, Melvin L., James H. Johnson, Jr. and Walter C. Farrell, Jr. (1993), 'Anatomy of a Rebellion: A Political-Economic Analysis', in Robert Gooding-Williams (ed.), *Reading Rodney King: Reading Urban Uprising*, New York: Routledge.

Osborn, Ralph (1992), 'Police Recruitment: Today's Standard and Tomorrow's Challenge', *FBI Bulletin* (June).

Pate, Anthony M. and Edwin E. Hamilton (1991), *The New York City Police Cadet Corps: Final Evaluation Report*, Washington, D.C.: Police Foundation.

——— (1991), *The Big Six: Policing America's Largest Cities*, Washington, D.C.: Police Foundation.

Pate, Anthony M. and Lorie A. Fridell (1993), *Police use of force: Official Reports, Citizen Complaints and Legal Consequences*, Vol. I, Washington, D.C.: Police Foundation.

Pate, Anthony M. (1994), 'Civil Disorder: Some disputed stereotypes and one indisputable fact', in *Civil Disorder: What do we know? How should we prepare?*, Washington, D.C.: Police Foundation.

Patterson (1989), 'How to make mistakes in Computerizing', *The Police Chief* (June).

Peak, Kenneth (1993), *Policing America*, Engelwood Cliffs: Regents/Prentice Hall.

Pearson, Allen and Robert Bradley (1989), 'Pitfalls in Agency Automation', *Law Enforcement Technology* (April).

Pennsylvania Crime Commission (1974), *Commission Report*, Harrisburg (PA).

Philadelphia Police Study Task Force (1987), *Philadelphia and its Police: Toward a New Partnership*.

Police Commissioners (1992), '*The City in Crisis: Report on Civil Disorder in Los Angeles*', Los Angeles: Special Adviser to the Board of Police Commissioners.

Police Foundation (1992), *Reconciling Higher Educational Standards and Minority Recruitment: The New York City Model,* Washington, D.C.

——— (April 1993), *Civil Disorder: What do we know? How should we prepare?,* Washington, D.C.

Pursley, Robert D. (1991), *Introduction to Criminal Justice*, New York: Macmillan.

Pynes, Joan E. (1994), 'Police Officer Selection Procedures: Speculation on the Future', *American Journal of Police,* Vol. 13 (2).

Raghavan, R.K. (1989), *Indian Police: Problems, Planning and Perspectives*, New Delhi: Manohar.

Rahman, M. (1993), 'Why Bombay burned, And Bhiwandi Didn't', *India Today* (15 January), New Delhi.

Rajgopal, P.R. (1987), *Communal Violence in India*, New Delhi: Uppal.

——— (1987), *Social Change and Violence: The Indian Experience,* New Delhi: Uppal.

Rana, N.S. (1993),'Delhi Police Nagrik Raksha Samithi Project', Paper presented at the Indian Police Science Congress, Nasik (May).

Rand, Michael (1990), 'Handgun Crime Victims', *BJS Special Report,* Washington, D.C.

Reddy, P.V.K. (1992), 'International Drug Trafficking Scenario', *National Police Academy Journal* (July-Dec.).

Rivlin, Alice M. (1992), *Reviving the American Dream,* Washington, D.C.: The Brookings Institution.

Rosenbloom, David H. (1994), 'Civil Service', *Encyclopaedia of the American Presidency*, New York: Simon & Schuster.

Roth, Jeffrey A. (1994), 'Firearms and Violence', *Research in Brief,* Washington, D.C.: National Institute of Justice.

Rowan, Roy (1986), 'The 50 Biggest Mafia Bosses', *Fortune* (10 November).

Saksena, N.S. (1978-9), *Notes circulated to the National Police Commission,* New Delhi.

Samaha, Joel (1988), *Criminal Justice,* St. Paul (Minn): West.

Santa Ana Police Department (1994), *Annual Report,* Santa Ana (Ca.).

Sewell, Bill (1988), 'Criminal Suspects Identified through Computerized Photo-Quality Composites', *The Police Chief* (May).

Shane, Paul G. (1980), *Police and People*, St. Louis: C.V. Mosby & Co.

Sharp, Arthur G. (1996), 'Computers are Law Enforcement's Future', *Law and Order* (August).

Sherman, Lawrence (ed.) (1974), *Police Corruption: A Sociological Perspective*, Garden City (NY): Anchor Books.

——— (1975), *Controlling Police Corruption: Final Report,* Washington, D.C.: National Institute of Justice.

——— (1992a), 'Police and Crime Control', in Michael Tonry and Norval Morris (eds.), *Modern Policing*, Chicago: University of Chicago Press.

Sherman, Lawrence (ed.) (1992b), *Policing Domestic Violence*, New York: Free Press.

Silberman, Charles E. (1980), *Criminal Violence*, New York: Vintage,

——— (1993), 'Why crime control is not reactionary', in David Weisburd and Craig Uchida (eds.), *Police Innovation and Control of the Police*, New York: Springer-Verlog.

Skogan, Wesley G. (1976), 'Citizen Reporting of Crime', *Criminology* 13 (Feb.).

——— (1976), 'Crime and Crime Rates', *Sample Surveys of the Victims of Crime*, Cambridge (MA): Ballinger.

——— (1989), 'Social Change and the Future of Violent Crime', in Ted Robert Gurr (ed.), *Violence in America*, Newbury Park (California): Sage.

Skolnick, Jerome H. and David Bayley (1986), *The New Blue Line*, New York: The Free Press.

——— (1988), *Community Policing: Issues and Practices Around the World*, Washington, D.C.: National Institute of Justice.

Sparrow, Malcom (1988), 'Implementing Community Policing', in *Perspectives in Policing*, Washington, D.C.: National Institute of Justice.

Sparrow, Malcom, Mark H. Moore and David M. Kennedy (1990), *Beyond 911: A New Era for Policing*, New York: Basic Books.

Srinivas, M.N. (1980), *India: Social Structure*, New Delhi: Hindusthan Publishing Corporation.

Srinivas, M.N. (ed.) (1996), *Caste: Its Twentieth Century Avatar*, New Delhi: Viking Penguin India.

Staufenberger, Richard A. (1980), *Progress in Policing: Essays on Change*, Cambridge (MA): Ballinger.

Sullivan, John J. and Joseph L. Victor (eds.) (1988), *Criminal Justice 1988/89*, Guilford (Conn): Dushkin.

——— (1990), *Criminal Justice 1990/91*, Guilford (Conn): Dushkin.

Swanson, C., L. Territo and R. Taylor (1993), *Police Administration: Structures, Processes and Behaviour*, New York: Macmillan.

Sylvester, John T. and John H. Stafford (1991), 'Judicial Acceptance of DNA Profiling', *FBI Law Enforcement Bulletin* (July).

Systems Development Corporation (1983), *The Emergency Command Control Communications System*, Los Angeles.

Thibault Edward, A., Lawrence M. Lynch and R. Bruce McBride (1985), *Proactive Police Management*, Englewood Cliffs: Prentice-Hall.

Tonry, Michael and Norval Morris (eds.) (1992), *Modern Policing*, Chicago: University of Chicago Press.

Trivedi, S.D. (1993), 'The Origin and Development of Police Organization in Ancient India', in S.K. Ghosh and K.F. Rustamji (eds.), *Encyclopaedia of Police in India*, New Delhi: Ashish Publishing.

Trojanowicz, Robert C. (1982), *An Evaluation of the Neighborhood Foot Patrol in Flint, Michigan,* East Lansing: Michigan State University.

———. (1992),'Building Support for Community Policing', *FBI Law Enforcement Bulletin* (May).

Trojanowicz, Robert C. and R. Bucqueroux (eds.) (1990), *Community Policing: A Contemporary Perspective*, Cincinnati: Anderson.

Tunnell, Kenneth D. and Larry K. Gaines (1992), 'Political Pressures and Influences on Police Executives: A Descriptive Analysis', *American Journal of Police*, Vol. XI (1).

Uchida, Craig (1993), 'The Development of American Police: An Overview', in Roger Dunham and Geoffery Alpert (eds.), *Critical Issues in Policing*, Prospect Heights (Ill.): Waveland Press.

United Nations Asia and Far East Institute and the Australian Institute of Criminology (1996), *Crime Trends in Asia and the Pacific,* The Fourth United Nations Survey.

US Congress (1994), 'Crime Control: The Federal Response', *Congressional Digest* (June-July), Washington, D.C.

US Department of Justice (1993), *International Factbook of Criminal Justice (Draft)*: Washington, D.C.

US Department of States (1995), *Patterns of Global Terrorism.*

Venugopala Rao, S. (1981), *Dynamics of Crime*, New Delhi: Indian Institute of Public Administration.

Vernon & Lasley (1992), 'Police Citizen Partnership in the Inner City', *FBI Law Enforcement Bulletin* (May).

Walker, Samuel (1983), *The Police in America*, New York: McGraw Hill.

Walker, Samuel and Vic W. Bumphus (1992), 'The Effectiveness of Civilian Review: Observations on recent trends and new issues regarding the civilian review of the police', *American Journal of Police,* Vol. XI (4).

Walters, Samuel (1992), *Policing Philosophy*, Santa Ana Police Department.

——— (1993), 'A Blend of Strategies', *FBI Law Enforcement Bulletin*.

Wasserman, Robert and Mark H. Moore (1988), 'Values in Policing', *Perspectives on Policing,* Washington, D.C.: National Institute of Justice (November).

Watson, Elizabeth M. and William A.Young (1991), 'Criminal Investigation Trends', in John W. Bizzack (ed.), *Issues in Policing: New Perspectives,* Lexington: Autumn House.

Webber, Alan M. (1991), 'Crime and Management: An Interview with NY City Police Commissioner Lee P. Brown', *Harvard Business Review* (May-June).

Weiner, Neil Alan and Marvin E. Woolfgang (1985), 'The Extent and Character of Violent Crime in America, 1969-82', *American Violence and Public Policy,* New Haven: Yale.

Weisheit, Ralph (ed.) (1990), *Drugs, Crime and the Criminal Justice System,* Cincinnati: Anderson Publishing Co.

Willis, Rod (1986), 'White Collar Crime, The Threat from within', *Management Review* (June).

Wilson, James Q. (1968), *Varieties of Police Behaviour: The management of law and order in eight communities,* Cambridge (MA): Harvard University Press.

——— (1985), *Thinking about Crime,* New York: Vintage.

Wilson, James Q. and George L. Kelling (1982) 'Police and Neighborhood Safety: Broken Windows,' *Atlantic Monthly* (March).

Wilson, James Q. and Richard J. Herrnstein (1985), *Crime and Human Nature,* New York: Simon and Schuster.

Wolfgang, Marvin E. and Franco Ferracuti (1967), *The Sub-culture of Violence: Toward an integrated Theory in Criminology,* London: Tavistock.

Worsnop, Richard L. (1991), 'Police Brutality', *Congressional Quarterly Researcher* (Sept).

——— (1993), 'Community Policing', *Congressional Quarterly Researcher* (Feb.).

——— (1994), 'Gun Control', *Congressional Quarterly Researcher* (June).

Wright, James D. (1989), 'The Armed Criminal in America', in Sullivan John J. and Joseph L. Victor (eds.), *Criminal Justice 1988/89*, Guilford (Conn): Dushkin.

Zahn, Margaret (1989), 'Homicide in 20th Century', in Ted Robert Gurr (ed.), *Violence in America* (Vol. 1), Newbury Park (California): Sage.

Zhao, Jihong, Quint C. Thurman and Nicholas P. Lovrich (1995), 'Community-Oriented Policing across the U.S. Facilitators and Impediment to Implementation', *American Journal of Police*, Vol. XIV (1).

Author Index

Subject Index